T5-DIJ-640

THE UTILITY OF INTERNATIONAL
ECONOMIC SANCTIONS

The Utility of International Economic Sanctions

Edited by
DAVID LEYTON-BROWN

ST MARTIN'S PRESS
New York

 For information, write:
Scholarly & Reference Division,
St. Martin's Press, Inc., 175 Fifth Avenue, New York, NY 10010
First published in the United States of America in 1987
Printed in Great Britain

Library of Congress Cataloging-in-Publication Data

The Utility of International economic sanctions.

Bibliography: p.
Includes index.
1. Economic sanctions. I. Leyton-Brown, David, 1946-
JX1246.U85 1987 341.5′8 86-14627
ISBN 0-312-00369-2

Contents

Contents

Contents

List of Tables

PREFACE

Earlier versions of the chapters in this volume were presented at a Conference on the Utility of Economic Sanctions as a Policy Instrument, held at York University in Toronto, Canada, 24-25 March 1983. The support of the Social Sciences and Humanities Research Council of Canada for the conference is gratefully appreciated.

I wish to express my appreciation to the contributors to this volume. They brought their impressive individual expertise to bear on a set of common questions, and collectively produced a work of both scholarly and policy relevance.

I am particularly grateful for the assistance provided by Rod Byers and the staff of the York University Research Programme in Strategic Studies. Kirsten Semple and Marianne Weide worked long and hard on the preparation of the manuscript. Special thanks must go to Michael Slack, without whom this volume would never have been produced.

David Leyton-Brown
Toronto, June 1986

Chapter One

INTRODUCTION

David Leyton-Brown

International economic sanctions have recently enjoyed an upsurge of governmental and public attention. Over the last decade various governments, but especially those of the United States and other Western countries, have imposed or threatened economic sanctions in a wide variety of conflicts. In democratic societies there have been even more frequent demands from the public for the imposition of sanctions against foreign targets. At times it appears that economic sanctions are being looked upon as an instrument of first resort - an easy way out for governments anxious to act, and to be seen to act, whether or not the economic sanctions can and do achieve the objectives claimed for them.

This preoccupation raises important questions about the utility of international economic sanctions as a policy instrument. This volume seeks to address this issue of utility and to clarify what international economic sanctions can and cannot usefully do. If properly designed and effectively applied, international economic sanctions offer the opportunity to act firmly in pursuit of policy goals without resort to the use of military force. If not, excessive rhetoric can lead to exaggerated public expectations, which if not realised can threaten to devalue the policy instrument and diminish its utility even where it would otherwise be appropriate.

International economic sanctions are deliberate government actions to inflict economic deprivation on a target state or society, through the limitation or cessation of customary economic relations. These involve trade and financial measures, including controls upon exports to the target, restrictions upon imports from the target, and interruptions of official or commercial finance, such as cutting off aid or freezing assets. For the purposes of this study, economic sanctions will be considered only as a subset of the larger category of instruments of economic statecraft.[1] This book will focus only upon economic sanctions as tools in specific peace-time conflict situations. Though there have been many instances of the imposition of economic sanctions as part of an overall war effort, the interest here is in economic sanctions as an alternative to military force, rather than a complement to it. Economic sanctions will be distinguished from positive economic inducements, from ongoing differentiation of economic treatment in monetary or commercial relations, and from non-economic sanctions, such as the suspension of cultural exchanges or diplomatic relations.

The fundamental question most often raised about economic sanctions is, 'Do they work?' That in turn raises other analytic questions about the purposes, practices and consequences of sanctions. This volume seeks to offer systematic comparative analysis of major individual cases of the imposition of international economic sanctions, in order to examine the utility of sanctions in each case and to draw general conclusions about the future prospects of economic sanctions as a policy instrument in international conflict.

The cases examined here are by no means exhaustive,[2] but do represent the major instances of the imposition of international economic sanctions and the major consequences associated with international economic sanctions in the post-Second World War period. To ensure comparability of analysis, each author was asked to address the following questions:

1. What were the objectives which the sanctions were intended to achieve (which may involve a distinction between rhetorical and real purposes)?
2. What particular sanctions were adopted?
3. What was the effect of the sanctions on the target?
4. What was the degree of success in realisation of the objectives?
5. What factors contributed to or militated against the realisation of the objectives?
6. What unintended consequences resulted from the application of sanctions?

The various chapters have been edited to ensure uniformity of style, but each author is responsible for the accuracy of the content and footnote references.

Part one of the book examines the application of international economic sanctions by multilateral organisations. Kim Nossal contrasts the underlying philosophical purposes of economic sanctions in the Covenant of the League of Nations and the Charter of the United Nations. Douglas Anglin explores the experience of the United Nations in its two major exercises of the imposition of economic sanctions against South Africa and Rhodesia.

Part two deals with Western economic sanctions in

East-West conflicts, which is perhaps the most prominent and ongoing category. Paul Evans examines the Western, and especially Canadian, experience with economic sanctions against the People's Republic of China. Sergio Roca considers the case of economic sanctions against Cuba. Peggy Falkenheim assesses the Western sanctions against the Soviet Union following its invasion of Afghanistan. Paul Marantz evaluates the Western economic sanctions in the Polish crisis.

Part three concerns examples of international economic sanctions by non-Western states, in non-East-West conflicts. David Dewitt analyses the Arab boycott of Israel, while Roy Licklider studies the 1973 Arab oil embargo of the United States.

Part four shifts focus from the effect of economic sanctions on the target to some of the collateral or unintended effects. These two chapters assess the impact of economic sanctions on the initiator. Robert Paarlberg evaluates the consequences for the participants, especially the United States and Canada, of the 1980-81 grain embargo of the Soviet Union initiated following the invasion of Afghanistan. Bernard Wolf studies the economic impact on the United States and on US multinational corporations of the Siberian gas pipeline sanctions in 1981-82.

Part five investigates the impact of economic sanctions on third parties. Howard Stanislawski examines the economic impact on Canada and the United States of the Arab boycott of Israel, and the different legislative and regulatory responses in those two countries to the effects of the boycott. David Leyton-Brown assesses the legal and political problems which arise from the extraterritorial application of US trade sanctions, and the possible responses of affected goverments. John Kirton reviews the problems of alliance consultation and Canadian involvement in four Western sanctions cases: the Iranian hostage crisis, the Afghanistan crisis, the Polish crises, and the Falklands/Malvinas war.

Part six draws conclusions about the utility of international economic sanctions as a policy instrument. Lawrence Brady provides a most useful indication of the policy-thinking in the Reagan Administration. Finally, David Leyton-Brown clarifies lessons which may be learned about the purposes, application and effects of international economic sanctions, and offers policy prescriptions for the effective design and implementation of sanctions in the future.

Notes

1. David A. Baldwin, Economic Statecraft (Princeton University Press, Princeton N.J., 1985).

2. See Gary Hufbauer and Jeffrey J. Schott, Economic Sanctions in Support of Foreign Policy Goals (Institute for International Economics, Washington D.C., October 1983).

PART I

ECONOMIC SANCTIONS BY MULTILATERAL ORGANISATIONS

7-21

Chapter Two

ECONOMIC SANCTIONS IN THE LEAGUE OF NATIONS AND THE UNITED NATIONS

Kim Richard Nossal

The purpose of this chapter is not to survey the several attempts during the twentieth century of international organisations to deter aggression by states, to change the behaviour of members of the international system, or to punish transgressions by imposing economic sanctions against members of the society of states. That history forms the basis of an extant literature of considerable size,[1] to which a brief chapter as this could not do justice.

Rather, this chapter will discuss the mechanisms used by the two universal international organisations this century to formulate a means of securing compliance to international law. It begins by examining the distance that has grown between our understanding of sanctions in the latter part of the twentieth century, and the understanding of sanctions that underlay both the Covenant of the League of Nations and the Charter of the United Nations. The provisions of the League and the United Nations with regard to economic mechanisms of compliance will be examined in an attempt to contrast the differences between the interwar and postwar regimes.

At this juncture, it should be noted that for the purposes of this chapter I have sought to differentiate those mechanisms of compliance that are grounded in universal international organisations from those which are taken in either a multilateral or a unilateral framework. What I term in this chapter as 'universal sanctions' are those measures adopted by either the League or the United Nations. By contrast, 'multilateral sanctions' might better be thought of as those measures which are adopted under the aegis of one of the many international organisations that do not have, as one of their characteristics, the goal of universal membership and universal adherence to their norms or codes of operation. Thus, measures initiated by a regional collective security organisation such as the North Atlantic Treaty Organisation, by such groups as the Organisation of Oil Exporting Countries, or by a regional development bank would fall under the rubric.

Similarly, unilateral sanctions are those measures introduced by one state. The state initiating these measures might seek to use its multilateral ties to add more weight to the effect of these sanctions, or to legitimise its actions by seeking support from those multilateral organisations of which it is a member. But the impetus for the sanctions is essentially unilateral.

Finally, the chapter will offer a perspective on the inutility of universal economic sanctions as a means of extracting compliance to the law from the states. The inutility of universal sanctions, it will be argued following most analytical perspectives on international law, lies in the very nature of the inter-state system, which traditionally has been fractured by contending sovereignties and politico-military rivalries, a condition that precludes either the emergence of a king of Kantian universal interest or a more Hobbesian mechanism for sanctioning transgressions of law by states. While it is hardly a conclusion that has not been drawn by others, it nonetheless should serve to remind us of the fragility of international law and the essential inability of the society of states to sanction transgression of that law.

A Semantic Digression

Semasiological quibbles may often contribute to a better understanding of a subject: David Baldwin's recent examination of the uses and abuses of the word 'interdependence' is an illustration.[2] More often than not, however, inquiries into the meaning of words may obfuscate more than they illuminate, for the inexorable tendency of those who take semantic digressions is to seek to impose evangelistically <u>their</u> understanding of a word on etymological heretics. The resulting debate is rarely edifying.

By engaging in an introductory discussion of the etymology of the word 'sanctions', I seek neither to impose a meaning of the word that does not accord with current accepted usage, nor to divert attention from an examination of the phenomenon of economic sanctions in international politics that is rooted in contemporary political reality. My purpose is to clarify how an understanding of sanctions must be rooted in the context of their application, as I will show.

How are sanctions generally understood today? If one looked to current popular usage, one would conclude that by 'economic sanctions' are meant those instruments of national policy intended to deprive other target states of the benefits of economic intercourse in order to effect a change in the target state's behaviour.

Indeed, the underlying assumption that sanctions need only involve deprivation for the target state pervades popular usage. Thus, if one looks to recent historical events, one sees a litany of attempts at deprivation: the UK attempt to deprive the Argentines of normal channels of economic intercourse after the Argentine invasion of the Falklands/Malvinas in April 1982; the attempt by the US government to induce change in both the Polish military authorities and the Soviet Union after the imposition of martial law in December 1981 by seeking to deny them access to economic and commercial benefits; the efforts of the Carter Administration to secure release of the US hostages in Iran by depriving the government in Teheran of the benefits of normal economic intercourse in the spring of 1980; and, finally, the attempts by the United States to deprive the Soviet Union of both economic and other benefits after the invasion of Afghanistan in December 1979.

In each of these cases, these economic measures were imposed for a constellation of reasons. The first, and most easily recognisable, was punition: the desire of those states taking these measures to punish the target state or states for their behaviour. The second motivation for instituting such measures was deterrence: a desire to signal that similar behaviour - by the target state or by other states - would have recognised attendant costs, and thereby deter such behaviour. A third objective was compellence: seeking to change the target state's behaviour by depriving that state of something it values, in essence forcing it to abandon the behaviour offensive to the initiating state or states.

Each of these recent cases is not dissimilar to other instances of what are popularly known as economic sanctions: the attempts by the US government to deprive the Cuban government of Fidel Castro or the Chilean government of Salvador Allende of access to unrestricted commercial intercourse; the coercive efforts of the Arab states to deter both the Canadian government - and of course others - from moving the Canadian embassy from Tel Aviv to Jerusalem by threatening sanctions; attempts in 1973 on the part of the Arab states to secure a change in Western policy vis-a-vis Israel; and earlier attempts by the US government to isolate the People's Republic of China and the governments of North Korea and North Vietnam by the imposition of restrictions on economic intercourse.

Each of these cases involves the use of economic measures by states to secure political ends. These measures - which have come to be called sanctions - are regarded simply as belonging to the repertoire of a state's foreign policy. The denial of the value of economic transactions (by boycott, embargo, restriction, regulation, seizure, etc.) is seen as merely a tool of state craft, albeit a non-violent (or, for those who would argue that there is violence in deprivation, more properly, non-forceful) tool.

In each of these cases punition was a cardinal motivating force in prompting the imposition of these economic tools of state craft against specified targets. It could be argued that the desires for deterrence or compellence were in each case distinctly secondary considerations in the minds of those who initiated the sanctions. For example, when imposing sanctions against Argentina in April 1982, Mrs Thatcher did not do so in the expectation that General Galtieri would immediately surrender; US sanctions against the Soviet Union in the wake of the imposition of martial law in Poland were not imposed in the expectation that General Jarulzelski would step aside to allow Solidarity to conduct its national referendum of confidence in the Communist Party. Indeed not: these measures were taken to punish the perpetrators.

Punishment itself suggests a hurtful penalty or reprisal (indeed the English 'pain' comes from the Greek _poine_, payment) imposed for a transgression or violation. But it is not at all clear what constitutes a transgression or violation. In each of these cases, we have a transgression that is first and foremost arbitrarily and not automatically defined. Thus it was a transgression worthy of the sternest of rhetoric and the strongest of economic reprisals from the US government when the Soviet Union invaded Afghanistan in 1979, but when four years earlier Indonesia committed an act that was in substance no different, there was neither moral outrage nor economic sanctions imposed on the government in Jakarta by the US government. When the Vietnamese overthrew the Kampuchean government of Pol Pot in early 1979 and replaced it with a government more to its liking, Hanoi was punished - by military action and economic reprisals. But when the Tanzanians, two months later, overthrew the government of Idi Amin in Uganda and replaced it with one more to its liking, there was barely any negative reaction internationally. In short, there appears to be little possibility for an objective definition of transgression. Whether a transgression has even occurred, or whether there should be punishment of that violation depends on the subjective and _ad hoc_ judgement of each state. One is forced to conclude, by the inconsistent behaviour of states, that the action found offensive is an action that they regard as a violation of _their_ interests, not necessarily actionable because it is a violation of law.

There is little doubt that the kinds of economic reprisals imposed in response to transgressions against a state's interests can be (and indeed are) described as 'sanctions'. At the same time, it can be argued that such a usage - one that ignores the etymological roots of the word - does not reflect adequately either the original intent of the word or the sense in which it must be understood in the context of universal international organisations.

Traditional usage of the word 'sanction' tends to retain the original meaning inherited from Latin. *Sanctio* referred to the exacting of a specified penalty for violation of a sacredness or for violation of a law or decree. It appears that until the late seventeenth century, the word had only a punitive or vindicatory sense - punishment for breaking the law. Its meaning was, however, extended to include those rewards provided for obedience to the law - or remuneratory sanctions.[3]

The juristic or legal interpretation of sanctions thus always involves either deprivation or reward, but it is inexorably bound, either through coercion or inducement, to the enforcement of law. By contrast, a looser interpretation of the notion of sanction appeared by the mid-1700s. This interpretation, which did not insist upon a legalistic focus on deprivations or rewards for obedience or disobedience to the law, was more akin to the sense in which it is used today. The focus is not on the lawfulness or otherwise of an agent, but simply on the *behaviour* of that agent and how that behaviour may be changed by rewards and punishments. In this latter sense, it is important to recognise, there is no necessity that sanctions must be related to a delict by an agent against whom sanctions are taken.

Such a distinction between a juristic interpretation of sanctions and what is characterised as an ethical view of sanctions is not simply a matter of semantics if the discussion focuses on the sanctions employed by international organisations to enforce international law. For, as I will argue, the major shift that took place in the area of sanctions employed against states by the international community from the League to the United Nations was rooted in a move from a legal to a less strict notion of sanctions.

Obligation and Enforcement under the League

The juristic interpretation of sanctions underlay the entire structure and *raison d'etre* of the League of Nations, and underwrote the Covenant signed at Versailles.

While the Covenant did not make war a delict under all circumstances, it did circumscribe the legitimate or rightful use of force by states. War could not be used as an instrument of national policy until a set of prescribed arbitral procedures had been fulfilled; the use of force could be employed against states which had violated the terms of the Covenant, but only that which was 'necessary for the maintenance of right and justice' (Article XV.7) and to be 'used to protect the covenants of the League' (Article XVI.2).

The Covenant did not outlaw resort to arms, but did make certain types of use of force a delict. Article X committed members to specific ends, thereby creating an obligation on the part of those states:

> The Members of the League undertake to respect and preserve as against external aggression the territorial integrity and existing political independence of all Members of the League.

Article XII, XIII and XV further specify obligations of member states to submit disputes to arbitration or judicial settlement, and to refrain from the use of force for a special period of time.

Thus the Covenant specified the legal obligations of states: if a state disregarded the obligation established by law - in other words, if it violated the provisions of the Covenant - it would ipso facto commit a delict, and be subject to the sanctions specified for that delict.

The sanction for violation of the obligations of states under the Covenant was laid out in paragraph 1 and 2 of Article XVI, though it was not termed a sanction:

1. Should any Member of the League resort to war in disregard of its covenants under Articles XII, XIII or XV, it shall ipso facto be deemed to have committed an act of war against all other Members of the League, which hereby undertake immediately to subject it to the severance of all trade or financial relations, the prohibition of all intercourse between their nationals and the nationals of the Covenant-breaking state, and the prevention of all financial, commercial or personal intercourse between the nationals of the Covenant-breaking state and the nationals of any other state, whether a member of the League or not.

2. It shall be the duty of the Council in such cases to recommend to the several Governments concerned what effective military, naval, or air force the Members of the League shall severally contribute to the armed forces to be used to protect the covenants of the League.

It would appear, then, that Article XVI was a sanction well within the juristic sense: an obligation had been clearly spelled out by the law; the penalty for a violation of that law was with equal clarity specified. Use of force that was not rightful was to be met with the penalty of immediate and comprehensive measures to break all intercourse with that state, and, if necessary, the legitimate use of force by other members of the international community.

It might be noted that this conclusion is at complete variance with the conclusions of the Report of a Group of Members of the Royal Institute of International Affairs (RIIA), issued in 1938. Their view was that:

> The Covenant of the League of Nations is based on the view that the object of sanctions is purely that of preventing the success of aggression. It lays down no penalties for the violation of international law or the breaking of the peace. It merely prescribes the methods which States Members are bound to follow in rendering assistance to the victims of aggression and upholding the Covenant of the League.

On the one hand, it is possible that the RIIA's interpretation was the result of the context in which it was written. This conclusion appeared in the context of seeking to establish the differences between 'national' and international law. It might be suggested that they were hesitant to equate the 'methods of rendering assistance' - with the five-to-ten style of penalty associated with sanctions under municipal law. Indeed, they conclude that if an accepted definition of a sanction is 'an evil incurred, or to be incurred, by disobedience', then 'whilst fitting enough for the sanctions of national law, lays more stress on the penal character of sanctions than is appropriate in world affairs'.

On the other hand, it is equally possible that the RIIA group simply did not see the measures prescribed in Article XVI as penalties of any kind. Clearly, they saw the main purpose of these measures as preventive - as deterrents to those states who would rationally choose to avoid incurring these measures. Punition is not mentioned in the discussion of their understanding of sanctions.[4]

Not that punition and prevention are unrelated: prevention is predicated on the assumption that an agent will fear the costs of punition more than he will desire the benefits of transgression. And, in turn, punition is specified clearly for a transgression to encourage prevention.

If we can indeed conclude that the measures outlined in Article XVI constitute sanctions in the juristic sense, we are nonetheless left with a problem. For the formulation of this article, as Kelsen has pointed out,[5] does not specify who is to judge if a delict has taken place. A sanction, by its very nature, cannot under law simply be imposed also automatically - whatever a literal reading of Article XVI suggests. There must first be a judicial ascertaining that indeed there has been a violation of the law, and only then may the specified sanction be applied. There was no provision under the Covenant for a centralised locus where such a judicial decision would be rendered. As a consequence, Kelsen argues, the only possible juristic interpretation of Article XVI was that each member was required to make the determination as to whether a delict had been committed. And only if the member answered in the affirmative, was it obligated to apply the sanctions outlined in paragraph 1.

Despite this considerable flaw identified by Kelsen, the Covenant of the League stands out as a revolutionary development in the law of states. For while treaties between states may specify particular penalties for non-performance, and while some international undertakings before 1919 had included general guarantees,[6] the Covenant was the first instance where specified acts were prohibited and a general penalty or sanction imposed for transgression. (There is some similarity here with the different types of delicts and sanctions under municipal law - compare the difference between a tort and a crime.) Importantly, the sanctions specified under the Covenant were sanctions in the classical sense of the term, and it was this feature of the Covenant that, it will be argued below, led to its eventual failure.

The United Nations and 'Sanctions'

If the Covenant of the League provided that specifically identified transgressions be punished by specific penalties, the Charter of the United Nations (which does not employ the word 'sanctions') takes a considerable step away from the notion of vindicatory punishments for specified delicts. For the Charter of the United Nations provides for only two sanctions. The first is contained in Article 6:

> A Member of the United Nations which has persistently violated the Principles contained in the present Charter may be expelled from the Organization by the General Assembly upon the recommendation of the Security Council.

While the provisions of Article 6 are exceedingly vague (which principles have to be violated? is it permissable to expel a member for persistent violation of one principle? how many times is persistently? etc.), they do constitute a recognised sanction, though, as Kelsen is quick to point out, the 'evil' associated with this sanction from the perspective of the expelled state is questionable.[7] It might also be noted that the Security Council is, in the first instance, given the responsibility of making that judicial determination that a delict has in fact occurred, and the General Assembly is also given a role in making the assessment of whether the determination of the Security Council warrants the imposition of this sanction.

The other sanction provided for in the Charter is to be found in Article 19:

> A Member of the United Nations which is in arrears in the payment of its financial contributions to the Organization shall have no vote in the General Assembly if the amount of its arrears equals or exceeds the amount of contributions due from it for the preceding two full years. The General Assembly may, nevertheless, permit such a Member to vote if it is satisfied that the failure to pay is due to conditions beyond the control of the member.

This provision of the Charter was designed to deter delinquency by providing the sanction of automatic suspension of voting rights in the General Assembly. (It might be noted, en passant, that juristically, it suffers the same problem as Article XVI.1 of the Covenant of the League: there is no determination that a delict has occurred, being in arrears assumed to be self-evident.)

If these are the two explicit sanctions provided for in the Charter,[8] there is no shortage of obligations that the Charter places on those states which are signatory to it. In the first instance, it places an obligation on members neither to use force nor to use the threat of force to settle disputes; it permits the use of force for 'individual or collective self-defence' - but only if 'an armed attack occurs' and only 'until the Security Council has taken measures necessary to maintain international peace and security' (Article 51).[9] Besides being obligated to behave peacefully, members are also under an obligation to refrain from acting 'in any other manner inconsistent with the Purposes of the United Nations' (Article 2.4). In addition, members undertake to assist the United Nations in preventive or enforcement actions, and not to give aid to those against whom the United Nations is acting (Article 2.5). In short, the principles enumerated in Article 2 of the Charter provide a weighty set of obligations - and, of course, an equally weighty set of possible delicts.

If there are a plethora of transgressions which can be committed, there are no sanctions outlined in the Charter (save for those mentioned above). Indeed, Chapter VII of the Charter does not even mention 'Charter-breaking' states as did the Covenant of the League. Article 39 of the Charter reads:

> The Security Council shall determine the existence of any threat to the peace, breach of the peace, or act of aggression and shall make recommendations, or decide what measures shall be taken...to maintain or restore international peace and security.

In other words, the Security Council is given the discretion to identify delicts, to target offenders, and to take whatever action it deems fit for the purposes. And Articles 41 and 42 provide the Security Council with appropriate enforcement mechanisms to give effect to their decisions.

But the enforcement measures outlined in Articles 41 and 42 are not sanctions. In particular, the economic measures outlined in Article 41 - 'complete or partial interruption of economic relations and of rail, sea, air, postal, telegraphic, radio, and other means of communication' - which are the universal 'sanctions' as popularly understood, cannot be considered as penalties, since no delict is specified, no punition is outlined and no target is mentioned. Article 41 gives the Security Council the necessary legal authority to exercise coercive interference in the sphere of a state which has committed a delict (and that may constitute the 'evil' necessary for a definition of sanction), but it is not itself a sanction in the juristic sense of the word.

The Retreat from Legalism

That the Charter of the United Nations only includes minimal juristic sanctions to be imposed on members reflects a major change from the basic approach used by the Covenant of the League of Nations as a means of entrenching the rule of law in the international system.

The governments which established the League of Nations in the wake of the First World War had been conditioned by the prevalent acceptance of the use of force as a morally and legally acceptable (and accepted) tool of state craft. Even aggressive war which defied all the requisites of jus ad bellum of an earlier era was not considered a delict under pre-war general international law. But in the wake of the Great War, and inspired by the idealism and legalism of President Woodrow Wilson, the statesmen gathered at Versailles were prepared to accept the idea of making certain uses of force illegal - or, put another way, to create an obligation on the part of members of the international system not to use force as a tool of state craft.

To enshrine this, they employed a device or jurisprudence: they made contrary behaviour - in other words, using force - the condition of a sanction. In the case of a state which committed a delict - aggressive war of violation of the Covenant - the sanction was to be economic ostracism by all other states and potentially the use of armed force by the international community.

By contrast, the sanctions included in the Charter are concerned with what might be thought of as peripheral issues to the major questions of the prevention of war and the maintenance of peace. The end remained the same for the statesmen gathered at San Francisco as it had been for their predecessors a generation earlier, but they sought rather different means to that end.

The United Nations Charter is not a jurist's document - Hans Kelsen spent 990 pages in 1950 picking apart the amphibology of the Charter. It does not seek to impose on the maintenance of order and peace in the international system the same kind of relationship between obligation, delict and sanction that is enmeshed in the maintenance of order within the state, and that was transposed, with but minor changes, onto the regime created at Versailles. And thus, the United Nations brings to the problem of the maintenance of peace and order internationally a very different perspective.

The obligations of states are retained - and indeed expanded. Signatories to the United Nations Charter, and even non-members, are required to behave in a way consistent with the general thrust of the lofty principles enshrined in the opening articles of the Charter. But delicts are undefined; the sanctions few and reserved for minor matters or for the truly recalcitrant state.[10]

The approach is a political rather than a legal one. It is designed to side-step all the problems encountered by a legalistic system which, to have effect, must ultimately depend on enforcement of sanctions. And universal sanctions, if rested solely on a framework of legalism, are, quite simply, ineffective. By ineffective in this context, I mean that they do not serve to punish, and therefore they do not deter states from committing the delict for which the sanction is specified. In the case of the League, of course, the failure to punish the Japanese or Italian states for their clear violation of its obligations under the Covenant meant that any preventive or deterrent effects that the relationship between obligation, delict and sanction are supposed to have were lost.

The United Nations maintains the underlying idea of universal sanctions in the political rather than juristic sense. The obligation to assist UN enforcement efforts, and the proscribing of assistance to the target of such efforts, creates - in theory, at least - the possibility of concerted and collective economic (if not military) enforcement measures against a state which disregards its obligations under the Charter. But the idea of punition, which is in its essence juristic, does not appear to be part of the underlying philosophic rationale of the Charter or the potentially wide powers given to the Security Council.

By contrast, effecting a change in behaviour *is* part of the rationale for universal economic sanctions under the Charter: the universal sanctions imposed against Rhodesia were not designed to punish the white minority regime, but to cause it to collapse; the purpose behind the Year of Sanctions against South Africa is not to punish either the state or the white minority but to cause change - either an evolutionary (but slightly more rapid) change in the attitudes and policies of the Afrikaner minority or a more radical transformation of the South African system.

(By contrast, multilateral sanctions appear to be driven by the desire to punish and deter more than by the expectation that economic or other sanctions will produce a change in the offending state's behaviour: see p. 10 above.)

In adopting what is in essence a political rather than a legalistic regime for the imposition of economic sanctions, the United Nations has avoided the more spectacular failures of the League. When the Soviet Union invades Afghanistan, for example, which is a delict under the Charter, and would have been a delict under the Covenant, there are no sanctions *required* by the Charter; all member states are not *ipso facto* at war with the Soviet Union; the United Nations is not confronted, as the League was, with the dilemma of having to impose a set of specified sanctions on a Covenant-breaking member and yet knowing, in political terms, that such a course of action would be unworkable. So, the international community, when confronted with a violation such as the invasion of Afghanistan, has the benefit of flexible response: some members may embrace economic sanctions - unilaterally or multilaterally - to punish, to deter or to compel; some members may express condemnation - a form of moral sanction; and yet others may say and do nothing. Importantly, the universal international organisation need not be involved, for its Charter does not require that it be involved.

The retreat from legalism has thus meant that if the universal international organisation imposes sanctions - economic or other varieties - it does so because there *is* wide-spread political support for such measures. While in practice this means that the great powers are always immune from UN sanctions, it does allow pressure to be brought to bear on smaller states, not as punitive measures for wrong-doing, but as an attempt to compel change. The prospect for such wide-spread support is, it is true, limited. But at the same time, the political requirement that the United Nations achieve consensus before proceeding has no doubt contributed to the continuing relevance of that organisation in international politics.

Conclusion

This brief essay has highlighted the fundamental philosophic differences that underlay the Covenant of the League and the Charter of the United Nations on the question of sanctions. It has argued that the notion of sanctions must be seen in both a classical - or juristic - sense as well as in its contemporary - or political - sense in order to distinguish between universal sanctions under the aegis of the League and sanctions under the United Nations.

In either case, however, universal sanctions will continue to fail. If employed in a juristic sense, as under the Covenant of the League, they will founder on the rocks of great power politics. If pressed upon great powers which commit delicts, at best the universal international organisation will cease to be universal, as the offending power will leave and, one assumes, will take its allies with it. At worst, the imposition of universal sanctions will become a casus belli, and the international system will drift or drop into general war.

If employed in a political context, as under the Charter of the United Nations, universal sanctions will atrophy as a means towards that larger end of the maintenance of peace and order in the international system. Only when there is wide consensus - a sufficient consensus to produce no negative vote from one of the permanent members of the Security Council - will the universal international organisation be able to impose universal sanctions on offending states. Rarely will there be the kind of constellation of circumstances that permits the relatively swift imposition of universal sanctions on a state like Rhodesia.[11] A more likely outcome is the continuation of the trend observed since 1946: the atrophy of this mechanism as a means to secure order.

Under either (one is tempted to say any) philosophic construct, universal sanctions are likely to founder because of the very nature of inter-state relations. Universal sanctions - like universal collective security to which sanctions are intended to contribute - depend for their success on Kantian assumptions about the interests of the political entities that compromise any international system. The rivalries of the major powers at the apex of the system persistently refuse to abate - in the contemporary era or in previous epochs. While there may be, as Hedley Bull convincingly shows,[12] some sense of community among the members of a states system, there is sufficient divergence of interest to bedevil attempts to secure a workable system of universal sanctions - juristic or political. Sixty-four years after the genesis of the initial experiment with universal sanctions, the interstate system remains as fractured as ever, each state jealously guarding that prized possession - its autonomy and its ability to define its interests independently.

Faced with a continuation of that basic condition, universal sanctions are likely either to collapse, League-like, in shambles, or simply to wither from disuse.

Notes

1. See, inter alia, Margaret P. Doxey, Economic Sanctions and International Enforcement rev. edn. (Oxford University Press, Toronto, 1980); Donald L. Losman, International Economic Sanctions: The Cases of Cuba, Israel and Rhodesia (University of New Mexico Press, Albuquerque, 1979); Royal Institute of International Affairs (RIIA), International Sanctions (Oxford University Press, London, 1938); M.V. Naidu, Collective Security and the United Nations (Macmillan, London, 1974), Ch. 4; Leonard T. Kapungu, The United Nations and Economic Sanctions Against Rhodesia (D.C. Heath, Lexington Mass., 1973).

2. David Baldwin, 'Interdependence and power: a conceptual analysis', in International Organization 34 (Autumn 1980).

3. For a juristic discussion of sanctions, see Hans Kelsen, The Law of the United Nations (Praeger, New York, 1950), pp. 706ff.

4. The Royal Institute of International Affairs, International Sanctions, p. 13.

5. Kelsen, Law of the United Nations, p. 726.

6. For a brief survey of these, see The Royal Institute of International Affairs, International Sanctions, pp. 10-12.

7. Kelsen, Law of the United Nations, pp. 711-12.

8. Ibid., pp. 720-4; Kelsen identifies two more, though, in his view, they do not rank as clear sanctions: one is the sanction imposed for refusing to comply with a judgement of the International Court of Justice (the Security Council can 'decide upon measures to be taken to give effect to the judgement' (Article 94.2)); the other is the sanction for the non-registration of treaties ('No party to any such treaty or international agreement which has not been registered in accordance with the provisions of paragraph 1 of this Article may invoke the treaty of agreement before any organ of the United Nations.' (Article 102.2)).

9. See Leland M. Goodrich, Edvard Hambro and Anne Patricia Simons, Charter of the United Nations: Commentary and Documents, 3rd rev. edn. (Columbia University Press, New York, 1969), pp. 342-53, for a discussion; also Kelsen, Law of the United Nations, pp. 708-9.

10. However, compare Kelsen, Law of the United Nations, pp. 735-7, who admits another interpretation: since general international law allows forcible interference into a state's sphere, either in the form of reprisals or in the form of war, only if a law has been broken (i.e. as a sanction), then the enforcement measures of Article 39, 41 and 42 'must be interpreted as sanctions if the Charter is supposed to be in conformity with general international law'.

11. See Kapungu, United Nations and Economic Sanctions, pp. 138-41; and Losman, International Economic Sanctions, pp. 121-3, for conclusions regarding Rhodesia.

12. Hedley Bull, The Anarchical Society: A Study of Order in World Politics (Columbia University Press, New York, 1977).

Chapter Three

UNITED NATIONS ECONOMIC SANCTIONS AGAINST SOUTH AFRICA AND RHODESIA

Douglas G. Anglin

Recent experience with the employment of external economic sanctions to effect domestic political change has seriously shattered the popular myth that they offer a cheap and easy (and not just morally acceptable) alternative to war as an instrument of national policy. Yet, paradoxically, the early 1980s have witnessed Western governments, faced with flagrant aggression and gross violations of human rights, responding with financial, food and other forms of economic leverage with increasing frequency. Iran, Afghanistan, Poland and the Falklands/Malvinas have all occasioned recourse to collective economic reprisals, while public pressure for coercive action against El Salvador, Israel and especially South Africa continues to mount. Despite the signal failure of international economic measures to topple the rebel regime of Ian Smith in Rhodesia 'within weeks not months', as Prime Minister Harold Wilson had rashly predicted,[1] faith in the persuasive potential of material deprivation remains surprisingly strong. Where doubts exist, they mainly concern the sufficiency of political will rather than the efficacy of the weapon itself.

This chapter seeks to probe the lessons of the Rhodesian sanctions experience, and apply them, where relevant, to an explanation of the possibilities of instituting meaningful enforcement measures against South Africa.

Rhodesian Sanctions

Part of the persisting appeal of sanctions is no doubt the opportunity they offer to indulge legitimately in a little bloodless headbashing. However, a more substantial argument in their defence is their overall record. This is not as dismal as sceptics generally assume, or as the victims pretend. Few targets of economic coercion have escaped unscathed from the encounter, and few potential targets would accept the prospect of sanctions with equanimity. Even in the case of Rhodesia, sanctions ultimately developed a healthy bite, and thus contributed significantly - though not decisively - to weakening the will and ability of the rebel regime to resist. The reason sanction efforts have acquired such a widely held reputation among the public for failure can often be traced to confusion surrounding their objectives. Certainly, conflicting perceptions of the purpose of the Rhodesia exercise proved a major cause of misunderstanding. Similar controversy continues to underlie much of the debate over sanctions against South Africa.

Objectives

Rarely has a rebellion received such advance publicity as Rhodesia's action in declaring independence from the United Kingdom unilaterally. When, following several false alarms during the course of 1964 and 1965, Ian Smith finally proclaimed Unilateral Declaration of Independence (UDI) on 11 November 1965, the decision came almost as an anti-climax. Yet, despite the months of warning, when the deed was eventually done, no firm consensus existed within the international community on how to respond to the challenge, beyond a vague determination to implement economic sanctions in some form. Basic to the problem of forging a credible and coherent strategy was lack of agreement between the United Kingdom, as the nominal colonial power, and a majority of United Nations members on what the proposed enforcement measures were intended to achieve.

Sanctions can be designed to serve a number of distinct and not necessarily mutually exclusive purposes. In practice, any particular package of measures is likely to embrace more than one objective, if only as the price of compromise. Moreover, however clearly the collective will may be expressed, individual states - in this case, notably the United Kingdom - almost invariably have national interests of their own that they seek to pursue. A further complication in defining the purpose of sanctions is that, if their application is prolonged as it was against Rhodesia, their rationale may evolve over time in response to changing circumstances. Nevertheless, analytically, it is possible to envisage five broad policy objectives that might serve to motivate the institution of sanctions measures. Not all are equally applicable to the Rhodesian situation.

1. Protest

In some circumstances, sanctions may be conceived as having no more than symbolic significance. Support for them becomes merely a means of expressing moral outrage, showing solidarity, upholding a vital principle, or boosting the national ego - without any serious expectation of their exerting any real pressure on the target state or perhaps even their being fully implemented. In this respect, they would be essentially no different from resolution rhetoric, public petitions, street demonstrations and unofficial boycotts - not that such gestures can be dismissed as unimportant. This is clearly not what the sponsors of Rhodesian sanctions had in mind, at least initially. By the early 1970s, however, by which time it had become painfully apparent that sanctions were not having their intended effect, the justification for their continuance had changed. Sanctions acquired an almost sacrosanct character. Any suggestion that they had outlived their usefulness generated fierce opposition, not least among those who were most vocal in decrying their ineffectiveness.[2] Prolonging the pretence was judged preferable to allowing the Rhodesians the psychological satisfaction and propaganda advantage they would gain from an open confession of failure.

2. Deterrence

A second possible purpose is as a preventive measure: the use of exemplary economic pressure - perhaps in the form of a slow turning of the screw or merely credible threats - as a signal to alert a prospective transgressor of the consequences and futility of breaching accepted norms of behaviour. As cognitive dissonance theory indicates,[3] human beings demonstrate an amazing capacity to see what they believe. Accordingly, a short, sharp shock in the form of carefully-designed psychological sanctions may be a prerequisite if individuals are to overcome their inherent reluctance to face reality and thereby restore a measure of cognitive consistency. Prior to UDI, suggestions that sanctions be imposed - and not merely threatened - in an attempt to deter rebellion were routinely rejected as likely to provoke the very outcome they sought to prevent. Consequently, Prime Minister Wilson confined himself to warning Mr Smith privately that any illegal seizure of independence would mean 'economic war'. Even so, much of the sting was taken out of his threat by his simultaneous undertaking not to intervene militarily.[4] Similarly, subsequent threats to use sanctions to check the increasing South African and Portuguese proclivities for sanction-breaking were consistently sidetracked.

3. Damage Control

Throughout the UDI crisis, suspicions concerning UK motives in Rhodesia ran deep, and justifiably so. African fears were fanned early by London's insistence on retaining responsibility for its wayward colony while, at the same time, pleading its inability to intervene effectively. When, therefore, the UK Labour government rushed to the Security Council in the immediate aftermath of UDI with a paltry package of sanctions proposals, critics promptly accused it of seeking to pre-empt any serious UN response. While subsequent UK initiatives to tighten the sanctions net helped to mollify African frustrations, there can be little doubt that a significant element in UK sanctions strategy was a determination to counter more sweeping (and more efficacious) proposals, especially the repeated and insistent demand for the use of force to crush the rebellion. As Prime Minister Wilson confessed to the House of Commons immediately after the UDI announcement:

> I think that the problem will be to avert excessive action by the United Nations. As for the economic sanctions, I think that it will be right for us to concentrate on trying to get others to follow our lead rather than seeing them get too far ahead of us.[5]

Accordingly, at each stage in the sanctions saga, the UK reaction was to concede only the bare minimum necessary to disarm critics and maintain a modicum of respectability. Subsequent revelations concerning massive UK collusion in oil sanction-busting[6] have vindicated African suspicions concerning the sincerity of successive UK governments in opposing the Smith regime vigorously. At the very least, they confirm the limited nature of the UK commitment, particularly once it became evident that a 'quick kill' was not feasible.

4. Reform

The declared aim of UK government policy was to persuade Rhodesian whites to repent, or at least reform. If Mr Smith and his supporters proved intractable, then perhaps sanctions could help to undermine his regime and contribute to the emergence of a more amenable successor leadership. As Sir Saville Garner, head of the United Kingdom's Commonwealth Relations Office and a principal architect of the sanctions strategy, explained, the objective was to bring about a 'change of heart in Rhodesia' by inducing

> a revulsion of feeling in the territory leading to the overthrow of the regime and its replacement by a government of moderates. Both the Governor and other well-placed observers were convinced that, if only the British showed that they meant business, loyalist opinion would rally and that there would be a popular demand for a change....Many of those most experienced in politics...were emphatic that Smith was a man of straw and did not have the support to lead

the country into rebellion.

More specifically, the United Kingdom appealed for a renunciation of rebellion, a 'return to legality', and a resumption of negotiations to work out a basis for independence 'acceptable to the people of Southern Rhodesia as a whole'. In Mr Wilson's mind, this did not necessarily imply majority rule. 'We seek no conclusion in Rhodesia,' he declared, 'except an honourable return to constitutional rule...with malice toward none, with no recrimination, in no punitive spirit'.[7] Although in 1966, much against his will, he was compelled, in the face of African threats to break up the Commonwealth as well as Mr Smith's incurable intransigence, to concede no independence before majority rule (NIBMAR), within a year he had succeeded in weaselling out of his solemn commitment.[8] In this connection, it is important to appreciate that the United Kingdom's overriding concern was not to reassert its (nominal) authority in Rhodesia, rather to disengage as rapidly as possible from its last major African colony, preferably with some semblance of dignity. Hence, the anxiety with which successive UK governments were prepared to settle or sell out on any terms that they felt they might get away with internationally.

Although the struggle for the hearts and minds of whites did not preclude the imposition of significant sanctions, it did require - in the opinion of London strategists - that they be introduced gradually and selectively, monitored closely, and reinforced by the judicious proferring of positive sanctions as inducements to change. The whole purpose of the exercise was to convert rather than to alienate those it was hoped to win over.[9] Yet, however rational and sophisticated this strategy might be, it was not an easy policy to sell to those sceptics who were already persuaded of UK half-heartedness, if not outright duplicity.

5. Coercion

For those who regarded Rhodesian whites as incorrigible racialists, incapable as well as unworthy of redemption, mere abandonment of independence was insufficient atonement for their sins. The cardinal issue in the conflict was racialism, not illegality. Accordingly, the only appropriate response to UDI was action to crush the minority regime swiftly, surely and decisively - preferably by military means, but otherwise by economic strangulation - whatever the cost to the Rhodesian economy. In some circles, there was also a demand for retribution - coercion for its own sake on the grounds that rebel perversity deserved severe punishment. Certainly, any settlement short of unconditional surrender and genuine black majority rule would amount to appeasement bordering on racialism. Hence, the insistence of a majority of UN members, led by the African states with the backing of the rest of the Third World as well as the Soviet bloc, that sanctions should be comprehensive, mandatory and immediate. The ensuing clash of ideologies and interests ensured that debates over the implementation, extension and termination of sanctions were long, bitter and frequently inconclusive.

Implementation

The three actors of primary importance in the implementation of Rhodesian sanctions were the United Kingdom (the evicted colonial power), Zambia (Rhodesia's most prosperous black neighbour and major market), and the UN Security Council (the executive arm of the organised conscience of the international community).

The United Kingdom

The United Kingdom was first off the mark with its schedule sanctions. Within hours of the UDI proclamation, Prime Minister Wilson banned the importation of Rhodesian tobacco and sugar (which accounted for 71 per cent of Rhodesian exports to the United Kingdom), withdrew Commonwealth tariff preferences and export insurance cover, expelled Rhodesia from the sterling area and blocked its assets in London, and barred it from access to capital markets. Subsequently, sanctions on additional strategic imports and financial transactions were tightened (1 December), an embargo on oil shipments was instituted (17 December), and the ban extended to other UK exports (30 January). In addition, the United Kingdom, in exercise of its formal legal sovereignty, assumed direct rule (on paper) over Rhodesia. It then proceeded to assert its theoretical authority by taking over the Reserve Bank of Rhodesia, repealing press censorship there, banning key Rhodesian exports to any destination, and indulging in other acts of fantasy which had some legal significance but no practical importance.[10]

Although competence was not the outstanding characteristic distinguishing London's conduct of economic warfare against Rhodesia,[11] the United Kingdom did have a reasonably coherent strategy it was attempting to pursue. This comprised four related elements:

1. Sanctions were concentrated on Rhodesian exports (and financial transfers) rather than imports with the intention of eroding foreign exchange earnings, precipitating a balance of payments crisis, inducing a reces-

sion and unemployment in the export sectors, and thereby threatening the inflexible consumption patterns and comfortable life-style of luxury-loving Rhodesian whites.[12]

2. Specific sanctions were selected with a view to their impact on interest groups in a position to exert effective pressure on the regime, in particular, the tobacco farmers (who formed the backbone of the ruling Rhodesian Front (RF)) and the business community (who were assumed to wield significant economic clout). The difficulties with this political diagnosis were twofold: the tobacco growers, though badly hit financially, were in no position to abandon either their livelihoods or their leader; and the capitalist class had already been largely excluded from power, having consistently opposed UDI and backed unsuccessful opposition challenges to the RF's monopoly of power.[13]
3. Imports which constituted key inputs into the economy were singled out for sanctioning, notably oil and foreign capital (though crucially and consciously not intra-firm transfers).
4. Finally, the selection and pace of introduction of sanctions was dictated by a concern to avoid a political backlash in Rhodesia (as well as in the United Kingdom), to steer clear of any confrontation with South Africa, and to minimise damage to the Rhodesian economy, on the optimistic assumption that the crisis would be ended and normality quickly restored.[14]

Zambia

Rhodesia's land-locked black neighbours posed a particular dilemma. Not only were some of them among its most important trading partners, they were also highly vulnerable to Rhodesian retaliatory action. Zambia's situation was especially difficult. It provided a market for more than one-quarter of Rhodesia's exports (Table 3.1), and an even higher proportion of its manufactured goods. At the same time, Zambia was dependent on Rhodesia Railways for the carriage of 65 per cent of its imports and 96 per cent of its exports, principally copper. In addition, Rhodesia supplied all Zambia's oil (from the Feruka refinery) and coal (from Wankie) as well as 69 per cent of its electricity (from Kariba).[15]

With the intimate economic interdependence of these neighbours north and south of the Zambezi - a legacy of the defunct Federation of Rhodesia and Nyasaland - Zambian participation became essential to the success of any sanctions undertaking. Yet, Zambia could survive a confrontation, even as a seige economy, only if it were sustained by a massive international rescue operation, as envisaged in

TABLE 3-1

RHODESIAN DOMESTIC EXPORTS, 1964-1981

Year	Indices: 1964=100 Volumes	Value	Value Rh$m.	Destination: Value (Rh$m.) and Percentage Zambia		Britain		South Africa	
1964	100.00	100.00	$230.4	$61.6	26.8%	$61.0	26.5%	$18.00	7.8%
1965	112.8	104.1	278.4	71.1	25.5	62.4	22.4	26.9	9.7
1966	72.3	94.6	171.0	46.4	27.1	9.1	5.4		
1967	75.0	91.4	169.9	32.2	19.0	0.3	0.2		
1968	74.0	93.3	167.5	22.6	13.5	0.2	0.1		
1969	84.5	99.3	212.2	21.8	10.3	0.1	0.1		
1970	92.1	102.2	245.1	20.6	8.4				
1971	101.6	103.9	266.3	21.1	7.9				
1972	121.7	104.4	322.2	10.6	3.3				
1973	124.3	113.9	377.8	6.9	1.8				
1974	129.5	149.2	482.1	0.5	0.1				
1975	121.2	159.5	477.7	-	-				
1976	121.8	166.5	518.2	-	-				
1977	115.7	173.2	500.8	-	-				
1978	120.3	184.2	558.7	-	-				
1979	118.7	211.7	645.4						
1980	113.0	280.6	787.5	3.8*	1.3	18.7*	6.6	59.4*	21.0*
1981	106.9	307.8	888.1	35.3	4.0	61.3	6.9	192.2	21.6

*August-December 1980; total exports for that period: $282.6m

Sources: Economic Survey of Rhodesia for 1965; Rhodesia/Zimbabwe, Monthly Digest of Statistics; Zambia, Annual Statement of External Trade.

Article 49 of the UN Charter. Although contingency planning for such an eventuality had been underway with the United Kingdom and subsequently the United States for nearly a year, UDI found Zambia without any solid assurance that the necessary support would be forthcoming. In any case, President Kenneth Kaunda was properly sceptical that sanctions could succeed and, accordingly, pressed the United Kingdom strongly to intervene militarily. Nevertheless, spurning Mr Smith's seductive offer to spare Zambia economic disaster on condition that it opted out of sanctions, President Kaunda bravely, even rashly, agreed to put his country and his people at risk in the greater interest of Rhodesian liberation.

The initial instalment of Zambian trade and financial sanctions, although modest, were neither insignificant nor painless. Repeal of Commonwealth preferences, for instance, had an immediate impact on the cost of living. The full application of sanctions, however, depended on three conditions being met: first, an emergency oil airlift; second, the development of alternative road and rail routes; and, finally, a guarantee that, when the crunch came, Zambia would not be allowed to collapse while waiting for Rhodesia to surrender. The first condition was met by a hastily mounted Berlin-style Anglo-American-Canadian airlift which, at great expense, enabled Zambia to survive the first critical months following Rhodesia's act of reprisal in cutting off oil supplies to Zambia in retaliation for the imposition of UN oil sanctions. The United Kingdom also, somewhat grudgingly, assisted Zambia materially and financially to reorganise its lifelines to the sea, though few other countries offered support, except rhetorically. Where plans came unstuck was over the projected operation 'quick kill', timed for 15 February 1966 and intended to bring Mr Smith to his knees 'within weeks not months'. Faced with the awesome implications of such an endeavour, the UK government simply opted out. Consequently, the deadline for Zambia to cut off all trade with Rhodesia passed uneventfully.[16] Despite this setback, Zambia continued to reduce its economic and other ties with Rhodesia until 1973, when it finally closed its southern border (until 1978, when a serious maize crisis compelled a partial reopening) (Table 3.2).

United Nations

Meanwhile, the United Nations had entered the sanctions arena. Its increasing involvement was marked by three fairly well-defined stages. Although the United Kingdom took the initiative in raising the issue in the Security Council, armed with the veto they fought a skilful rear-guard action to ensure that control of the operation did not

TABLE 3-2

RHODESIAN IMPORTS, 1964-1981

Year	Indices: 1964=100 Volumes	Value	Value Rh$m.	Source: Value (Rh$m.) and Percentage Zambia		Britain		South Africa	
1964	100.00	100.00	$216.6	$10.8	5.0%	$66.8	30.8%	$53.4	24.7%
1965	106.9	103.5	239.6	8.6	3.7	72.8	30.4	54.0	22.5
1966	68.7	114.0	169.5	4.1	2.4	5.5	3.2		
1967	76.0	113.8	187.1	1.5	0.8	2.1	1.1		
1968	85.4	112.0	207.1	0.7	0.4	1.4	0.7		
1969	80.8	114.1	199.5	0.3	0.2	1.4	0.7		
1970	91.0	119.2	235.0	0.5	0.2	0.9	0.4		
1971	102.7	127.1	282.5	0.3	0.1	1.1	0.4		
1972	102.0	124.4	274.7	1.0	0.4	1.1	0.4		
1973	110.0	129.6	308.6	0.3	0.1				
1974	114.6	176.6	438.3	0.3	0.1				
1975	109.3	195.1	461.9	0.4	0.1				
1976	79.9	221.1	382.7	0.2	0.1				
1977	73.6	243.6	388.1	-	-				
1978	67.3	276.9	403.7	9.0	2.2				
1979	66.4	379.0	549.3						
1980	91.4	406.1	809.4	10.4*	2.7	32.2*	8.4	104.7*	27.4
1981	114.1	403.6	1027.7	24.6	2.4	101.9	9.9	279.7	27.2

*August-December 1980; total imports for that period: $382.2m

Sources: Economic Survey of Rhodesia for 1965; Rhodesia/Zimbabwe, Monthly Digest of Statistics; Zambia, Annual Statement of External Trade.

slip from their hands and sanctions become dangerously effective. Nevertheless, they were gradually compelled to retreat in the face of UN pressure. Whereas initially the Security Council merely called upon all states 'to do their utmost in order to break all economic relations' with Rhodesia (S/RES/217, 20 November 1965), the failure of voluntary sanctions forced the Security Council a year later to impose selective mandatory sanctions in a precedent-setting decision that declared the Rhodesian rebellion 'a threat to international peace and security' under Article 39 of the Charter (S/RES/232, 16 December 1966). Then, in May 1968, following a particularly flagrant instance of Rhodesian defiance of world public opinion, the list of mandatory economic measures was made 'comprehensive' (S/RES/253, 29 May 1968). Nevertheless, at UK insistence, important omissions including postal and telecommunication ties remained. The real defect, however, was the absence of any provision to compel the more notorious sanction-breakers to respect their legal obligations to comply with Security Council orders.

Impact

On paper, Rhodesia approximated to the ideal target for the application of sanctions. It was a small, land-locked country with an open and fairly sophisticated economy and a white population of only 225,000. By all the standard coefficients of economic dependence, it was unusually vulnerable to external pressure and, at the same time, incapable of creating by way of reprisals more than a minor inconvenience for any of its principal trading partners, with the single exception of Zambia. Exports accounted for 38 per cent of Rhodesia's gross national product (GNP) and imports represented 34 per cent (compared with 23 per cent and 21 per cent in the case of Canada). Moreover, trade was heavily concentrated on a few partners and a limited range of products: Zambia and the United Kingdom provided markets for 48 per cent of exports, and the United Kingdom and South Africa supplied 53 per cent of imports. In terms of commodities, tobacco represented 46 per cent of exports, and machinery and transport equipment 32 per cent of imports. If ever there was an opportunity to demonstrate the efficacy of sanctions, the Rhodesian rebellion appeared to be it.[17]

The theory of sanctions postulates a dual linkage: between external trade and economic deprivation, and between economic deprivation and political change.[18] The effectiveness of sanctions in practice can, therefore, be appropriately assessed in terms of their impact on the material well-being of Rhodesian whites and, more importantly, the extent to which sanctions induced a greater measure of political flexibility and realism. In each case, the results were problematic.

Economic Deprivation

The capacity of the Rhodesian economy to absorb the shock of sanctions varied over time and from sector to sector. Three phases can be distinguished (Tables 3.1 to 3.3).[19] Until 1969 exports declined steadily in volume (by 27 per cent) and in value (by 42 per cent), with agricultural products (notably tobacco and sugar) particularly severely hit. On the other hand, manufacturing suffered a less serious slump, and mining was scarcely affected at all. With respect to white employment and incomes, the overall impact was modest and certainly less than had been feared.Moreover, by defaulting on its overseas debts and blocking the payment of dividends owed to overseas investors (but not South Africans), the country ironically actually succeeded in profiting from financial sanctions to improve its balance of payments situation. The government was also able to exploit the valuable breathing space that the leisurely adoption of sanctions provided to devise effective countermeasures and restore business confidence. As a result, by the end of the 1960s, all the economic indicators pointed to the corner having been turned. Between 1968 and 1974, GNP recorded an impressive average annual increase of nearly 9 per cent. Rhodesia, according to one analyst,

> was one of the world's boom economies....The value of mineral production was increasing rapidly. There was a healthy trade surplus and a rapid increase in tourism. By this time a steady increase was also being achieved in overall employment...[20]

The domestic manufacturing sector, in particular, appeared positively to prosper under adversity. Even the depressed tobacco industry continued to acount for 10 per cent of the world market, compared with its previous 27 per cent share,[21] with the shortfall more than compensated for by diversification into maize, wheat, cattle and especially cotton.

By the mid-1970s, however, the cumulative strain of a decade or more of economic warfare was beginning to take its toll. The rebel regime's final five-year lease of life saw stagnation set in with per capita incomes falling by 12 per cent in real terms, 'thus wiping out much of the real improvements in standards of living' made since 1966.[22] Virtually every other indicator of economic performance recorded similar disturbing declines, despite the cushioning effect of South African soft loans.

Only a fraction of this downturn can be attributed to

sanctions biting belatedly. More critical, undoubtedly, were the world recession following the escalation in the cost of oil (which led to a reintroduction of gasoline rationing in February 1974 after having been abandoned in 1971) and especially the intensification of the liberation struggle which, among other things, increased defence expenditures 'at a rapid annual rate of 35 per cent between 1972 and 1980'.[23] Nevertheless, the contribution of sanctions cannot be entirely discounted. While they were not the decisive weapons their authors anticipated, neither was their impact negligible, especially in the long run. It seems likely, however, that it was not so much trade sanctions *per se* that wore down the Rhodesians, as the shortage of foreign exchange for capital renewal. As *The Economist* has argued:

> It was Rhodesia's inability to raise long-term credit on the international capital market that put the biggest economic strain on its resources and this, together with the civil war, brought its recalcitrant politicians to the negotiating table.[24]

A number of attempts have been made to quantify the real costs of sanctions. D. G. Clarke has conservatively estimated the loss of investment capital resulting from the necessity to pay a 15 to 20 per cent premium on imports and to absorb a similar discount on exports at Rh $915 million or over one-quarter of the actual net capital inflow. He concludes that the cumulative effect - albeit long delayed - of the forfeiting of this potential investment on profits, employment and poverty was economically very damaging.[25] E. G. Cross, adopting a different approach based on lost export earnings, has assessed sanctions-induced costs considerably higher at $3,600 million or 38 per cent. However, he notes that gross national income declined only $1,500 million or 6 per cent. 'This represents $10 per capita per annum and suggests that the programme had little or no effect on the population group against which the sanctions programme was directed and who were responsible for UDI.'[26]

Political Change

Measuring the extent of political behaviour modification attributable to sanctions is even more hazardous than calculating their economic impact. Nevertheless, two criteria suggest themselves: the degree of stability of white support for Mr Smith; and the willingness of the regime to negotiate an end to the impasse.

With respect to the political loyalty of the electorate, the evidence is overwhelming that sanctions proved counter-productive to change - precisely as Galtung predicted.[27] Far from demoralising or dividing white opinion, they encouraged a hardening of hawkish attitudes, a closing of racial ranks and a greater willingness to accept sacrifices. Even the internal business opposition 'quickly wilted under pragmatic necessities, compliance requirements under new legislation, and potential or implied threats from the administration'.[28] By 1968 the judiciary too had conceded de jure recognition to the illegal regime.[29] The one measure of white morale that did reveal some degree of dissatisfaction, though only during the later years of the rebellion, was the trend of figures on those that voted with their feet (Table 3.3). During the first seven years of 'independence', the rate of emigration actually declined and, except for 1966, immigration numbers increased annually. However, by 1972 emigration figures began to climb, eventually forcing the government to cut back on emigrants' remittances. This was followed, in 1976, by a fall-off in immigration. Since then, the annual net outflow of whites has been substantial. Nevertheless, over the period of UDI, 133,000 settled in Rhodesia - nearly half the white population - compared with only 121,000 who abandoned the country (usually for the security of South Africa).

Almost from the outset of UDI, the United Kingdom sought to coax Ian Smith back to the conference table and, on three occasions - in 1966, 1968 and 1971 - he consented. In each instance, it can be argued, he acted under a certain measure of economic compulsion induced by sanctions. In 1968 Mr Smith even publicly confessed a willingness to resume negotiations 'in order to try and terminate the economic war which is being waged between Britain and Rhodesia to the detriment of both countries'.[30] Yet the pressure was never great enough to compel him to qualify his absolute rejection of 'unimpeded progress toward majority rule'. Rather, it was a case of a confident Smith 'talking without negotiating'[31] with the frustrated United Kingdom, in its increasing impatience to disengage, offering successively more retrogressive concessions. Only Mr Smith's blind intransigence saved the United Kingdom from outright sell-outs in 1966 and 1968, while in 1971 it was the unexpected militancy of the African majority - which for the first time was consulted concerning its fate - that vetoed the notorious Home-Smith agreement to legitimise UDI. Thereafter, other actors entered the arena and negotiations became more complicated. Nevertheless, in the fierce political jockeying that characterised the years 1974 to 1979, the state of the economy was a powerful constraint on Rhodesia's room for manoeuvre. A significant part of the credit for whatever verbal concessions Mr Smith was forced to voice must go to sanctions. Moreover, the maintenance of sanctions proved a critical ingredient in the success of

TABLE 3-3

RHODESIAN ECONOMIC INDICATORS, 1964-1980

YEAR	GROSS NATIONAL PRODUCT constant (1965) prices		VISIBLE BALANCE OF EXTERNAL TRADE				EUROPEAN MIGRATION
	total Rh$m.	per capita Rh$	Rh$m.	Commercial Agriculture (1964 prices)	Manufacturing volume	Mining volume	net recorded
1964	$ 678	$155	$ 58.2	100.0	100.0	100.0	-8,710
1965	711	158	83.2	93.2	108.9	110.8	2,280
1966	692	149	18.6	113.4	98.9	108.2	-2,090
1967	798	167	1.3	117.7	107.7	116.4	2,050
1968	812	164	-14.8	97.4	117.8	114.8	6,210
1969	929	181	31.3	129.6	132.9	139.8	5,040
1970	985	182	23.8	122.3	148.7	158.7	6,331
1971	1098	195	7.8	154.9	160.3	169.5	9,407
1972	1204	206	74.4	168.0	184.3	174.8	8,825
1973	1241	206	80.5	140.1	199.3	192.3	1,682
1974	1357	220	92.8	174.7	213.2	186.9	580
1975	1338	213	69.4	169.4	211.2	189.0	1,928
1976	1319	203	174.7	182.7	199.1	205.8	-7,072
1977	1221	182	162.7	168.8	187.4	196.3	-10,908
1978	1183	171	205.6	167.1	182.5	186.2	-13,709
1979	1187	166	166.4	164.8	202.1	185.3	-9,557
1980	1370	186	99.8	185.0	232.2	181.4	-10,833*

*includes Blacks

Source: Zimbabwe Monthly Digest of Statistics; Renwick, Economic Sanctions, p. 99

the final Lancaster House negotiations. Thus, sanctions can claim to have contributed to the defeat of minority rule, but not to have determined the outcome. The decisive factors were undoubtedly the economic impact of the war, the oil price hike and Pretoria's penchant for flexing its economic muscle periodically as a reminder of its regional hegemony.

Influences

United Nations sanctions against Rhodesia were adopted and applied more extensively, intensively and over a longer period of time, than on any other occasion in history. Yet, despite the apparent vulnerability of the target to external pressure, the most that can be said of the great experiment is that - whatever its assumed objectives - it proved less than completely successful. How can this comparative failure be explained? Two broad sets of factors conditioned the course of events: the ingenuity of Rhodesians in devising counter-measures, and the sins of omission and commission of powerful international actors.

Counter-measures

A basic element in the sanctions strategy employed against Rhodesia was the conviction that production and consumption patterns were inflexible. This assumption proved surprisingly wide of the mark. In part, this was due to the piecemeal implementation of sanctions that provided the country with a valuable breathing space during which to adapt economically and psychologically to its new circumstances. As a result, the UDI years witnessed dramatic structural changes in the Rhodesian economy. Internally, an imaginative import substitution drive and diversification programme, especially in manufacturing but also in agriculture, along with stringent import controls and some belt-tightening, enabled the country to contain its chronic foreign exchange problem within manageable proportions. In addition, deliberate and effective action was taken to shift the burden of sanctions, especially redundancies, onto the black majority. At the same time, remarkable resourcefulness was displayed in circumventing sanctions and capitalising on the inability of foreign entrepreneurs, corporations and governments to resist the temptation to profit from Rhodesia's plight. Falsification of certificates of origin, inaccurate bills of lading and other unethical practices became standard procedures.

Evasions

Three principal motives appear to account for the systematic and wide-spread evasion of sanctions: political sympathy, commercial greed and the costs of compliance. Apart from the United States - whose Congress, responding to powerful pro-Rhodesian interests, adopted the Byrd Amendment which lifted the ban on the importation of Rhodesian chrome between 1972 and 1977[32] - the major countries to flout sanctions openly were (Portuguese) Mozambique and especially South Africa. Each of these neighbours of Rhodesia had ideological and strategic as well as economic reasons to fear the success of sanctions and, therefore, was prepared to risk defying world opinion. Their support proved decisive; without it, it is inconceivable that the rebellion could have survived many weeks, let alone months. Just how dependent Salisbury was on Pretoria's goodwill, especially following the collapse of the Portuguese colonial regime in 1974 and the closure of the Mozambique-Rhodesia border two years later, became apparent in August and September 1976 when Prime Minister Vorster briefly imposed crippling economic (and military) sanctions on Mr Smith to compel him to accept - verbally - the Kissinger formula for a transition to majority rule within two years.[33]

The behaviour of most sanction violators was much less complicated. Although some UK Conservatives retained close personal and political ties with Rhodesia, the motivation of most UK businessmen involved in sanction-busting, along with their counterparts in the Federal Republic of Germany, Italy, France, Japan, Switzerland and elsewhere, including the Soviet bloc, was totally unprincipled and mercenary. In their scramble to outstrip each other in cheating, they acted in open contempt of their governments' supposedly solemn commitments to honour their moral and legal obligations and, as often as not, worked in secret collusion with these governments. The whole sorry tale must surely rank as one of the shabbiest and most shameful episodes of this century.The UK Labour government's carefully concealed double-dealing was the most deceitful of all countries involved in sanctions violations, though not the most successful.

Costs

Although the United Kingdom contributed its share to sabotaging sanctions, it ultimately paid a heavy price for them. What the final bill amounted to is probably impossible to calculate. Prime Minister Wilson, on one occasion, assessed the loss during the first year of UDI alone at over $250 million.[34] Certainly, the steadily escalating cost of the Rhodesian commitment was a constant concern to London, especially with the rebellion apparently dragging on indefinitely and the UK economy staggering from one sterling crisis to another. This preoccupation with cost seriously constrained the government's ability to act boldly and effectively. It also severely soured relations with Zambia.

Zambia was without any doubt the principal casualty of sanctions. Although President Kaunda had little faith in them, he was *faute de mieux* prepared to play the UK game - provided London assumed responsibility for its fair share of the financial burden. The United Kingdom, however, insisted that there should be a ceiling on its contribution. Its grudging attitude so enraged the Zambian government that, on one occasion in June 1966, its spokesman bluntly accused them, with considerable justification, of waging economic warfare 'with limited commitments...with limited determination and with limited sincerity'.[35]

Since the United Kingdom was ultimately unwilling, or possibly unable, to provide Zambia with the minimum life-support necessary to survive in a showdown with Rhodesia, it was forced to abandon its strategy of looking to Mr Kaunda to administer the *coup de grace* in the sanctions campaign. Despite this, Zambia continued, at great cost to its development hopes, to disengage progressively from Rhodesia as rapidly and completely as possible (Tables 3.1 and 3.2) and, at the same time, to increase its support for Zimbabwe liberation movements. When in January 1973 Prime Minister Smith somewhat precipitately closed his northern border as a punitive measure, President Kaunda decided without hesitation - much against UK advice - to keep it closed (until compelled by a threat of starvation to reopen it in 1978). According to an official UN estimate, the cost to the country of this defiant action totalled some $800 million.[36]

If President Kaunda had expected the international community to rally to his assistance, he was soon disabused. United Kingdom contingency aid, while never adequate, compared very favourably with the meagre contributions from other states. Although Zambia (unlike Botswana and Portugal) never formally sought exemption from UN sanctions under Article 50 of the Charter, it did appeal to the world for assistance 'as a matter of priority' in overcoming the 'special economic problems' it faced in implementing sanctions fully.[37] There was no lack of sympathy for Zambia's dilemma. In addition to the United Nations, the Organisation of African Unity (OAU) and the Commonwealth regularly called on their members to come to Zambia's aid, and both set up special committees to mobilise international resources. The response, however, in financial and material terms was almost inconsequential. Certainly, it came nowhere near to matching the need. Moreover, at the same time as Zambians were accepting sacrifices in the common cause, many UN members were shamelessly violating sanctions with profit and impunity.

Enforcement

No country campaigned harder to ensure that other UN members lived up to their sanctions obligations than the United Kingdom. In undertaking this unpopular task, it received little support from either the African states (which had always been sceptical of sanctions succeeding) or other Western European states and Japan (which, apart from the Nordic countries, felt only a limited commitment to respect sanctions, especially as they suspected - correctly - that the United Kingdom itself was guilty of wide-spread evasion). Admittedly, the United Kingdom could claim more successful prosecutions of individuals and firms indulging in sanction-busting than in the whole of the rest of the world - including Canada, where both a defective law and a lackadaisical enforcement agency made the exercise something of a farce. Yet, most of those caught in the UK net were comparatively small fry. The big fish - notably Shell-BP - escaped unscathed, with the government excusing its monumental incompetence (to state it most charitably) on the feeble grounds that the guilty companies had failed to report their illegal activities. No effective action was taken to interfere with the 'business as usual' operations of UK subsidiaries in Rhodesia. To do so would have required the Labour government to declare war on the City of London. This it felt unable to do. As a result, UK firms were conspicuous in propping up virtually every sector of the Rhodesian economy.[38]

The UK government's suspicions that its friends and allies were winning the race to circumvent sanctions was an important factor in its reluctant decision to abandon its opposition to mandatory sanctions.[39] Its original objection, however, remained. Accordingly, it was adamant that sanctions, though mandatory, should not be enforced against the two principal offenders: South Africa and Mozambique.[40] This immunity also left UK firms in these countries free to trade with Rhodesia. The reason for the United Kingdom's scandalous laxity was more economic than ideological; the state of the UK economy was too precarious to withstand a severing of 'the South African connection'. For a majority of UN members, however, Pretoria and Lisbon were the prime targets. When successive attempts to extend sanctions to sanction-breakers, or at least to blockade Maputo in addition to Beira, fell foul of UK vetoes or threats,[41] there was little enthusiasm left to make the UN Sanctions Committee effective. Despite the enormous effort that went into the committee's twelve annual reports,[42] it never managed to so much as name the chief villains. The most thorough investigations into the character and scale of the international conspiracy against sanctions were undertaken by journalists and church groups, with the assistance of aberrant tycoons such as LONRHO's Tiny Rowland and Mozambique's Jorge Jardim, both of whom were themselves deeply implicated.[43]

Global Economy

The implications for the success of sanctions in light of the weakness of the UK economy highlights a final factor - the state of the world economy - which influenced the outcome of the operation. Since Rhodesia was incapable of achieving complete self-reliance, it continued to be powerfully affected by global economic forces, notably the deterioration in the terms of trade, the escalation in the price of oil and the deepening recession of the 1970s. Indeed, the forces of supply and demand, as reflected in the import premiums and export discounts it was compelled to accept, impinged on Rhodesia with amplified effect. Those contemplating sanctions would do well to remember that the global economic climate can inject a further hazardous element, essentially beyond the control of any of the actors, into the calculation of costs and benefits.

Unintended Consequences

The 14 years of economic warfare against Rhodesia were rich in unforeseen developments. Almost nothing went according to expectations. This was as true of the implementation of sanctions internationally as of their impact on the target regime. The lesson learned from this experience must surely be how uncertain an instrument of foreign policy the sanctions weapon can be in the hands of amateurs.

Impact

Sanctions proved neither as decisive as anticipated nor as swift in taking effect as intended. In fact, almost a decade transpired - by which time most people had abandoned hope for their success - before they began to bite economically, let alone politically. Even then, the results were not quite what had been predicted. The effects were felt as much or more in the spheres of employment and investment as on trade.[44] As an official Zimbabwean assessment explains, the 'relative failure' of sanctions can be attributed 'in large measure...to the relative failure in making a significant impact on the balance of payments question'.[45] Controversy also continues concerning their precise contribution, as compared to other influences, notably the guerrilla war. Certainly, when the regime eventually began to crumble, it was not because the white electorate or its leaders had finally been persuaded of the merits of majority rule. Rather, it was a case of all other options having been foreclosed. The optimistic Wilson scenario that envisaged moderate whites waiting in the wings, ready and 'anxious to make themselves known at the right moment' and take over the reins of power never materialised. As Sir Saville Garner later conceded, the hope of 'replacing the illegal regime' was based on a complete miscalculation at least in any short term'.[46] In any case, if the intention was to encourage a liberal revival - which was never a realistic possibility - driving the Rhodesians further into the arms of the South Africans, politically as well as economically, did not help.[47] On the other hand, it must be conceded that resource constraints did check the efforts of RF ideologues intent on reorganising Rhodesian society more on the pattern of apartheid South Africa.

Perhaps the greatest single surprise was the comparative ease with which the Rhodesians not only managed to minimise the adverse impact of sanctions on their economy, but appeared to prosper positively in the process. During much of the first decade, Rhodesia was an embarrassingly 'high performer'. The secret of its success has important implications for the development strategies of other Third World countries. According to one white Zimbabwean:

> The main lesson of the Rhodesian experience in terms of the impact of foreign trade flows on the domestic economic activity is that the static marginal gains from international trade are limited....[This] points to the need to go beyond simply encouraging foreign investment in export-oriented industry if the real economic potential of a nation is to be realized...strict control over the use of foreign exchange to limit the import of non-essential goods and food...can play a major role in the development of local industry.[48]

Of course, one reason the white sector of the economy was able to escape the full rigours of sanctions was its skill in shifting the burden to the African majority, and especially the peasant population, through 'fiscal changes, direct subsidies, a move towards indirect taxation, and state support for affected enterprises and potentially unemployed persons' in the 'political target group'.[49] The hardships that sanctions imposed on the African masses did not, however, dampen their nationalist fervour, as the United Kingdom found to its chagrin when the Pearce Commission sounded out opinion in 1972.[50]

Instrument

The naivete of those who launched the sanctions exercise is bound, in hindsight, to occasional amazement. To begin with, they seriously underestimated the incentive which sanctions offered unscrupulous interests prepared to take advantage of the restraint of others to engage in sanction busting. They also failed to face up squarely to the need to assert physical control over the sources of supply and especially the communication routes on which Rhodesia relied. The pathetic charade of the Royal Navy dutifully blockading Beira for nine long years (at a cost of $250 million), while completely ignoring Rhodesia's flourishing trade through nearby Maputo, is only the most dramatic illustration of the contradiction that bedevilled the whole botched operation. Another fundamental weakness in the implementation of sanctions was the culpable behaviour of governments in declining to control the economic activities of their multinationals, especially those that continued to operate inside Rhodesia.[51] As the Rhodesian Minister of Transport and Power once bragged: 'whatever any particular government says, of course, is quite different to what their businessmen do and this is precisely how Rhodesia...is winning the war'.[52]

If the UK government had foreseen that sanctions would remain in force for 14 long years, it is doubtful if it would have embarked on them quite so readily and confidently. Their long life had several serious and unwelcome consequences, not least the cumulative costs that participants incurred. Economic sanctions did not prove the cheap (or quick and easy) weapon their sponsors had counted on. The price Zambia has paid has been particularly steep; it has emerged from the encounter permanently scarred, with its economy unlikely ever to recover fully.

On the other hand, sanctions can claim some credit for the fact that the rebellion was ultimately defeated. Moreover, Prime Minister Wilson's alarmist fears that UDI would open the door to Soviet and Chinese penetration of Zimbabwe have proved unfounded.[53] In the end, the Western powers succeeded in extricating themselves from the shambles of sanctions remarkably skilfully and unscathed. Their interests have, in fact, been salvaged substantially intact - more so than their dubious record on sanctions observance entitled them to expect. It is unlikely, on present indications, that they can count on similar luck when the day of reckoning comes in South Africa.

South African Sanctions

The issue of sanctions against South Africa has been hotly debated for two decades or more, with little likelihood of it being resolved in the foreseeable future.[54] Certainly, the United Nation's proclamation of 1982 as the 'International Year of Mobilization of Sanctions against South Africa' failed to advance the cause very far. Yet, although there is no immediate possibility of serious sanctions being adopted, as long as apartheid persists demands for international action to end it will continue and intensify. Within South Africa, the attitude of the government to the prospect reveals considerable ambivalence, if not paranoia. The official line is that they pose no threat, practically or economically; sanctions will not work and cannot work. At the same time, the enormous international propaganda effort devoted to ridiculing them or, alternatively, to claiming that the blacks would suffer most, indicates the extent to which Pretoria is almost pathologically preoccupied with the issue. Foreign Minister Pik Botha has even warned South Africans to expect the inevitable. 'It is time we must accept', he declared in 1980, 'that sanctions are going to come.'[55]

The South African government has provided ample provocation to invite sanctions upon itself. Apart from its deplorable record as the leading sanction-buster in Rhodesia, its continued illegal 'belligerent occupation' of Namibia, its systematic efforts to destabilise its black neighbours through military incursions, subversion and economic domination, and its ever more rigorous enforcement of apartheid domestically despite the facade of reform, could all qualify as 'threats to international peace and security' in terms of Chapter VII of the UN Charter. Indeed, in the aftermath of the Soweto massacres, the Security Council, on the initiative of its Western members, did declare in 1977 that South Africa's massive military build-up constituted such a threat, and accordingly imposed a mandatory arms embargo on it - the only occasion on which the United Nations has applied obligatory enforcement measures against one of its members. Since 1963 the ban had been merely voluntary and, as often as not, observed in the breach. At the same time, the Western powers once again vetoed African demands for a total economic blockade on the grounds that it constituted a counsel of despair.[56]

The stubborn refusal of successive UK and US governments, regardless of party, to contemplate meaningful economic measures against South Africa imposes severe limitations on what is presently politically possible. In these circumstances, rather than approaching the problem in terms of what is ideally desirable, it may be more profitable to explore what can be achieved with the restricted arsenal of economic weapons which are realistically available. Pending a reassessment of Western priorities, pursuit of the perfect may prove the enemy of the possible, and the alternative to doing nothing may mean settling for the barely satisfying rather than the fully satisfying. In surveying the range of sanctions options, three criteria define the parameters of the possible:

1. their political acceptablity to the major Western powers;
2. the likelihood of the principal economic actors

concerned actually implementing the designated measures; and

3. their prospective impact on the target population, economically and in other respects.

In considering these conditions in the context of South Africa, it is useful to compare the difficulties likely to be encountered with those experienced in Rhodesia.[57] Despite their geographical propinquity and shared histories, the situations of the two countries are in many respects quite different. In some respects, South Africa poses fewer complications. Its economy is more modern and complex and, therefore, more vulnerable to external pressure (and sabotage). More important, it has no friendly neighbours ready and able to come to its rescue. There might be some slippage through border states, especially Mozambique which, even prior to the Nkomati Accord, regularly served as a conduit for illicit trade with Africa and elsewhere. However, in general, physical control of communications with the outside world should prove easier than in the case of Rhodesia. On the other hand, South Africa is a much bigger nut to crack with a white population of 4.5 million compared with under a quarter of a million, and has a much stronger and more diversified economy. Most coefficients of trade concentration indicate that South Africa is less dependent on external partners than was Rhodesia. Admittedly in the case of trade as a proportion of GNP, the difference is not great: 65 per cent as compared with 72 per cent. A more significant measure is the country concentration. Here, the two major markets account for only 14 per cent of exports (instead of 48 per cent) and the two principal sources of supply provide only 22 per cent of imports (instead of 53 per cent). Moreover, for the past 20 years, Pretoria has been stockpiling strategic commodities, developing domestic industrial capabilities, promoting substitutes, and otherwise preparing for the eventuality of sanctions. Although the business community is increasingly uneasy over the high cost of these programmes,[58] the country is now surprisingly self-sufficient in most (but not all) essentials.

A further consideration is that South Africa is a much more valuable economic prize, with a much greater Western economic stake, thus ensuring that sanctions there would prove costlier and sanction-breaking even more rewarding and tempting than was the case in Rhodesia. Although South African threats to deny supplies of strategic minerals to the West in the event of sanctions can safely be discounted,[59] the same cannot be said of the merciless military and economic retaliation that Pretoria has promised to visit upon the helpless hostage states on its borders. Despite their attempts to appease Pretoria by promising to ignore sanctions, they are not likely to be allowed to escape its fury quite so easily.[60]

Objectives

What worthwhile purpose, then, could sanctions against South Africa reasonably be expected to achieve? In an attempt to answer this, the five objectives outlined earlier will be considered in reverse order. To begin with, there is little hope, in present circumstances, of any action capable of inflicting crippling damage on the system or even measures intended to induce fundamental reform - though neither eventuality can be entirely ruled out in the long run. The time may eventually come when Western governments and multinational corporations will be compelled in their own interests to increase the costs of apartheid to the point where meaningful change - on which there is as yet no consensus in the West - emerges as the least unpalatable option open to Pretoria. That moment of truth may not arrive until a credible guerrilla threat arises as a stark alternative to serious sanctions.

More promising as an interim prospect is the third possibility: Western acquiescence in limited economic measures as a diplomatic ploy to contain pressures for more sweeping sanctions. This is what stirred the Western powers to propose a mandatory arms embargo in 1977, after having vetoed it in each of the previous two years. The same situation could recur again, since the West is rapidly running out of viable and credible alternative strategies for genuinely progressive change in South Africa.[61] Persuasion through negotiations, or the 'candid friend' approach exemplified by the Contact Group on Namibia, has been notable mainly for the unlimited opportunity it has afforded Pretoria to prolong discussions and postpone decisions indefinitely.[62] Nor has 'constructive engagement', especially as practiced by the present US Administration, produced the leverage predicted.[63] As President Reagan ought to have anticipated, unilateral concessions and professions of friendship have evoked only a token response. More importantly, they have supplied South Africa with an incentive repeatedly to demand more, as it continues to do. Nevertheless, Western governments are not yet ready to confess their failure and revise their strategies. On the contrary, they have fallen willing victims to Pretoria's slick misinformation campaign which has projected its constitutional entrenchment of apartheid and its intensification of repression and forced removals as racial reforms, and portayed its brutal subjugation of its weaker neighbours as a 'peace process'.

A fourth possible purpose - deterrence - offers some scope for intervention. Indeed, Western reminders of the automatic nature of air sanctions against states harbouring aerial hijackers was decisive in securing the hurried rearrest and subsequent conviction of Major Mike Hoare and his mercenary gang, despite the inevitable embarrassment of court revelations concerning South African complicity in the plot to overthrow the Seychelles government in November 1981.[64] Similar threats or exemplary acts might be effective as limited constraints in instances of particularly reprehensible South African behaviour, such as unusually flagrant abuses of human rights or savage assaults on neighbouring states.

Finally, sanctions can serve a useful, if subsidiary purpose as symbols, providing a warning to the oppressors and some comfort to the oppressed. The belated institution of an obligatory arms embargo in 1977 had, as South African spokesmen were quick to assert with some exaggeration, more symbolic value than substance, since the country was now virtually self-sufficient in arms.[65] A number of unofficial boycott campaigns - against Paarl wines, Granny Smith apples, Outspan oranges, gold Krugerrands, etc. - also come within this category. The most significant of these is the international sports boycott, accorded formal sanction by the Commonwealth in the June 1977 Gleneagles declaration on racism in sport.[66] None of these measures could conceivably bring the citadel of apartheid crashing down. Yet, they all help to drive home to white South Africans, in a particularly poignant way more effectively than mere words could, their increasing international isolation. South Africa's exclusion from world-class cricket and rugby was felt particularly keenly, since sport for whites is almost a religion. While their pariah status was resented, it forced them to face up to the fact that they could no longer ignore world opinion.

Opportunities

What then is the range of sanction possibilities which can realistically be regarded as politically acceptable - if not immediately, at least in the foreseeable future - and do they add up to anything worth while? Four areas of action offer some promise. In the first place, opportunities exist for governments to act individually or collectively to achieve 'limited but concrete and short-term results' through pressure - possibly in the form of carrots as well as sticks - at critical moments and at sensitive points in the South African economy.[67] 'I think the weight of our investments there,' Jimmy Carter declared slightly naively in the immediate aftermath of his election as President, 'the value South Africans place on access to American capital and technology can be used as a positive force in settling regional problems.'[68] Certainly, Mr Kissinger's ruthless manipulation of the gold price in the mid-1970s as a means of pressuring Mr

Vorster to put the squeeze on Mr Smith,[69] and President Carter's cancellation of US shipments of enriched uranium destined for South Africa's first nuclear power plant (in protest against Pretoria's refusal to sign the Treaty on the the Non-Proliferation of Nuclear Weapons), as well as his ban on the sale of computer technology to the South African security forces,[70] are examples of initiatives that might usefully be undertaken more often. Bilateral bargaining, precisely because it can be issue-specific, flexible and short-term (thus allowing no time for countermeasures to take effect), is a particularly effective instrument of influence when wielded with intelligence, imagination and conviction.

Second, there is further scope for psychological sanctions targeted on the privileged white minority with a view to accentuating its sense of isolation. Reinforcement of the sports boycott is an urgent necessity if it is not to succumb to erosion in the face of the powerful and well-financed South African counter-campaign designed to undermine it. Perhaps even more dramatic and relatively easy to implement would be a ban on all air communications with South Africa. Such a move the African states could initiate on their own - if only they could muster the political will to act in unison to implement the many OAU (as well as UN) resolutions adopted on the subject since 1964. The co-operation of the Frontline States, Kenya, Cape Verde and the Ivory Coast would be especially necessary. Australia's initiative in 1977 in unilaterally cancelling Qantas flights to Johannesburg merits emulation.[71]

Third, there is the whole area of financial disengagement: disinvestment (or, at least, no new investment or business contacts),[72] divestment, bans on bank loans and export credits, restrictions on technological transfers, etc. In the recent past, opportunities to exercise some financial leverage have been missed through timidity. During 1977 and 1978, in the shadow of Soweto, the Western powers came close to accepting a mandatory ban on all government support for the promotion of new investment in South Africa, but in the end backed away from even this mild measure.[73] More recently, the 1982 $1.07 billion International Monetary Fund loan was a classic instance of dereliction of duty on the part of Western governments in failing to insist - as they could have done quite legitimately - on major reforms in the fields of labour, internal security and the public service, as conditions for at least the stand-by credit portion of the loan. Each of these elements of the apartheid structure was an important contributing cause to the country's balance of payments crisis.[74] Crucial to the success of any financial sanctions would be increased overseas government control over the operations of their multinationals in South Africa. This would have the added advantage of facilitating general sanctions if ever they should be attempted at a later date. According to D. G. Clarke, an 'extremely important fact' of direct relevance both to the failure of Rhodesian sanctions and the debate on South African sanctions, is that 'trade and financial boycotts were not accompanied by actual disinvestment'.[75]

Finally, consideration could be given to the advantages of focusing on a single critical import or export commodity. Traditionally, oil has been identified as the Achilles' heel of modern economies and, for this reason, it has acquired a certain symbolic significance as a test of sincerity. Although oil is the one energy source on which South Africa is externally dependent, there is considerable controversy concerning the effectiveness of an embargo, in view of the government's well-publicised claim that it has stockpiled at least two years' supply.[76] Knowledgeable analysts, however, contend that the exercise would be technically feasible and economically justified. The obstacles to its implementation are political.[77] A second possibility is agricultural produce, especially sugar and fruit. This and an embargo on air transport were the two measures which, in a move to counter growing demands for comprehensive sanctions, a Western working group advised in October 1978 was both politically realistic and capable of having an immediate substantial impact on the economy and lives of South Africans.[78]

The catalogue of sanctions outlined above is far from formidable. Even if every measure proposed were fully acted upon, their cumulative impact would scarcely shake the target regime to its foundations or cause it to institute fundamental reforms. Moreover, experience north of the Limpopo is a reminder that, even in more favourable circumstances, sanctions are not the cheap, easy and speedy answer to political change that is often assumed. Certainly, in the case of South Africa, the international community is not yet prepared to impose its will on Pretoria, not least because no consensus exists as to the remedies to prescribe beyond an abandonment of apartheid. On the other hand, if the immediate aim of the exercise is defined more modestly than complete social transformation, the measures available appear less insignificant. Collectively, they provide an opportunity to exert a limited but nevertheless worthwhile influence on the course of events in South Africa. In this case, a slice of a loaf can be better than no loaf at all, provided the slice is real and not a sleight of hand. Moreover, once the process of pressing for meaningful change has begun, there is a greater chance that the momentum will be maintained and even increased. Fear of this is, in fact, one of the arguments advanced in opposition to taking any initiative.

Critics of Western inaction on apartheid undoubtedly

exaggerate the extent to which South Africa is responsive to external pressure. On the other hand, Western powers are not as helpless to influence policy in Pretoria as they like to claim. Practical political realities dictate a pragmatic incrementalist approach to the festering sore of South Africa. Both humanitarian concerns and material interests demand that the process should begin without further delay. Assuming the West is sincere in its opposition to apartheid, it should take the lead in introducing selective sanctions with energy and intelligence - and a realistic appreciation of both their possibilities and their limitations.

Notes

1. Harold Wilson, A Personal Record: The Labour Government, 1964-1970 (Little, Brown, Boston, 1971), p. 196.
2. Harry R. Strack, Sanction: The Case of Rhodesia (Syracuse University Press, Syracuse, 1978), pp. 36, 135.
3. Leon Festinger, A Theory of Cognitive Dissonance (Tavistock, London, 1957), p. 3.
4. Southern Rhodesia: Documents relating to the negotiations between the United Kingdom and Southern Rhodesian Governments, November 1963-November 1965, (Her Majesty's Stationery Office, London, 1965), Cmnd. 2807, pp. 83-4, 111, 113-15.
5. United Kingdom, House of Commons Debates, 1965-66, vol. 720, col. 361, 11 November 1965.
6. Jorge Jardim, Sanctions Double-Cross: Oil to Rhodesia (Intervencao, Lisbon, 1978); Martin Bailey, Oilgate: The Sanctions Scandal (Hodder and Stoughton, London, 1979); T. H. Bingham and S. M. Gray, Report on the Supply of Petroleum Products to Rhodesia (Her Majesty's Stationery Office, London, 1978).
7. Joe Garner, The Commonwealth Office, 1925-1968, (Heinemann, London, 1978), pp. 391, 393; United Kingdom, House of Commons Debate, 1965-66, vol. 722, cols. 771-2, 10 December 1965; The Times (London) 15 Dec. 1965, p. 11.
8. Robert C. Good, UDI: The International Politics of the Rhodesian Rebellion (Princeton University Press, Princeton, 1973), pp. 170, 176, 191, 201-2, 220-1, 226, 253-4, 269, 271.
9. Ibid., pp. 67, 69, 72, 97, 322.
10. Ibid., pp. 65-70.
11. Hugh Thomas (ed.), Crisis in the Civil Service, (Anthony Blond, London, 1968), pp. 97-8; Chapman Pincher, Inside Story (Sidgwick and Jackson, London, 1978), pp. 108-9; Wilfred Beckman (ed.), The Labour Government's Economic Record, 1964-1970 (Duckworth,

London, 1972), p. 144; Richard Deacon, The British Connection (Hamish Hamilton, London, 1979), p. 260.

12. Richard C. Porter, 'Economic Sanctions: The Theory and the Evidence from Rhodesia', Journal of Peace Science 3(2) (Fall 1978), pp. 96-7, 107; Good, UDI, pp. 69-71; D. G. Clarke, 'Zimbabwe's Economic Position and Aspects of Sanctions Removal', Journal of Commonwealth and Comparative Politics 18(1) (March 1980), pp. 29-30.

13. Kees Maxey, 'Labour and the Rhodesian Situation', African Affairs 75(299) (April 1976), p. 158; Good, UDI, p. 69. Prime Minister Wilson specifically denied that tobacco farmers were singled out for their political views as opposed to their economic importance. United Kingdom, House of Commons Debates, 1965-66, vol. 720, col. 634, 12 November 1965.

14. Good, UDI, pp. 72, 97, 322.

15. Douglas G. Anglin and Timothy M. Shaw, Zambia's Foreign Policy: Studies in Diplomacy and Dependence, (Westview Press, Boulder, 1979), pp. 198-203.

16. Good, UDI, pp. 113-15, 123-5.

17. Johan Galtung, 'On the Effects of International Economic Sanctions: With Examples from the Case of Rhodesia', World Politics 19(3) (April 1967), pp. 384-7; Economic Survey of Rhodesia for 1965, C.S.R. 35-1966, pp. 17-22, 28.

18. Strack, Sanctions, p. 15; Galtung, 'On the Effects of International Economic Sanctions', p. 388.

19. Robin Renwick, Economic Sanctions (Harvard University Center for International Affairs, Cambridge, 1981), pp. 31-46; E. G. Cross, 'Economic Sanctions as an Instrument of Policy', International Affairs Bulletin 5(1) (1981), pp. 20-4; Ministry of Economic Planning and Development, Annual Economic Review of Zimbabwe, Cmd. R.Z.11 (August 1981), pp. 10-12; Good, UDI, pp. 211-18.

20. Renwick, Economic Sanctions, p. 43.

21. Strack, Sanctions, p. 94.

22. Annual Economic Review of Zimbabwe (August 1981), p. 11.

23. Ibid., p. 14.

24. The Economist, 19 July 1980, p. 16.

25. Clarke, 'Zimbabwe's Economic Position', pp. 36, 40, 41-2.

26. Cross, 'Economic Sanctions as an Instrument of Policy', pp. 22-4.

27. Galtung, 'On the Effects of International Economic Sanctions', pp. 388-90.

28. Clarke, 'Zimbabwe's Economic Position', p. 31.

29. Good, UDI, p. 250.

30. Renwick, Economic Sanctions, pp. 34, 40, 44; Good, UDI, pp. 270, 301-3; Rhodesia, Parliamentary Debates, vol. 72 (28 August 1968). See also, Zimbabwe

Rhodesia, 'The Benefits of Lifting Sanctions: Statement from the Prime Minister's Office', *'For the Record'*, no. 3 (28 July 1979).

31. Robert O. Matthews, 'Talking without negotiating: the case of Rhodesia', *International Journal* 25(1) (Winter 1979-80), pp. 91-117.

32. Strack, *Sanctions*, pp. 146-64.

33. Martin Meredith, *The Past is Another Country: Rhodesia, 1890-1979* (Andre Deutsch, London, 1979), pp. 242, 249, 259-60; David Martin and Phyllis Johnson, *The Struggle for Zimbabwe* (Faber and Faber, London, 1981), pp. 238, 248, 250.

34. Good, *UDI*, pp. 171-2, 185. Cf. United Kingdom, *House of Commons Debates, 1972-73*, vol. 858, cols. 304-5 (26 June 1973); and Guy Arnold, 'Rhodesia sanctions have brought some benefits to the UK', *African Development*, no. 60 (September 1972), pp. 16-17.

35. Richard Hall, *The High Price of Principles: Kaunda and the White South* (Penguin, Harmondsworth, 1973), pp. 167-8.

36. United Nations document A/33/343, 1 November 1978, p. 1.

37. United Nations document S/RES/253, 29 May 1968; Vernon J. Mwaanga, *An Extraordinary Life* (Multimedia Publications, Lusaka, 1982), pp. 121-3; Good, *UDI*, p. 252.

38. See Note 6.

39. Renwick, *Economic Sanctions*, pp. 34-5, 37, 38.

40. Good, *UDI*, pp. 203-7, 253, 290. Effective enforcement of sanctions would have required the blacklisting of all delinquent governments and companies, as the United Kingdom did with considerable success in wartime under the Trading with the Enemy Act - which was never invoked against Rhodesia.

41. *Yearbook of the United Nations, 1969*, pp. 119-20; *Yearbook of the United Nations, 1972*, pp. 120-1; *Yearbook of the United Nations, 1973*, p. 116.

42. For the final report, see *Twelfth Report of the Security Council Commitee established in pursuance of Resolution 253 (1968) concerning the Question of Southern Rhodesia*, United Nations Security Council Official Records, 35th Year, Special Supplement No. 2 (1980), 2 vols., S/13750. In addition to the UN Committee, the European Community and the Commonwealth also set up committees. The Commonwealth Sanctions Committee was the earliest and most active.

43. See Note 6; and *The Oil Conspiracy: An investigation into how multinational oil companies provide Rhodesia's oil needs* (Center for Social Action, United Church of Christ, New York, 1976).

44. Clarke, 'Zimbabwe's International Economic Position', pp. 36, 39, 42.

45. Annual Economic Review of Zimbabwe, August 1981, p. 14.

46. United Kingdom, *House of Commons Debates, 1965-66*, vol. 722, col. 780, 10 December 1965; Garner, *The Commonwealth Office*, p. 391.

47. Good, *UDI*, pp. 314-22.

48. Cross, 'Economic Sanctions as an Instrument of Policy', pp. 28, 29, n.3.

49. Clarke, 'Zimbabwe's International Economic Position', p. 31; Cross, 'Economic Sanctions as an Instrument of Policy', p. 24.

50. *Rhodesia: Report of the Commission on Rhodesian Opinion under the Chairmanship of the Rt. Hon. the Lord Pearce*, Her Majesty's Stationery Office, London, 1972), p. 81.

51. Harry R. Strack, 'The Influence of Transnational Actors on the Enforcement of Sanctions against Rhodesia', International Studies Association, Toronto, 25-29 February 1976, (mimeo.), pp. 6-14; Clarke, 'Zimbabwe's International Economic Position', p. 31.

52. Rhodesia, *Parliamentary Debates*, vol. 67, col. 229, 26 April 1967.

53. United Kingdom, *House of Commons Debates, 1965-66*, vol. 720, cols. 636-37, 12 November, 1965.

54. Ronald Segal (ed.), *Sanctions against South Africa* (Penguin, London, 1964); Barbara Rogers and Brian Bolton, *Sanctions Against South Africa: Exploding the Myths* (Manchester Free Press, Manchester, 1981); *Economic Sanctions against South Africa* (Scandinavian Institute of African Studies, Uppsala, 1981), 13 vols.

55. *The Star* (Johannesburg), weekly ed., 22 Nov. 1980, p. 5; Tony Koenderman, 'Sanctions', South Africa Foundation, *Briefing Paper*, no. 11, November 1978; Theo Malan, 'South Africa and Economic Sanctions', Supplement to *SA Digest*, Pretoria, 13 March 1981.

56. S/RES/181, 7 August, 1963 and S/RES/418, 4 November 1977, *Yearbook of the United Nations, 1977*, pp. 141-6.

57. James Barber and Michael Spicer, 'Sanctions against South Africa - Options for the West', *International Affairs* 55(3) (July 1979), pp. 388-90.

58. *Financial Times* (London), 31 Jan. 1983, p. 4,and 7 Oct. 1983, p. 19.

59. *Financial Times* (London), 19 Nov. 1980, p. 3, and 26 May 1981, p. XI; John Kane-Berman, 'Botha waves his double-edged sword', *South* (London), 4 (January 1981), p. 17; Robert M. Price, "Can [South] Africa afford not to sell minerals?,' the *New York Times*, 18 Aug. 1981, p. A21; *South Africa: Time Running Out* (University of California Press, Berkeley, 1981), pp. 318-22, 449-54.

60. *The Economist*, 22 January 1983, p. 60; *The*

Times (London), 23 June 1982, p. 7, and 11 Mar. 1982, p. 9; 'Southern Africa: The oil weapon', Africa Confidential 24(7) (30 March 1983), pp. 1-3. On Mozambique's position on South African trade and sanctions (prior to Nkomati), see AIM Information Bulletin (Maputo), no. 62 (August 1981), pp. 9-10.

61. Barber and Spicer, 'Sanctions against South Africa', pp. 390-5.

62. 'Namibia: The Elusive Settlement', IDAFSA Briefing Paper, no. 6 (November 1981); Africa Contemporary Record, 1982-83, pp. A24-31; Randolph Vigne, 'The Namibia File', Third World Quarterly 5(2) (April 1983), pp. 345-52.

63. Chester Crocker, 'South Africa: Strategy for Change', Foreign Affairs 59(2) (Winter 1980-81), pp. 325-7, 345-51; John Dugard, 'Silence is not golden', Foreign Policy 46 (Spring 1982), pp. 37-48; John Seiler, 'Has Constructive Engagement failed?', South Africa International 13(3) (January 1982), pp. 420-33; Christopher Coker, 'The United States and South Africa: Can Constructive Engagement Succeed?', Millenium 11(3) (Autumn 1982), pp. 223-41.

64. Douglas G. Anglin, 'South Africa: Skyjack sanctions should be imposed', Citizen (Ottawa), 10 Dec. 1981, p. 9.

65. Africa Research Bulletin (PSC) (1977), pp. 4623, 4655.

66. African Contemporary Record, 1977-78, pp. C48-9.

67. Newell M. Stultz, 'Sanctions, Models of Change and South Africa', South Africa International 13(2) (October 1982), p. 125; David Baldwin, 'The Power of Positive Sanctions', World Politics 24(1) (October 1971), pp. 19-38; Galtung, 'On the Effects of International Economic Sanctions', p. 414.

68. Africa Research Bulletin (EFT) (1976), p. 4059.

69. R. W. Johnson, How Long Will South Africa Survive? (Macmillan, London, 1977), pp. 215-42.

70. South Africa: Time Running Out, pp. 415-16; The Economist, 15 November 1980, pp. 91-2.

71. 'Implications of a boycott of airlines flying to and from South Africa, with special reference to action by African states', United Nations document A/AC.115/L.481, 6 December 1977.

72. South Africa: Time Running Out, pp. 424-8.

73. Toronto Star, 15 Sep. 1979, p. 1.

74. Financial Times (London), 7 Oct. 1982, p. 16, and 25 Jan. 1983, p. 4.

75. Clarke, 'Zimbabwe's International Economic Position', p. 31; Barber and Spicer, 'Sanctions against South Africa', p. 400.

76. According to the official report on the 1979 Salem oil fraud, following the fall of the Shah of Iran, 'crude oil

importers literally lived from hand to mouth, they had to purchase in the highly unfavourable spot markets and, furthermore, had to conceal deliveries to the Republic of South Africa'. ('Memorandum on the Salem Tanker compiled by the SFF Association [Proprietory] Limited at the request of the Minister of Mineral and Energy Affairs to be laid upon the table of the House of Assembly', 9 March 1983, p. 1).

77. Bernard Rivers and Martin Bailey, South Africa's Oil Supply: Its Importance, How it is Obtained, and How the Existing Embargo could be made Effective, UN document A/CONF.107/6, 1981; 'South Africa: Vital oil flows', Africa Confidential 24(1) (5 January 1983), pp. 1-4; Stanley Uys, 'South Africa: Prospects for an Oil Boycott', Africa Report 25(5) (September-October 1980), pp. 215-18.

78. Guardian (London), 23 Dec. 1978, p. 1.

PART II

ECONOMIC SANCTIONS IN EAST-WEST CONFLICTS

Chapter Four

CAGING THE DRAGON: POST-WAR ECONOMIC SANCTIONS AGAINST THE PEOPLE'S REPUBLIC OF CHINA

Paul M. Evans*

In scope and duration the various economic sanctions imposed against the People's Republic of China (PRC) represent the most extensive post-war effort to alter a target's political behaviour by economic means. They stood in place for more than two decades, involved more than 60 nations, and were conducted under the auspices of at least four international organisations. They raise several fundamental questions about the utility of sanctions as a tool of state craft, the motives of participants, and the conditions under which multinational co-operation can be maintained.

My concern here is the variety of import, export and credit restrictions, controls over Chinese foreign assets, and limitations on trans-shipments of goods to the PRC which have been instituted since 1949. The line between economic warfare and 'sanctions' conceived of in a moral or juridical sense is thin indeed with reference to the various actions taken against the PRC. Even the restrictions imposed under United Nations auspices during the Korean War barely fit the definition of a globally-endorsed collective action to punish or deter a transgressor state for the simple reason that a substantial number of countries, especially but not exclusively in the Soviet bloc, refused to participate in them. We can investigate the diverse range of actions only by considering 'sanctions' in the currently accepted realpolitik sense of the word, which refers to state interference in normal cross-national commercial intercourse, either unilaterally or in concert with other states, with the intention of influencing the political behaviour of a target nation. While the various participants invoked a variety of justifications to support their actions, questions of justice and dispassionate, impartial application of the rules of international law are little informed by the case study at

* Professor Evans wishes to thank the Social Sciences and Humanities Research Council of Canada for the funding which made this study possible.

hand.

It is not a simple matter to disentangle the comparatively common action, on the one hand of imposing export restrictions on specific hazardous goods such as nuclear materials from, on the other, interference in normal trade patterns that are designed to alter the external behaviour or internal character of a potential or real adversary. What distinguishes the case of the PRC is the scope of goods embargoed and the motivations for the restrictions which were frequently couched in the vocabulary of deterrence or punition.

A striking number of nations have at some point since 1949 placed restrictions on commercial relations with the PRC for overtly political reasons. The focus here, however, will be primarily the Western bloc activities - 'Western' here interpreted also to include Japan, Australia, New Zealand and a number of other countries in Asia - and will disregard the politically-inspired restrictions imposed by the Soviet Union and its allies beginning in the fall of 1960. Finally, 'China' will be used to refer to the People's Republic of China. Several countries, including the United Kingdom and Canada, placed restrictions on the export of strategic materials to Taiwan, but the restrictions were less inclusive and intended to achieve different objectives than those imposed on China.

While there is little monographic material on the China sanctions, we do have a handful of studies which deal with various national perspectives on the embargoes as well as the larger subject of their place in the framework of East-West economic conflict.[1] This study draws heavily on these previously-published works and also incorporates the results of an examination of material located in the Department of External Affairs and the Privy Council Office in Ottawa that is related to Canadian participation in the sanctions.[2]

My general argument is that the sanction effort against China involves motivations and manoeuvres that are more complex than generally acknowledged. In answering basic questions about the effectiveness of the sanctions, the reasons for their imposition and the techniques by which they were implemented and co-ordinated, there emerges a heady array of inconsistencies, unintended consequences, confusions and partial compromises which suggest policy, both in formulation and application, was far less rational and unified than is normally assumed.

Further, the sanctions offer an interesting insight into the workings of the Western Alliance system during the height of the Cold War. Since the Sino-Soviet split, if not before, China has not fitted easily into a simple model of 'East-West' confrontation. As opponent it has at different moments been perceived as both more and less of a threat to Western interests than the Soviet Union. This fact is attested to by the vigour of US efforts in implementing a far greater range of economic penalties against China than the Soviet Union until the mid-1970s, and is why, later, the situation has been reversed. This not only suggests some of the reasons why it is difficult to address dispassionately the broader legitimacy of the sanctions, but also raises the critical matter of the context of images and assumptions in which policy-makers in Washington and other capitals considered various courses of actions.

Historical Survey

The sanctions fall into at least four distinct phases which embrace considerable variation in the number of 'sanctioners', the instrument of legitimation and co-ordination, the extent of the goods and services proscribed, as well as the ostensible objectives.

1. Summer 1949 to June 1950. Even prior to the formal establishment of China in October 1949, the Truman Administration applied limited export restrictions on materials destined for Communist-held areas of the mainland. Multilateral controls on trade in strategic goods with China first were instituted in March of 1950. They represented efforts begun in November 1949 as a corollary to military defence plans instituted by the NATO allies. Several NATO members, responding to US initiatives, created the Consultative Group (CG) through an unusual, unwritten 'gentleman's agreement'. Daily operations were administered by the Co-ordinating Committee (CoCom) based in Paris. Originally composed of the United Kingdom, the United States, Italy, the Netherlands, Belgium, Luxembourg and France, it expanded to include Norway, Denmark, the Federal Republic of Germany and Canada in 1950, Portugal and Japan in 1952, and Greece and Turkey in 1953 - all of the members of NATO except Iceland.[3]

CoCom has functioned as a regular and confidential forum for discussion of matters related to the establishment and maintenance of a multilaterally-acceptable list of goods that are subject to collective embargo against export to Communist countries except Yugoslavia and Cuba. It has operated on the basis of consensus and unanimity rather than majority voting. Its decisions are not formally binding on the participants but have been adhered to with few exceptions. Both of these characteristics point to its inherent fragility and, paradoxically, its durability which has been based upon pragmatism, flexibility and a variety of mechanisms for granting special exemptions to member states.

Reflecting an explicit compromise between unrestricted trading and a total trade ban, it created three different lists: the first specifying items subject to complete embargo; the second (discontinued in 1956) containing material not entirely prohibited but subject to aggregate quantitative limits and the third enumerating items subject only to surveillance. The lists, which became effective January 1950, functioned as a lowest common denominator and participating countries, especially the United States, often unilaterally imposed controls more rigorous and extensive than the CoCom lists. In March 1950, following the signing of the Sino-Soviet Treaty of Friendship, Alliance and Mutual Aid, its members agreed to apply them to mainland China.

It is arguable whether the CoCom lists can be considered 'sanctions'. They were not intended to alter specific aspects of Chinese policy, but instead were designed to deprive a perceived enemy of materials that could be of benefit in competition with the West. Nor did they indicate that China had violated any principle of international law. They can only be seen as sanctions in the sense that they represented multilateral efforts to put economic pressure on a Communist government by depriving it of specific goods and technologies. In this sense they differed from customary unilateral forms of trade restrictions on strategic goods of the kind imposed, for example, by US officials on the export of fissionable material to India, Iraq or Israel.

2. June 1950 to July 1953. With the outbreak of the Korean War, the CoCom lists were immediately expanded to cover some 350 items deemed to be of military value. Several of the Western allies took stronger measures. The United States stopped all trade with North Korea in June 1950 and, following the Chinese intervention in the war in late October, imposed a ban on virtually all trade with China which would stay in effect for two decades.

While only a handful of nations moved as far as the United States in prohibiting all exports, freezing all Chinese assets and forbidding its ships to enter Chinese waters, US officials were successful in consummating a series of agreements and bilateral understandings which broadened the embargo on trade in strategic goods with China to include most of the non-Communist world. Most important of these was the creation of the China Committee, CHICOM (also known as CHINCOM), a cognate to CoCom under the nominal authority of the Consultative Group, which would establish and administer a special set of embargo lists for China, Korea and, later, North Vietnam. Formally established in September 1952, CHICOM included all of the CoCom members and proceeded to draw up lists far more restrictive than the CoCom lists of 1950. The complete embargo list (List I) appears to have contained more than 500 items, including various kinds of munitions, atomic materials and 'other products' encompassing metal working equipment, specified chemical and petroleum products, rubber, electronic machinery, and specified minerals and metals. Items on the CHICOM but not the CoCom lists included such things as rubber tubing, paraffin wax, refinery equipment, all forms of trucks and tractors, barbed wire, telescopes and binoculars, electrical motors, internal combustion engines and locomotives.

CoCom-CHICOM served as the hub of the embargo campaign but other international organisations also became involved. The Organisation of American States (OAS) endorsed China sanctions by passing a resolution on 7 April 1951 which supported export restrictions along the lines established at CoCom. At the same time, under a Commonwealth agreement, New Zealand, South Africa and Australia undertook parallel action in circumscribing their China trade.

The most publicised, though not necessarily the most effective, aspect of the international effort took place under the auspices of the United Nations. It followed from the February 1951 General Assembly resolution that declared China to be 'an aggressor nation' and a further resolution of 18 May 1951 which called on all members to apply voluntary embargoes on the shipment to China and North Korea of 'arms, ammunitions and implements of war, atomic energy materials, petroleum, transportation materials of strategic value, and items useful in the production of arms, ammunition and the implements of war'. Soviet-bloc countries did not participate in the vote, and the resolution passed 47-0, with eight abstentions (Syria, Sweden, India, Pakistan, Burma, Afghanistan, Egypt and Indonesia). While the resolution called for measures less restrictive than those already implemented by the CoCom members, it represented the most important legitimation of the 'sanctions' effort, and perhaps the only component of the overall restrictions that can be considered 'sanctions' from the perspective of international law. Unlike CoCom and CHICOM lists, the UN sanctions were applied in response to a specific Chinese military action and, accordingly, were to be removed at such time as the Chinese intervention in Korea came to a halt.

By the fall of 1952, more than 55 countries were participating in the sanctions as co-ordinated by CoCom, the United Nations, the OAS, the Commonwealth, or arranged in bilateral agreements between individual states and the US government. The United States clearly played the principal role as catalyst, watchdog and enforcer. It would be unwise, however, to subscribe too closely to the suggestion by Gunner Adler-Karlsson that other governments supported the effort solely, or even primarily, as a result of US pressure and fear of losing US aid.[4] The origins of the sanctions lay in something more pervasive than US arm twisting. Several of the participating countries, including Canada, Australia and New Zealand, were not recipients of

US assistance. Canadian accounts of discussions at CoCom-CHICOM indicate as well that the member-states agreed on the virtue of at least a minimum control list. It is instructive, moreover, that none of the governments withdrew from CoCom-CHICOM after they stopped receiving aid from the United States.

The specific mechanisms for legalising and implementing trade and other controls varied from country to country. Not surprisingly, the most extensive and complicated control system developed in the United States, where at least five distinct pieces of legislation applied to the China sanctions.[5] The first two were the Munitions Control Act administered by the State Department and the Atomic Energy Act administered by the Atomic Energy Commission. The Foreign Assets Control Regulations (FACR), which grew out of the Trading with the Enemy Act of 1917, constituted the third component. These regulations, overseen by the Treasury Department, were designed to deprive the target country of US products while simultaneously preserving equity between US corporations based both in the United States and abroad. Their invocation by President Truman in December 1950 effectively froze Chinese assets in the United States and imposed penalties on US citizens who as individuals or through corporate activity engaged in trade with China. This action, of course, had direct extraterritorial implications for US-controlled enterprises, including branch plants, which operated in Canada, the United Kingdom, France, Belgium and elsewhere.[6]

The Export Control Act of 1949 constituted the fourth dimension of the legal framework. Administered by the Department of Commerce, it empowered the President to place restrictions on the export of any US-produced goods as well as to prohibit their re-export from their original destinations to proscribed countries. Fines and a blacklist gave teeth to its provisions. Canada was the only country to which these trans-shipment controls did not formally apply.

Finally, the Mutual Defense Assistance Control Act, the most controversial component of the control system, had been enacted to enlist international co-operation with US trade restrictions. Better known as the Battle Act, it gave the President the discretion to curtail foreign aid to countries that exported strategic goods to Communist-bloc countries. While its provisions were only applied to a recalcitrant third party on one occasion, they did give the President a potent weapon for extending the embargo umbrella. In 1951 more than 60 countries received US aid, the total value of which exceeded by several times the combined worth of its recipients' trade with China. To the relief of the governments of these states, in most instances it was the CoCom and CHICOM lists, rather than the far more restrictive US list, that were applied as the standards of reference in interpreting the Battle Act provisions.

The co-ordination of these various departments and regulations fell to three executive organisations: the Advisory Committee on Export Policy; the Joint Operating Committee; and the Economic Defense Advisory Committee (EDAC). The latter is probably the most important, and involved the participation of at least 15 separate agencies. Chaired through the 1950s by Averell Harriman and then Harold C. Stassen, the EDAC had a staff of more than 300 and oversaw the operations of several thousand more. Considering the various institutional interests at play, the 'pulling and hauling' within the committee must have been intense. Although the matter has not received detailed attention, at least one source suggests in understated fashion that within the EDAC 'bureaucratic disagreements are known to exist'.[7]

Other states implemented controls in less complicated and less public fashion. Most of the Western European governments surveyed by Gunner Adler-Karlsson did not pass new legislation but utilised existing executive powers. This, he suggests, reflected the fact that the China sanctions were unpopular in most of these states. 'The embargo would never have been feasible', he observes, 'if it had been put before the parliaments or ventilated in public discussion.'[8] Without reliable public opinion data it is difficult to assess the proposition, but he is certainly correct in emphasising that the sanctions against China and trade controls in general were rarely made high-profile issues outside the United States. In Canada, for instance, export controls were implemented without discussion in the House of Commons on the basis of a series of Orders in Council, the most important of which were issued on 22 August 1951 and 27 May 1954. Both were administered by the Department of Trade and Commerce in consultation with the Department of External Affairs. Legislation was not required because Canadian exporters already required a licence to export goods abroad. Officials in Ottawa did not make any major public announcements about the China sanctions except to express support for the UN resolution of May 1951. CoCom and CHICOM obligations were met by simply refusing to grant export licences on the proscribed items. Between 1950 and 1953 these proscriptions received broad interpretation and amounted to a virtual trade embargo.

3. <u>August 1953 to May 1957</u>. With the Korean ceasefire, the justification for a large-scale embargo became less compelling in the eyes of most but not all of the participants. United States leaders actively claimed that the cessation of hostilities did not mean the war against Chinese Communist aggression was at an end or the need for vigilance less precipitous. Within CHICOM, however, the

next four years were characterised by increasing dissatisfaction over the extent of the China sanctions, and by ever-increasing vociferous demands for expanded exemptions and fewer restrictions in trade with China.

If the allied sanctioners were slumbering in the same bed, they were dreaming very different dreams. Tensions were most pronounced on the issue of the 'China Differential', the distance between the CHICOM lists applied to China and North Korea and the CoCom lists which applied to the Soviet Union and Eastern Europe. The China Differential began with the creation of CHICOM and was enlarged by CoCom's decision in 1953 to reduce the number of items on its lists. One academic observer has stated that it amounted to 207 items in 1954, a figure slightly less than the 270 mentioned in an External Affairs memorandum of February 1956.[9]

The United Kingdom and the United States emerged as the main antagonists in the dispute within CHICOM on the China Differential. United States officials pushed hard for expanding the embargoes, reducing exemptions which permitted countries to violate the lists with the approval of the other members, and continuing the differential. Their UK counterparts, on the other hand, advocated a shorter list, more exemptions, and the eventual dissolution of the inequities between the CoCom and CHICOM lists. Part of the dispute focused on the definition of 'strategic'. The US leaders, in CHICOM and elsewhere, made a case for a strikingly broad interpretation. Bernard Baruch suggested, only partly in jest, that providing buttons to the Chinese supported their war effort for the simple reason that Chinese soldiers would be less effective in the field if at least one of their hands had to be firmly affixed to their trousers. Less frivolous was the claim that to deny China any industrial goods would have salubrious consequences because it would demand that scarce resources be diverted from projects that might have direct potential for war production. Even during the Korean War, CHICOM was divided by an intense and pervasive disagreement on the 'strategic' nature of specific products such as pharmaceuticals, motorcycles, spray painters and fork lifts.

Despite various attempts to achieve a compromise on the differential issue, including two bilateral summit meetings between US and UK leaders and various multilateral discussions, the United Kingdom finally moved unilaterally in May 1957 to disregard the China Differential and issued licences to its exporters. Within a few weeks all of the other participants in CHICOM, with the exception of the United States, Canada and Turkey, followed the UK lead. The fragile consensus destroyed, CHICOM was dissolved in early 1958 and the control of trade with China reverted to CoCom auspices and its less restrictive lists.

4. Post-1957. In the decade after the abolition of the China Differential, non-Communist trade with China rose rapidly. The increase in trade, the conclusion of the UN action, and the steady reduction of the CoCoM lists have frequently been interpreted as the end of the China sanctions. Only for a few months in the aftermath of the Sino-Indian border war of October 1962 did any appreciable number of nations circumscribe trade to protest a specific Chinese action. Again, it is debatable whether the continued US embargo, which remained virtually complete until its partial relaxation during the Nixon Administration, constituted 'sanctions' or simple economic warfare.[10] It seems unambiguous, however, that from the Chinese perspective and that of most allies of the United States, the effort to use economic means to alter China's political behaviour was not at an end. The distance between US policy and that of its allies created significant problems until the Sino-American rapprochement of the early 1970s. The Battle Act, for instance, continued to threaten the recipients of US aid and the FACR still held extraterritorial implications for US controlled corporations outside the United States.

The implications of FACR raised pressing problems in Canada, Japan and several of the countries in Western Europe where branch plants of US corporations resided. In Canada, for example, the effects of FACR aroused far more public attention than any other aspect of the China trade prior to 1961. Lester Pearson, Secretary of State for External Affairs between 1948 and 1957, was not unaware of the volatility of the situation, describing it in 1956 as potentially politically explosive when so many Canadian companies were branches of larger US concerns. Most celebrated were the exchanges beginning in 1958 between Canadian and US officials over the possible export to China of Ford trucks and Chrysler automobiles manufactured in Canada. Government files indicate that the Ford and Chrysler episodes were only the tip of the iceberg. Prior to 1958 there were numerous instances of US-owned, Canadian-based firms refusing Chinese orders for fear of legal action against the parent company by US authorities.

The actual effect of the regulations on the development of trade with China is difficult to assess. In Canada, for example, the wheat sales which began in 1961 were unaffected. United States legislation was enough of an obstacle, however, to lead two analysts to conclude that the regulations 'were sufficient to immobilise a significant portion of those manufacturing industries that otherwise might have been interested in developing trade with China'.[11] In addition to the legislative dimension of US pressure, another pair of commentators observed in 1972 that 'many Canadian firms have simply not bothered to explore sales to China because they were American subsidiaries or were reluctant to offend steady American customers'.[12]

The Objectives of the Sanctions

It is difficult to conceive of a justification or objective for imposing economic penalties that at least one of the major participants did not advance at some point. They were variously intended to punish calumnies past and present, to deter Chinese aggression, to compel the Chinese to alter either minor or major aspects of their foreign policy, to destabilise the Communist regime, to deprive an enemy of the wherewithal to conduct military operations, or to cause disruptions in the economic system of an adversary. In practice, there emerged two general conceptions of their objectives. We can label the first the 'minimalist' and the second the 'maximalist' conception. The minimalist view, generally associated with the UK position, accepted the need for restricting exports of goods which were of direct military significance to Communist countries, including China. In time of military conflict, such as the Korean War, the restrictions could be broadened for strategic and psychological purposes, but the general object was to minimise controls as far as feasible and re-establish free trade as quickly as possible.

The minimalist position on sanctions grew out of a broader set of ideas on the utility of economic tools of state craft and specific assumptions about Chinese intentions and foreign policy behaviour. While it was seen as desirable to deprive Mao's China of specific kinds of technology, these efforts were not designed to isolate China or to cripple or retard its industrial development. This minimalist view served as the base line of consensus on CoCom-CHICOM and appears to have been the common denominator of the UN effort. Sanctions, in other words, were less a sign of disapproval of the internal character of the regime than an attempt to deprive China of particular kinds of goods that had a military value and, on occasion, to protest against a specific Chinese action such as the military intervention in Korea.

The maximalist conception embraced a much broader range of objectives and political goals. First was to punish the Communist leadership in Beijing for past aggression and to deter it from similar action in the future. As stated by John Foster Dulles: 'We ought to do everything possible to subject China to a maximum economic strain in order to penalize her for her aggression, and make her give up her ways and to give up her aggression'.[13]

Second was the goal of slowing China's industrial growth by creating dislocations, bottlenecks and shortages in vulnerable sectors of the Chinese economy. This related to a recurrent hope that external pressures, including economic ones, would lead to the collapse of the regime. Trade, according to this view, represented a zero sum security game where Chinese advances would come at the expense of allied losses. Third, it was further hoped, that sanctions on strategic goods alone would retard aggregate economic growth by demanding that scarce Chinese resources be diverted from other tasks. Here resided the central argument for expanding the definition of 'strategic' items. In short, collective and unilateral sanctions were meant to achieve the broad objectives of altering the external and domestic policies of the Chinese state, if not precipitating its collapse.

Fourth, even ineffective sanctions, it was often argued, served as an important contribution to the containment of an expansive Chinese Communist regime. They signalled to non-Communist Asia the resolve of the Western allies as demonstrated by their willingness to absorb significant financial losses in caging the Chinese dragon, an enterprise that would boost morale among the Asian allies. According to this rationale, the greater the suffering endured by the sanctioners, the greater their credibility and worth. This complemented the position frequently advocated in US Congress that restrictions on trade with China and even its complete abolition were moral ends in themselves and defensible as such, whether or not they served other political purposes.[14]

The United States emerged as the most persistent and forceful exponent of the maximalist view. Its advocacy of multilateral sanctions and implementation of its own unilateral trade embargo were but two aspects of a broader policy which, for more than two decades, aimed at the diplomatic isolation and political and military containment of China. During this period China was viewed as not just another Cold War opponent but as an enemy of unique and menacing proportions. In considering strategic trade controls with regard to China, the US representative at CHICOM stated just after its inception in 1952 that the actual existence of hostilities in Korea was not the only governing factor. In his view, Chinese aggression in Korea was but the most obvious current manifestation of the aggressive expansionist designs of the brutal political ideology controlling China. He added that the leaders of the Chinese government were both imbued with aggressive doctrines that were interpreted and promulgated by the Kremlin and, further, convinced that these doctrines were correct and must be brought to prevail not only in Asia but throughout the world.

The origins of this policy and perspective are complex but certainly involved cultural elements, a calculation of strategic interest, and the domestic currents of party politics and public passions which emerged in the wake of the 'loss of China'. The sociological and political phenomenon we generally refer to as McCarthyism had a direct influence on the formulation and implementation of China policy. In addition to the loyalty and security hearings which destroyed the careers of most of the foreign service officers who had experience in China, the 1950s produced a durable consensus within government and the broader public on the virtues of a fierce stand against Mao's China. Thus, sanctions were not an alternative to more drastic diplomatic steps but a supplement to a policy of containment and isolation that had significant popular support.

On matters of tactics, however, the US consensus was less comprehensive. Congress and the executive tended to have significantly different approaches to the implementation of the embargoes. Considerable evidence suggests that Congress wished to pursue an even stronger position on the international enforcement of the sanctions than did the Truman Administration or its successors. Adler-Karlsson makes an interesting case that the CoCom-CHICOM arrangement and the implementation of the Battle Act tended to strengthen the hand of successive administrations intent on blunting congressional and public demands for more vigorous US pressure on its allies to tighten and expand the sanctions. While awaiting further work on the governmental politics of the US embargo policy, it is at least plausible to accept his general suggestion that the State Department was successful in attracting other countries into the sanctions effort through CoCom-CHICOM because it was able to deflect domestic opposition and adjust the Battle Act lists in accordance with the CoCom-CHICOM lists rather than the reverse. The secretive nature of the CoCom-CHICOM meetings gave the executive a further tool which, Adler-Karlsson adds, tended 'to blur the picture to interested right-wing Congressmen, and may also have diffused the responsibility for actual decisions taken, so as to provide the President with an excuse for not going as far as Congress wanted'.[15]

The View from Ottawa

The Canadian approach to the sanctions makes for an illuminating contrast and reveals an interesting disjunction between expressed policy and actual behaviour. Diplomatic intentions began giving way to other considerations even prior to the Communist victory. Contrary to a public commitment to maintain a 'hands-off' policy in the civil war, in 1947 Ottawa made available to Chiang Kai-shek's regime military equipment valued at roughly CDN $100 million.[16] On policy toward China, the official Canadian position was certainly closer to that of the United Kingdom than that of the United States. With reference to the UN-sponsored effort, for example, Lester Pearson stated in the House of Commons on 22 May 1951 that 'we have not put a complete embargo on all goods of any kind to China, but we have put an embargo on all goods that will assist China in any way in the prosecution of aggression in Korea'. Two weeks later he emphasised that 'trade had always been a major avenue for establishing relations with other countries' and that cutting off all commercial transactions was 'a final diplomatic step' that Canada was unwilling to make.[17] In Canada, unlike the United States, there existed a widespread consensus for keeping the trading door at least partially open, and for implementing the minimum number of controls compatible with assuring strategic security.[18] It is therefore interesting that during the fighting in Korea, Canadian officials interpreted the UN restrictions in the broadest possible fashion, granting almost no export licences at all.

A second difference, less visible to the public eye, concerned the diversity of opinion and the breadth of debate within the Canadian government, and the Department of External Affairs in particular, over the embargo policy and its relationship to Canada's China policy more broadly defined. Contrary to the rigid and cautious discussion of these issues within the US State Department at the time, the spectrum of debate within External Affairs was broad indeed on the tactics, utility and legitimacy of the international embargo and Canadian participation in it.[19] If the prevailing consensus throughout the 1950s came closest to the 'minimalist' position outlined above, there were also strong cases presented on behalf of the 'maximalist' view as well as an 'abolitionist' stance which advocated Canadian withdrawal from CoCom-CHICOM altogether.

Relations among CHICOM members were frequently turbulent. Even before the fighting in Korea had ended, it seemed clear to Canadian observers that a clash between the United Kingdom and the United States had become inevitable. The situation contained the ingredients of a major confrontation: the two sides espoused different principles; possessed different interests; were strongly supported by public and elite opinion at home; and, because the issue generated considerable publicity, simple avoidance seemed unlikely. The Charge d'Affaires at the Canadian embassy in Washington, for example, advised Lester Pearson in August 1953 that the parallel course under the compulsion of the Korean War would soon dissolve. Anticipating the division, the Charge suggested that there should not be any expectation of a change of heart on the US side where public opinion was strongly against trade with China. He advised that Canada not take a high profile on the matter, recommending that Canada should not regard its trade with China as so urgent that Canadian officials run the risk of a great divergence from US policy. Instead, he recommended that Canada attempt to exercise a moderating influence in the matter, which had in it the potentialities of a serious international dispute.

When the elephant and the lion stampeded, the gazelle stepped lightly. Canadian representatives on CHICOM heeded the Charge's advice and played a self-appointed role as mediator. They attempted to assert what they perceived to be their modest influence on the side of moderation, and to work always for a harmonising of conflicting attitudes, especially between the United States on one side, and the European countries and Japan on the other. Their basic position was that they desired the minimum controls over the trade with the Soviet bloc and China consistent with the paramount need to safeguard the vital security interests of Canada and the rest of the free world.

One of the principal points of ongoing tension which Canadian officials undertook to resolve concerned applications for special exemptions which permitted the sale of otherwise proscribed goods to China. The problem generated persistent conflict between the United States on one hand, and the United Kingdom, Japan, Portugal and several other European countries on the other. A representative example concerned a UK request in 1956 that it be given a special exemption by CHICOM to sell China 350 Land Rover jeeps valued at approximately half a million pounds sterling. The sum involved was not in itself inconsequential but represented only a small fraction of the total exemptions in 1956 which amounted to approximately $70 million. CoCom, the UK representative pointed out, had previously approved a similar request in 1952 for the export of the same vehicles to Taiwan.

Canadian officials initially opposed the UK request on the grounds that, contrary to UK arguments, the vehicles had direct military applications and that the exemption, if granted, would substantially weaken the control effort. The Canadian representative on CHICOM observed caustically that the United Kingdom was waging a guerrilla campaign against the basic principles of strategic control. Officials at home, however, came to a different conclusion in light of the intervention of the High Commissioner to London, Norman Robertson, who made a strong case for the salience of the issue to UK authorities. After weighing the mood in Washington on the matter, Lester Pearson recommended first that Canada support the UK request on a strictly ad hoc basis which did not establish a precedent, and second that the exemption procedure be thoroughly reviewed. Jules Leger, his Under-Secretary, lamented that it would not be a pleasant task to transmit this decision to

Washington and that a vigorous reaction was to be expected.

The Canadian Ambassador to the United States, A.D.P. Heeney, disapproved of the decision, indicating in a series of telegrams the vigorous response that he did indeed receive, drawing attention to considerable public and congressional pressures on the US Administration to oppose the exemption, and reiterating US arguments that the exemption would jeopardise the integrity of the control system and give a propaganda victory to Beijing at a time when it was still proving to be intransigent on the issues of returning prisoners of war and the off-shore islands conflict. Ambassador Heeney noted in passing that US diplomats were vitally concerned that they should not make any formal approval that could be construed at any subsequent congressional hearing to mean that the Department of State had started proceedings which were designed to lead to a lessening of China controls. CHICOM ultimately granted the United Kingdom the exemption. The US representative grudgingly concurred, but did so along the lines of the Canadian suggestion that the Land Rover sale be approved without conceding the principle that the vehicles did not constitute a strategic weapon. The resulting compromise was inherently unstable, leaving none of the major actors satisfied.

The dispute over the exemptions issue echoed a larger disagreement on the value and scope of the China Differential. Here again, as the dreams and objectives of a middle power gave way to other considerations, Canadian hopes, rhetoric and intentions did not always align with actual behaviour. There is little doubt that the vast preponderance of Canadian thinking in both External Affairs and Cabinet after the Korean cease-fire favoured the abolition of the differential. Various internal memoranda and private statements by senior policy makers, including the head of the Far Eastern Division, Arthur Menzies, described the differential and US support of it as unrealistic and unjustifiable.

Canadian and US officials quarrelled privately on numerous occasions on a variety of issues related to developments in the Far East and appropriate policy responses. Mr Menzies, for example, took the line that the wars in Korea and Indo-China were at least halted for the moment, that the crisis over Quemoy and Matsu were as much generated by the Nationalists as the Communists, and that there was still hope that China could be encouraged to lessen its dependence on the Soviet bloc.

Early in 1956, as the Anglo-American conflict heated up, Mr Leger sent a message to Mr Pearson which succinctly summarised the view that for some time the Department of External Affairs had felt that the very large China list was unrealistic and the inclusion of many items could not be justified on strategic grounds. It therefore would welcome a decision to review and reduce the list. On the other hand, External Affairs felt that it had not been under serious pressure from Canadian exporters on the issue and, in the face of adamant US opposition to any change, had done no more than inform US officials privately of its position.

The issue came to a head a year later. In the face of pressure from the United Kingdom and Japan in particular, the United States attempted to maintain the principle of a China Differential while reluctantly conceding that its scope might be reduced. Negotiations on specific items that could be eliminated from the list, however, proved to be unproductive. Canadian officials privately expressed sympathy for the UK position on the abolition of the differential through both normal diplomatic channels and during the March 1957 meetings between the newly-elected UK Prime Minister Harold Macmillan, Canadian Prime Minister Louis St Laurent and several of his cabinet ministers.

Canadian hopes ran high that a compromise could be found despite the intense level of feeling in both Washington and London on the matter. Mr Pearson had been momentarily heartened by a speech by a member of the Eisenhower cabinet in April 1957, which seemed to indicate a new flexibility on the problem following an Anglo-American summit meeting in Bermuda. At the same time, however, Mr Pearson was also sensitive to the fierce opposition to reducing the lists that frequently found voice in Congress and among leading State Department officials, including the indefatigable Under-Secretary for East Asia Affairs, Walter Robertson. Various telegrams from the embassy in Washington gave little reason for optimism. The Ambassador reminded Ottawa that the United States viewed itself to be carrying the burden of responsibilities in Asia, that aggressive and expansionist actions of China since 1949 added up to an objective to dominate the Far East by overt action or subversion, and that Communist Chinese military aggression was not over, merely suspended.

Attempts at mediation in the late spring failed, prompting Mr Leger to advise Mr Pearson that it would be unwise to take a bold stand on the matter. On 30 May the United Kingdom unilaterally renounced the China Differential, thereafter basing its restrictions on trade with China on the same criteria as its trade with other Communist countries. Other CHICOM members soon followed suit and within weeks it was clear that the China Differential and the rationale for maintaining a special committee had collapsed. Contrary to earlier views on the 'unrealistic and unjustifiable' nature of the differential, Canada was one of the three last states to abandon it. When in late summer it did so, it proceeded without making any kind of public statement on the matter, simply granting export licences on previously proscribed goods without making Canadian traders aware of the change in policy.

The ambiguous Canadian positions on the issues of both the exemptions and the differential grew out of a variety of factors. It is clear that Canadian officials did not support the China Differential in principle. Nor was there any major support for the idea that the embargoes were having a significant or salutary effect on Chinese behaviour. In several instances, top-level Canadian officials voiced the view that trans-shipment of goods from the Soviet Union and its allies negated the force of the special China list and moreover, that the embargo tended to strengthen rather than reduce Chinese dependence on the Soviet Union. Balanced against this, however, was a concern for alliance solidarity, a position which drew on the convictions of Mr Pearson and others that an embargo to be effective on even strategic goods must be collective.

Canadian sacrifices in the name of alliance solidarity exacted a very small political and economic price. Policy-makers in Ottawa frequently commented that, unlike their counterparts in Washington and London, they were subjected to little domestic pressure from the general public, Parliament or business interests, a fact which accorded them considerable flexibility for quiet diplomacy and changes of position. Further, unlike the United Kingdom which had a major stake in Asia through Commonwealth and empire ties, especially Hong Kong, unlike the United States which had extensive political and military investment in the region, and unlike some of the lesser powers that had a relatively significant China trade or administered colonies that did (e.g. Portugal and Macao), China did not rank high on the agenda of Canadian strategic priorities.

Nor was there overwhelming pressure from within government on the prospects of China trade. Most of the estimates in the mid-1950s, for example, on the prospects of exports to China were pessimistic. Few expected a 'gold rush' and, as was observed by many, including the Trade Commissioner in Hong Kong, the importance of the Chinese market was minimal. Concerns largely focused on the possibility of developing a China trade in future. Several officials even argued that specific sectors of the Canadian economy benefitted from the allied trade controls, finding, for example, a new Japanese market for iron ore and coal that traditionally had been purchased from Manchuria. The head of the Far Eastern Division noted that only a moral obligation not to press for freer trade with China until the UN resolutions were rescinded existed for Canada. Furthermore, it had not been demonstrated that Canada was suffering from the CHICOM embargo.

It is interesting, therefore, to compare Canadian perspectives on CHICOM between 1953 and 1957 with views expressed following the Sino-Indian border war in October 1962 which led to a brief suspension of Canadian exports to China. By 1962, of course, the Canadian government had established a large stake in the China trade in the aftermath of major grain sales a year earlier. While publicly proclaiming a tough embargo against China immediately following the Chinese incursion into northern India, the Diefenbaker government created a Cabinet-level mechanism for granting special exemptions to Canadian exporters and exempted grain exports altogether. The border situation was still not resolved in the summer of 1963, but the new Liberal government moved quickly to reduce the restrictions to those imposed by the CoCom lists. 'Experience has shown', argued Mitchell Sharp, the Minister of Trade and Commerce, 'that restriction of exports to Communist China of items which are not part of the Export Control List may cause resentment and ill-will on the part of Chinese state trading organizations and affect negotiation of future wheat sales'.[20]

A matter of ongoing concern was the interests and views of the United States. Canadian policy-makers were acutely aware of the multiple and forceful passions which the China issue provoked in their southern neighbour. Some Canadian diplomats, most often based in Washington, shared hard-line views on the military, political and economic containment of China. These perspectives appear to have been in a small minority, but they did reinforce the broader segment of elite opinion which was sensitive to the possibility of retaliation. There was concern about general congressional retaliation on bilateral trade issues as well as specific retaliations in the area of abrogating the special relationship by which US goods could be exported to Canada without the special export licences that were required to export goods to any other country. This general worry led to a special sensitivity to US concerns about the possibility of trans-shipment of US goods through Canada to China and in part explains why Canada delayed so long in dropping a China Differential. There prevailed, moreover, a pervasive belief that the United States should not be allowed to suffer a major defeat at CHICOM, a concern that grew out of a deep-seated fear that frustration on the China issue could lead to the collapse of the Western Alliance and the resurrection of US isolationism. On various occasions the argument reappeared that the value of Canadian trade with China paled against even a slight reduction in Canadian exports to the United States. C. D. Howe made this point in forceful fashion during a meeting with high-level UK officials in March 1957 at which time the matter of the China Differential was discussed.[21]

The People's Republic of China

With trade embargoes as with the larger problems of diplomatic recognition and the admission of China into the United Nations, the issue of timing was paramount to Canadian thinking. A. E. Ritchie, an Assistant Under-Secretary, made this point clearly in December 1955:

> We have for some time held the view, now put forward explicitly by the UK, that it is difficult or impossible to justify the maintenance of a separate China list on purely strategic grounds, and we have been unsympathetic to the moral and political arguments which underlie the US insistence on its preservation. We have not so far considered it worth while on balance, however, to challenge the US position in the Consultative Group, although the US has certainly been made aware of our attitude on an informal basis. For these reasons I do not believe that we will find ourselves opposed in any way to the UK's general objective of bringing the two lists into line primarily through the reduction of the special China list.
> On the other hand, there will no doubt be delicate problems of tactics and timing. The US public reacts so emotionally to anything which concerns China that the US authorities in an election year are almost certain to be seriously concerned at this development.[22]

Earlier, in February 1954, Arthur Menzies had advocated the principle that Canada support UK demands for the elimination of the China Differential, but suggested that it not be acted upon until the Panmunjom and Berlin negotiations were successfully completed. Waiting for the right moment for independent Canadian initiatives on trade embargoes, as on the larger questions of diplomatic relations, proved to be a frustrating enterprise for more than 20 years.

The Effectiveness of the Sanctions

Measurement of the political or economic effectiveness of the sanctions is a hazardous undertaking in part because of generic difficulties in measuring the effectiveness of sanctions in any situation and the complexities of the China case. In this case, first, we lack reliable statistics on the Chinese economy for much of the 1950s and, second, the objectives of the sanctioners differed so dramatically.

Several factors clearly limited the effective 'bite' of the embargoes imposed against China as seen from either the minimalist or maximalist perspectives. The most important is the nature of the Chinese economy which traditionally has been largely agricultural and largely self-contained. Trade, of course, is not unimportant to China but persistently represents only a very small fraction of its total gross national product. The inertia of the Chinese economic system and its comparative isolation from the world economy have made it peculiarly resistant, though not entirely immune, to external economic pressures. It is difficult to conceive of a more difficult target to influence.

Second, despite vigilant US efforts, the embargo was never universal or watertight, even with respect to strategic goods. The Soviet Union and its Eastern European allies served as alternative sources of supply for most of the embargoed items through the 1950s. Moreover, clandestine trans-shipments of Western products (often through the Gdanyi connection), special exemptions and exceptions approved by CoCom-CHICOM, and goods occasionally supplied by nations not formally committed to the sanctions (especially Sweden, Switzerland and India) represented major leaks in the control system. After trade with the Soviet bloc declined in the early 1960s, it was Western suppliers who relaxed controls sufficiently to sustain Chinese imports in most commodities.

Most academic analysts who have examined the sanctions tend to conclude that they were largely, even spectacularly ineffective. Margaret Doxey, for example, points to China's ability to reorient its foreign trade and argues that the Chinese sanctions were 'incomplete, indecisive and inconclusive'.[23] Alexander Eckstein, US economist, concluded that 'the practical consequence of the U.S. embargo and allied trade controls were negligible'.[24]

There is fragmentary evidence that if the Western embargo in the 1950s did not prevent Chinese authorities from turning to other suppliers, especially the Soviet Union, it did likely raise the cost of these substitutes. Eckstein and Feng-Hwa Mah both estimate that China might have paid as much as $940 million more than world market prices for its imports between 1955 and 1959.[25] Compared to the total volume of China's foreign trade for that period, the figure is not negligible but amounts to less than 1 per cent of the gross national product. The embargoes also hindered China's accumulation of foreign reserves, but only to an extent that Eckstein describes as 'minimal'. Overall, concludes another economist, externally-imposed obstacles did little to slow the aggregate growth of Chinese industry which between 1952 and 1959 expanded at an annual rate of almost 20 per cent, four times that of India and twice that of the Soviet Union.[26] There are further arguments that the Western embargoes facilitated the process of import substitution and inadvertently advanced the expansion of an indigenous steel industry.[27]

Aggregate data, while helpful, cannot help us evaluate the effect of the sanctions on specific sectors of the Chinese economy, especially the production of military equipment, or particular geographic regions. Without field study in China and internal US intelligence material, it nevertheless seems reasonable to speculate that, while the embargoes did not stunt overall economic development, they might well have created significant sectoral distortions. Eckstein suggests that Western controls, combined with the curtailment of Soviet bloc exports after 1960, had the effect of contributing to 'a marked deterioration in the equipment of the Chinese Communist armed forces', raised the costs of nuclear development, and postponed the acquisition of a nuclear capability by at least two years'.[28]

It is even more difficult to assess the extent to which the sanctions might have had political effects on the Chinese leadership. There is no evidence that they significantly altered the domestic or external goals of the Communist regime or contributed to a sense of national isolation or collective psychological guilt for the calumnies of aggression. We can confidently conclude that they did not lead to the collapse of the regime. Ezra Vogel and others who have examined the Chinese press in the 1950s generally suggest that external economic and political pressures tended to increase rather than harm the popularity of the Communist government and were in fact useful to the party in the Anti-Landlord campaign which ran concurrent with the fighting in Korea.[29]

Against these penalties inflicted on the target country can be weighed some of the expenses incurred by the participants in the sanctions. The most obvious was the loss of trade revenue which, of course, varied greatly from country to country. A second cost, often overlooked, was the direct expense of administration. We lack authoritative figures, but J. Wilczynski has estimated that the direct administrative expenses for screening East-West trade in the mid-1960s amounted to more than 50 million pounds sterling per year. He noted, for instance, that in 1964 the US Department of Commerce employed in excess of 300 people, at a cost of more than $4 million, to handle export controls. We do not know what portion of this figure can be attributed to the China sanctions alone, but the total sum was not negligible.[30] Canada's expenditure in 1952 to support its portion of CoCom's operating costs and its Paris personnel amounted to 90,000 francs per month.

Because of the global sweep and duration of the sanctions effort, the subject of its 'unintentional consequences' is potentially enormous. In addition to the problems of extraterritoriality already discussed, two in particular deserve attention. The first is the possibility that the sanctions, to the extent that they had any political effect, drove the Chinese deeper into the Soviet Union orbit in the early 1950s, and precluded the possibility that Mao's China might go the way of Tito's Yugoslavia. Certainly this surfaced as the most frequently mentioned <u>realpolitik</u> argument against the maximalist interpretation of the embargoes. A sharp exchange between Canadian and US officials in 1956 underscores the point. The controversy centered on the details of Sino-Soviet rail connections. US officials argued that the embargo tended to put unbearable strain on the rail system, and the Canadians countered that the actual effect of the Western embargo would be to promote the upgrading of the system and closer commercial integration of the two countries. The exchange indicates that the implications of the sanctions for the Sino-Soviet relationship were, to say the least, hard to evaluate, especially in light of the sceptical view that external economic pressures have little potence for influencing the main lines of Chinese foreign policy decision-making.

Second, China's Asian neighbours paid an undeniably heavy price. The cost to Hong Kong and Macao merchants, particularly during the period of the China Differential, was significant and led to the dramatic reorientation of the trade patterns of both colonies. Restrictions on exports, particularly of rubber, from Malaysia and Indonesia to China raised a thorny problem of 'imperialist manipulation'. Canadian officials, at least, paid particular attention to charges raised in 1953 that the CHICOM lists permitted the United Kingdom to manipulate to its advantage the price of rubber produced in Singapore by artificially restricting demand. Propagandists in Beijing were not unaware of the resentments that the embargo effort engendered. *People's Daily* on one occasion claimed that, 'as a big purchaser', the United Kingdom like the United States, 'uses every pretext to force down prices and raise customs to inflict great losses on those countries whose economy is dependent on exports'.[31] The specific problem of Singapore rubber exports was eventually resolved by a CHICOM exemption granted to the United Kingdom. This solution, however, was far from perfect. Indonesia, an independent nation not participating in CHICOM, was restrained from similar exports of rubber to China by Battle Act regulations which were based on the standing CHICOM lists and which did not take account of the special exemptions and exceptions made to member countries. If the sanctions did not drive a wedge between the major Western powers and their Third World colonies and allies, they tended to aggravate a running sore.

The obstacles to effective implementation, then, are easy to enumerate: disagreements among sanctioners; the impervious nature of the Chinese economy; the loose knit of the enforcement mechanisms; and the nature of the objectives often advanced as the ends of the allied effort. It is more difficult to account for the fact that the sanction effort held together as long as it did. The United States clearly provided the initiative and resources to keep the collective effort alive. It paid a heavy price in implementing its own embargo and in manipulating aid policies so that it could expand the geographic coverage of the sanctions. It showed skill, persistence and determination in extending the economic campaign through dozens of bilateral arrangements and several multilateral ones. Ironically, however, the blanket nature of the US embargo made it a blunt instrument for effecting measurable changes in Chinese behaviour. Unlike the kinds of economic sanctions subsequently placed on the Soviet Union, the treatment of China prior to the Nixon initiative lacked specificity and manipulable rewards.

CoCom and CHICOM deserve further study as mechanisms for international co-ordination and co-operation. Considering the various pressures and diversity of viewpoints of the members of CoCom-CHICOM, it is remarkable that the organisation has functioned as effectively as it has. United States leadership and pressure is one factor, though the organisation has continued to operate in a generally effective fashion even as US influence has declined. The nature of discussions, the exemptions procedure and a general consensus on the value of restricting some kinds of exports to real or potential adversaries are important ingredients in providing the flexibility that assured survival.

The final factor that cemented the sanction campaign can perhaps best be described as a fear of China. Contrary to those views of those who suggest that the economic actions against China were products of US animus alone, it is important to keep in mind the extent of voluntary co-operation with the US effort. The extent of co-operation varied considerably, but in addition to the countries that wished to get back to generally unrestricted trading as soon as possible, others such as New Zealand and Australia imposed unilateral embargoes that rivalled US embargoes in their comprehensiveness and duration. It is ironic that in the 1980s it is the United States that is pushing CoCom to relax, if not abrogate, restrictions on China trade. Now that US leaders have classified China as a 'friendly, non-aligned' nation, it is the United States that is advocating the sale of sophisticated military equipment to China.

Conclusion

What general conclusions can we derive from the sanctions effort against China? The first area concerns the matter of motivations. Our examination of the range of putative goals in Canada and the United States suggests that objectives are not necessarily coherent or consistent within or among participating states. Perhaps the most striking aspect of the entire undertaking was that from the US perspective, 'success', measured in the behavioural terms of influence on specific Chinese decisions, was largely unimportant. So far as the sanctions were seen as a deterrent against Chinese 'aggression', they were largely and admittedly unsuccessful. The fact that US leaders were willing to absorb substantial costs for more than 20 years indicates that the China sanctions fall into a special category where simple ends-means calculations are largely irrelevant.

In a related sense, the sanctions suggest that commonality of purpose and identity of thinking are not essential ingredients for mounting an extensive international effort. Despite acute differences in objectives and approach, at least minimal controls could be implemented on the basis of a general negative perception of the target nation, combined with the steadfast determination of a major power to promote and guide common action.

The most interesting and important questions about the historical context of the China sanctions inevitably lead to the doorstep of US motivations and influence. The degree of US resolve, unanimity and passion on the China question are probably without precedent in the post-war US experience. The general policy of militarily containing, diplomatically isolating and economically strangling Communist China exhibited remarkable durability for more than 20 years and drew support from a broad, bi-partisan elite and public constituency. Unlike various economic embargoes against Cuba, the Soviet Union and other states, the China sanctions engendered little domestic opposition and received overwhelming popular endorsement. This homogeneity of thinking and the political consensus it represented are rare occurrences indeed. The US crusade against China was so fundamental to the broader international sanction effort that it seems unlikely that such a large and costly undertaking will occur again.

The special nature of the US response to Mao's China coincided with the high point of US influence on the Western Alliance. While it would be inaccurate to suggest that the other participants in the sanctions were motivated solely or even primarily by overt US pressure, US leadership on the issue tended to extend the embargo effort further and longer than most of them wished. A small number of Canadian officials shared the US interpretation of Chinese intentions, the situation in Asia, and the appropriate policy response; most considered China a blindspot in the US approach to post-war international order. As Canadian actions indicate, the form of participation is only partially determined by the explicit objectives of national decision-makers. The distance between espoused principles and objectives on the one hand, and actual behaviour on the other, is revealing testimony about the nature and significance of US influence in the Cold War years.

Notes

1. See particularly Gunnar Adler-Karlsson, Western Economic Warfare, 1947-1967 (Almqvist and Wiksell, Stockholm, 1968); Alexander Eckstein, Communist China's Economic Growth and Foreign Trade (McGraw Hill, New York, 1966); Arthur Stahnke (ed.), China's Trade with the West: A Political and Economic Analysis (Praeger, New York, 1972); and John McIntyre and Richard Cupitt, 'East-West Trade Control: Crumbling Consensus', Survey 25, no. 2 (Spring 1980).

2. I am grateful to the Department of External Affairs, the Department of Industry, Trade and Commerce, and the Privy Council Office for the documentation and assistance they provided. The opinions expressed here, however, are mine alone. In preparing this chapter I have been given access to a variety of files in the Department of External Affairs, Ottawa. This access was granted, however, on the condition that I not quote from or cite the specific files which I have employed.

3. While there are several brief accounts of the origins and operations of CoCom, there exists no major monographic work on what is surely one of the more successful inter-governmental organisations of the post-war period. This unfortunate situation is probably the result of the secrecy which has surrounded the operations of the Committee. On recent developments at CoCom, see McIntyre and Cupitt, 'East-West Trade Control'.

4. Adler-Karlsson, Western Economic Warfare, Chs. 4 and 5, especially p. 56.

5. The literature on the US control system is extensive. The most useful account relevant to the China embargo is John R. Garson, 'The American Trade Embargo Against China', in Alexander Eckstein (ed.), China Trade Prospects and U.S. Policy (Praeger, New York, 1971).

6. On US views, see Garson, 'The American Trade Embargo', pp. 24-43. Canadian perspectives can be found in James Irvine Whitcomb Corcoran, 'The Trading With the Enemy Act and the Controlled Canadian Corporations', McGill Law Journal, vol. 14, no. 2, 1968; Chen Tungpi, 'Legal Aspects of Canadian Trade with the People's Republic of China', Law and Contemporary Problems, vol. 38, no. 2 (Summer-Autumn 1973), pp. 208-15; and Henry S. Albinski and F. Conrad Raabe, 'Canada's Chinese Trade in Political Perspective', in Arthur Stahnke (ed.), China's Trade with the West: A Political and Economic Analysis (Praeger, New York, 1972), pp. 99-102.

7. McIntyre and Cupitt, 'East-West Trade Control', p. 93.

8. Adler-Karlsson, Western Economic Warfare, p. 67.

9. Margaret Doxey, Economic Sanctions and Inter-

national Enforcement, 2nd edn. (Royal Institute of International Affairs, London, 1980), p. 18.

10. On the nature and objectives of the relaxation of US controls during the Nixon Administration, see Arthur Cahill, The China Trade and U.S. Tarriffs (Praeger, New York, 1979), pp. 8-11; Oliver M. Lee, 'U.S. Trade Policy Toward China: From Economic Warfare to Summit Diplomacy', in Arthur Stahnke (ed.), China Trade, pp. 33-87; and Henry Kissinger, White House Years (Houghton-Mufflin, Boston, 1979), Ch. XVIII.

11. Samuel Ho and Ralph Huenemann, Canada's Trade with China: Patterns and Prospects (Private Planning Association of Canada, Montreal, 1972), p. 24.

12. Henry A. Albinski and F. Conrad Raabe, 'Canada's Chinese Trade', p. 100.

13. Quoted in Oliver Lee, 'U.S. Trade Policy Toward China', p. 42.

14. On the role of Congress, see John R. Garson, 'The American Trade Embargo', pp. 10-23; and Philip J. Briggs, 'Congress and the Cold War: U.S.-China Policy, 1955', China Quarterly, no. 85 (March 1981).

15. Adler-Karlsson, Western Economic Warfare, p. 37.

16. See Kim Richard Nossal, 'Business as Usual: Relations with China in the 1940s', in Kim Nossal (ed.), The Acceptance of Paradox: Essays in Honour of John Holmes (Canadian Institute of International Affairs, Toronto, 1983). Additional information on subsequent sales of military equipment to the Nationalist governments in Nanking and Taipei is located in a Memorandum for Cabinet from Brooke Claxton, Acting Secretary of State for External Affairs, 13 April 1953., Cabinet Document 24-53, C-20-9-(a)-D, Privy Council Office Files.

17. As quoted in Denis Stairs, The Diplomacy of Constraint: Canada, the Korean War, and the United States (University of Toronto Press, Toronto, 1974), pp. 180-1.

18. For a more thorough discussion of Canadian views on trade with China, see John Holmes, 'Canada and China: The Dilemmas of a Middle Power', in A. M. Halpern (ed.), Policies Toward China: Views From Six Continents (McGraw Hill, New York, 1968); and Paul M. Evans and Daphne Taras, 'Looking (Far) East: Parliament and Canada-China Relations, 1949-1982', in David Taras (ed.), Parliament and Foreign Affairs (Canadian Institute of International Affairs, Toronto, 1985.

19. See James C. Thomson, Jr., 'On the Making of U.S. China Policy, 1961-9: A Study in Bureaucratic Politics', China Quarterly, no. 50 (April-June 1972), pp. 220-2; and A. T. Steele, The American People and China (McGraw Hill, New York, 1966), Ch. 10.

20. Mitchell Sharp, Memorandum to Cabinet, 27 May 1963, PCO File T-1-12-C1.

21. Canadian leaders including Prime Minister Louis St Laurent, Lester Pearson and C. D. Howe met with top UK officials including Prime Minister Harold MacMillan and Trevor Lloyd on the matter. During the session Mr Howe in particular expressed the view that he was not enthusiastic about pressing beyond the distance the United States was willing to go on the matter of the China Differential.

22. 12 December 1955, PCO File T-50-4-C.

23. Doxey, Economic Sanctions, p. 18.

24. Alexander Eckstein, Communist China's Economic Growth and Foreign Trade (McGraw Hill, New York, 1966), p. 247.

25. Eckstein, Communist China's Economic Growth, pp. 171-2 and Feng-Hwa Mah, 'The Terms of Sino-Soviet Trade', China Quarterly, January-March 1964, pp. 174-91.

26. As quoted in Adler-Karlsson, Western Economic Warfare, p. 207.

27. J. Wilczynski, The Economics and Politics of East-West Trade (Macmillan, London, 1969), p. 288.

28. Eckstein, Communist China's Economic Growth, p. 265.

29. Ezra Vogel, Canton Under Communism (Harvard University Press, Cambridge, 1973), Ch. 3.

30. Wilczynski, The Economics and Politics of East-West Trade, p. 289.

31. See Robert Boardman, Britain and the People's Republic of China, 1949-1974 (Macmillan, London, 1976), p. 108.

Chapter Five

ECONOMIC SANCTIONS AGAINST CUBA

Sergio Roca

The application of economic sanctions against Cuba by or at the behest of the United States encompasses more than two decades. In that period, significant variations have occured in the objectives pursued, in the sanctions applied and in the effects achieved. Seven US presidents, five Soviet leaders and one Cuban revolutionary have confronted that issue within a shifting triangular relationship and in the midst of changing world conditions. For these reasons, this chapter will attempt to concentrate on the salient features of the topic. Concluding remarks will deal with the current potential opportunity for the United States to enhance the effectiveness of its regional policy in the context of Cuba's foreign debt situation.

Intended Objectives

The objectives pursued by the United States in 22 years of economic warfare against Cuba, despite variations in design and scope, can be classified under two major headings: overthrow and containment.

In the early phase of the confrontation (roughly 1960 to 1963), the basic intent of US economic sanctions, in conjunction with military and diplomatic actions, was to overthrow the Castro regime. After his Administration cut the Cuban sugar quota in July 1960, President Eisenhower declared: 'This action amounts to economic sanctions against Cuba. Now we must look ahead to other moves - economic, diplomatic and strategic'.[1] In his memoirs, former US Ambassador Philip Bonsal concluded that 'the suspension of the sugar quota was a major element in the program for the overthrow of Castro'.[2] In his comprehensive review of events and attitudes leading to the 1961 formal break of US-Cuban relations, Cole Blasier assessed the sugar quota cut as an 'economic measure apparently designed to eliminate Castro politically'.[3]

According to Blasier, in addition to the 'decisive

motivation' related to Washington's perception that Premier Castro was becoming a conduit for Soviet political and military meddling in the continent and coupled with the Cuban leader's 'open and belligerent defiance of U.S. political primacy in the hemisphere', US economic sanctions were influenced by private economic considerations. He stated: 'Powerful vested interests in the U.S. and in some Latin American countries hoped to profit from Cuba's political difficulties and get part of the Cuban quota...and [they] contributed to the pressures on Congress and the President to cut the quota for reasons not related exclusively to public interests'.[4] Whatever the mixture of public and private, political and economic, diplomatic and military, ideological and personality considerations or motives, the early US economic sanctions were intended to overthrow the Castro government.

From about 1964 the basic objective of US economic warfare became the containment of the Castro revolution. In this shift, the nature of the US goal was transformed from specific to indeterminate. Writing in 1972, Lynn D. Bender, in his indispensable book, provided this assessment of the new policy:

> Nevertheless, still absent was a clear definition of the ultimate goal pursued by U.S. policy toward the Castro regime--a problem that even today is yet to be fully and satisfactorily resolved....
> The United States did come to the realization during this phase that the containment policy alone would not bring about the collapse of the Castro regime...,but also harbored the expectation that, in the long run, its over-all policy would be effective in creating the necessary conditions for the eventual overthrow of Castro.[5]

The particular objectives pursued by the containment policy were outlined by Under-Secretary of State, George C. Ball, in early 1964:

1. to reduce the will and ability of the present Cuban regime to export revolution and violence to the other American states;
2. to make plain to the people of Cuba and to the elements of the power structure of the regime that the present regime cannot serve their interests;
3. to demonstrate to the peoples of the American republics that Communism has no future in the Western Hemisphere;
4. to increase the cost to the Soviet Union of maintaining a communist outpost in the Western Hemis-

phere.[6]

With minor changes related mostly to modifications in the application of sanctions and not to revisions of substantive objectives, US economic policy toward Cuba remained virtually unchanged through 1980. The key element remained containment, the basic purpose was punitive, and the ultimate goal was still to be clearly defined. In fact, at a recent meeting of the US-Cuba Study Group, sponsored by the Council on Foreign Relations, participants (in and out of government alike) had difficulty articulating what goals the United States had been pursing vis-a-vis Cuba.

Subsequently, in the context of Cuban involvement in Angola and Ethiopia, in the aftermath of the Nicaraguan revolution, in light of renewed armed struggles in Central America, and with the advent of the Reagan presidency, US efforts were concentrated on limiting or reducing the effectiveness of Cuba's aggressive foreign policy in all its dimensions. Increasing threats against the island, some explicitly military, were voiced by high officials of the new administration, including Secretary of State Alexander Haig's reference about 'going to the source'. In that vein, Thomas O. Enders, Assistant Secretary for Inter-American Affairs, in enumerating the tasks for US policy in the hemisphere, declared:

> we will focus on the source of the problem....Cuba has become a misshapen society....Yet it plays Gurkha to the Soviet imperialists in Africa and threatens nearly all of its neighbors....Cuba has declared covert war on its neighbors - our neighbors....The United States will join with them to bring the costs of war back to Havana.[7]

It is clear that at present US policy is designed to increase the economic cost to Cuba and to the Soviet Union of pursuing their respective, often-times coincidental, comprehensive foreign policies. To Washington, the main irritants involve Cuban troops in Africa, Havana's support of Central American insurgents, and the very existence of the close Soviet-Cuban relationship.

Sanctions Adopted

The first major economic sanction imposed by the United States was the cutting of Cuba's sugar quota by 700,000 tons in July 1960, which resulted in about US $80 million in lost income to the Castro regime. Subsequent presidential proclamations extended the exclusion of Cuban sugar from the US market on a temporary basis.

On 3 February 1962 the formal US embargo on Cuban trade was implemented by Presidential Proclamation 3447.

Cuba

The legal foundation of the US embargo is essentially contained in three statutes: the Trading with the Enemy Act of 1917, the Foreign Assistance Act of 1961, and the Export Administration Act of 1969, all as amended. The provisions of the US embargo resulted in the following developments:

1. the banning of all trade (exports and imports) with Cuba, except for humanitarian reasons;
2. the requirement of approval by the US Department of Commerce for exports or re-exports to Cuba of commodities originating in the United States, including US subsidiaries abroad and even non-US firms engaged in triangular trade of US goods with Cuba;
3. the restriction of the use of US ports by foreign vessels trading with Cuba; and
4. the requirement of authorisation by the US Treasury Department for the few imports (books) allowed from Cuba.[8]

In July 1964 and September 1967, the US embargo was multilateralised through hemispheric approval and support at the Organisation of American States (OAS). The following OAS sanctions were imposed against Cuba:

1. the severing of diplomatic and commercial relations;
2. the suspension of all trade (direct and indirect), except for foodstuffs, medicines and medical equipment;
3. the suspension of all sea and air service to and from Cuba;
4. the establishment of passport restrictions on travel to and from Cuba;
5. the recommendation that government-owned or financed cargoes not be shipped on vessels sailing to Cuba; and
6. the general call to Western allies to restrict their trade and financial ties with the island.[9]

In the Western Hemisphere, only Mexico and Canada did not participate in the embargo; rather, they expanded their trade and financial relations with Cuba. Non-socialist countries such as Spain and Japan resisted US pressure and engaged in trade with the Caribbean island. By the late 1960s, the unified OAS embargo was broken when Chile and Peru resumed trade with Cuba. In 1973 Argentina re-established trade relations with the Castro regime and US subsidiaries in Argentina were authorised by US officials to export manufactured goods to Cuba. In July 1975 the OAS accord was relaxed to allow each country to pursue its own interests in determining the nature and extent of its diplomatic and commercial relations with Havana.

Based on the OAS resolution, the US State Department announced a modification of those aspects of US policy which affected third-country trade with Cuba. Under the revised regulations, foreign subsidiaries of US firms located in third countries, could be granted licences for the export of non-strategic foreign-made goods to Cuba.[10]

In addition, the United States lifted the suspension of US aid (credit and food) to countries that traded with the island or provided transportation services to Cuba. However, the total embargo on direct US-Cuban trade remained in effect.

The relaxation in the hostility level between the United States and Cuba achieved during the early years of the Carter Administration was concentrated on peripheral issues. These agenda items were important to the difficult process of normalisation of relations but were largely unrelated to the trade embargo. From 1977 to 1979 the two countries resumed diplomatic contact at the level of interests sections, signed fishing rights and maritime boundary agreements, and negotiated an anti-hijacking pact. Washington lifted the ban on US travel to Cuba and permitted the resumption of charter flights between the two countries. Havana allowed some 4,000 former political prisoners and their families to emigrate. But the embargo remained in effect.

Under the Reagan Administration, the application of US economic sanctions against Cuba has intensified. Economic warfare expanded its coverage and escalated in severity. In April 1982 the US Treasury Department, in order 'to reduce Cuba's hard currency earnings', limited travel to the island to official business, family visits, news gathering and research activities.[11] At the same time, the Financial Times (London) commented that the United States 'is tightening its economic pressures to add serious financial and commercial problems to Castro's government'.[12] In response to Cuba's external financial crisis, the United States tried to undermine the island's debt restructuring efforts by pressuring Western creditors to demand hard International Monetary Fund type terms.[13] At a minimum, the United States intended to raise the financial cost to Cuba of any accommodation with her creditors.

Effect of the Sanctions

This section will consider only the domestic economic impact on Cuba of economic sanctions imposed or sponsored by the United States. A distinction will be made between the total cost and the net cost of economic sanctions to the Cuban economy.

United States economic sanctions were just one of many factors which have contributed to Cuba's economic shortcomings. From the start, Cuban leaders and economic officials readily acknowledged the relative insignificance of the embargo's impact because there were several more persuasive explanations for the mounting economic difficulties. Ernesto Guevara railed in 1961 against explaining away every problem by blaming the US blockade and the increase in domestic consumption levels.[14] In 1963 Guevara chastised 'certain leaders' for 'our lack of courage in facing economic realities...we have followed an ostrich-type economic policy by blaming drought and imperialism'.[15] Alban Lataste, a Chilean economist who was investment director of Cuba's central planning board, wrote in 1964:

> It would be of little help to our economic tasks to remain bogged down in the apologies of previous years, never finding anything wrong and explaining all difficulties in terms of capitalist heritage, the imperialist blockade, or natural calamities.[16]

And later that year, Premier Castro stated that 'at first many times we blamed it all on imperialism and the imperialist blockade...but the blockade should not be a pretext ...it is clear that our inexperience, lack of ability, irresponsibility, and superficiality have also been responsible for many of our difficulties'.[17]

In later years, when the Cuban leadership was able to draw upon its own historical experience to evaluate successes and failures, the detrimental impact of the economic sanctions was still agreed to be relatively inconsequential. In December 1969 Premier Castro disclosed that 'we have had problems with spare parts from all capitalist and socialist countries, very serious problems...ranging from the purchase of the parts to their timely delivery... which combined with the inferior technical level of our operators and mechanics, and with our well-deserved reputation as equipment-wreckers...all these factors together constitute a real tragedy'.[18] In September 1973 President Osvaldo Dorticos, called for greater discipline and intensive effort so that

> in the not too distant future we could be able to show the world the prestige of a healthy economy, an efficient economy, with high productivity, scientifically managed, well-managed politically. We have yet to achieve this and we are just now starting to think about how to do it.[19]

Finally, in the main document of the First Congress of the Cuban Communist Party, which contained the official confession of 'mistakes made' in the early revolutionary period, Premier Castro asserted:

> But it is also necessary to admit that in many cases resources have not been used to the utmost. Our economic management has not been as efficient as it might have been. Economic direction methods that have been put into practice have not been the best possible. Generally, our administrative cadres do not have the required economic consciousness, the required concern for matters regarding costs and production efficiency in general....In guiding our economy, we have undoubtedly made idealistic mistakes and, at times, have ignored the reality that there are objective economic laws by which we must abide.[20]

However, to argue that economic sanctions had minimal impact is not to deny that they imposed certain costs on the Cuban economy. The embargo's total cost may be defined as the sum of: (1) losses in export income and/or markets; (2) additional costs of imports and/or transportation; and (3) indirect negative effects (e.g. difficulty in acquiring spare parts, need to expand warehouse capacity, technological incompatibility with new suppliers). This is a general definition which may be further refined.

The most comprehensive analysis of the impact of the Cuban embargo in its first decade is found in the work of Maryanna Craig Boynton.[21] Using an econometric model of price determination for world market sugar, she tested three hypotheses related to the issue of potential losses in markets and income:

1. The US boycott of Cuban sugar did not reduce the volume of Cuba's sugar exports (the income effect).
2. The US boycott of Cuban sugar did not depress the world price of sugar (the terms of trade effect).
3. Cuba's sugar diverted from the US market could not be sold on the world market.

Her conclusions were:

1. For the period 1962-64 the US boycott had a direct positive effect on the world sugar price through the US global quota sugar purchases in lieu of the Cuban quota. United States global purchases significantly increased the world sugar price in these years, but there may have been an indirect downward effect on the world sugar price after 1964 attributable to increased sugar stocks in the Western Hemisphere. Otherwise, hypothesis (2) cannot be rejected.
2. Cuba could not have sold the quantity of sugar

diverted from the US market on the world free market. Hypothesis (3) cannot be rejected.

3. Cuba's sugar exports show no significant trend effect from the US boycott. Trade creation occurred in the socialist bloc. Hypothesis (1) cannot be rejected.
4. Reduction of Cuban export volume on the free market cannot be attributed to buyers' complicity in the boycott. It can be attributed to one or all of the following: (a) increased production by other exporting nations; (b) increased beet production in Europe; (c) leftward movements along a supply curve for Cuban exports as world prices fell.

And furthermore, the commodity pattern of Cuba's exports and the level of Cuba's export earnings have not significantly changed as a result of trade warfare. No improvement or deterioration in Cuba's aggregate economic performance can be demonstrated. Cuba has regained ownership of its resources, but its foreign indebtedness is large.

In sum, Boynton's study and conclusions indicate that Cuban losses of export income and markets on account of US economic sanctions were insignificant.

Regarding the two other components of the embargo's total cost (additional import/transport costs and indirect effects), virtually all academic experts agree that such costs were relatively small and transitory. For example, Boynton concluded:

> The embargo against Cuba represented an intensification of trade warfare that caused production declines during 1961 that were at least in part due to shortages of spare parts and raw materials. By 1964 the socialist nations had rescued Cuba from the embargo's direct effects, and in 1964 Cuba's traditional trading partners, France, Japan, Spain, Canada, and the United Kingdom were also increasing their exports to Cuba. The spread of the embargo policy to include all Western Hemisphere nations except Canada, together with restrictions on commercial shipping, elicited a larger rescue response.[22]

Eric N. Baklanoff, writing in 1970, provided this assessment:

> Cuba after 1960 was unable to purchase in the United States spare parts for the maintenance of sugar mills, factories, refineries, railways, and automotive equipment. This serious problem resulted in stoppages and bottlenecks in the early 1960s....But the island was soon able to buy the necessary spare parts through triangular trade, particularly with Canada and some

> Western European nations....
> Still, the boycott and the embargo may have had some effect, for example, increased transportation costs due to the distance of Cuban trade partners and slightly increased costs and more time to obtain spare parts. But these are minor economic problems.[23]

In his evaluation of the first revolutionary decade, Carmelo Mesa-Lago concluded:

> United States economic actions (e.g., the cut of the sugar quota) and the embargo against Cuba have failed because the latter has been able to obtain needed spare parts from triangular trade, transportation equipment from Western Europe, and fuel, military equipment, machinery, and credit from the USSR and the socialist countries. The latter, in turn, have made agreements to buy Cuban products, mainly sugar. Also, Cuba's merchant marine rapidly expanded in the second half of the 1960s and today is one of the largest in Latin America.[24]

Finally, Jorge Dominguez, in his land-mark study, wrote:

> The United States embargo's economic effects were mixed. In the short term, the sugar purchases made by the United States to replace the lost Cuban supplies helped (along with the decline in Cuban production) to drive up the world price of sugar. More serious and longer-term effects arose from the difficulties Cuba faced in transferring its trading patterns to the socialist countries. Larger port facilities to handle long-haul trade were needed, as were Soviet shipping commitments to handle the trade and the adjustment of Cuban industry to new spare parts, new machinery, and new techniques. While this conversion was being carried out, the capacity of large segments of Cuban industry was underutilized for lack of spare parts and imported inputs.[25]

Additional evidence regarding the transitory nature of the economic burdens of the embargo can be presented. For their part, Cuban scholars and political leaders declared victory a long time ago. In 1967 Julio Le Riverend, one of Cuba's foremost economic historians, wrote:

> As a result of the changes made during 1961, 1962 and 1963, and of the victory of the people over the blockade which did not win general support in Latin

> America or the capitalist world, the Revolution entered into a maturing stage, which in 1964 was characterized by production growth...[26]

Addressing an international conference in 1969, Carlos Rafael Rodriguez, a high government official, stated: 'The blockade that the United States tried to impose upon us has totally failed....It no longer has any economic significance'.[27] Later that year, Premier Castro boasted about the increasing availability of foreign financial and material resources 'in the past four or five years' which reflected 'the loss of prestige of the imperialist blockade'.[28]

Probably the most resounding victory statement was made by Premier Castro in 1975 at the massive popular meeting held to celebrate the party's first congress. In reacting to US threats to abort the incipient process of bilateral normalisation, Premier Castro declared:

> At first they bothered us a lot with their cancellations...but now when we fortunately do not depend on them for anything, not for trade, not for supplies, for nothing; if we were victorious now after victory with what can they threaten us? With cancelling what thing which they have not cancelled before to no effect?[29]

Five years later, in enumerating the factors responsible for the unfulfilment of the first five-year plan targets (i.e. falling world sugar prices, worsening terms of trade with capitalist areas, high interest rates on foreign debt, increased shipping costs, plant and animal diseases, introduction of new planning and management systems), Premier Castro made no mention whatsoever of the US economic embargo.[30]

Recently, the advent of Cuba's foreign debt crisis has revived official interest in the embargo and its burden on the Cuban economy. In late 1982 a report by the Banco Nacional de Cuba cited an incomplete study by 'Cuban specialists in various fields' which estimated 'the economic effect of the blockade imposed on Cuba by the United States and of the concomittant measures of aggression and sabotage promoted by that nation's governments through December 1981.[31] The preliminary cost estimates ('only the capital cost and excluding financial elements') were:

Table 5.1

	Million US Dollars
Foreign trade and maritime transport	$ 5,285.6
Invisibles	890.7
National defence and domestic order	2,905.0
TOTAL	$ 9,081.3

Obviously, without knowing the assumptions and methodology used in reaching these estimates, it is impossible to assess their accuracy and validity. But the Cuban estimate of the total cost of US economic warfare will allow for the discussion of the net cost of the embargo.

The concept of the net cost of the embargo is based on the largely political-ideological nature of Cuba's international economic relations. Cuba's sugar specialisation may be based on comparative advantage, but the bulk of its output must be sold in protected markets accessible mostly, if not only, through political affiliation. As a small, strategically-located developing country, similar political considerations are likely to influence the flow of foreign aid and financial credits. Just as US economic sanctions were imposed because Cuba chose a given socio-economic system (with Castro's added idiosyncrasies), Soviet aid flowed to the island for the same reason. In other words, US economic sanctions and Soviet aid largesse were different and offsetting reactions to the same event - Cuba's choice of socialism.

It is highly doubtful that the United States would have imposed such costs and that the Soviet Union would have offered such aid if not for the Cuban choice. Thus, the net cost of the US embargo would be equal to the total cost of US actions minus the total aid provided by the Soviet Union. It is conceivable that such calculation may yield a net benefit, not cost, to Cuba. For example, using Mesa-Lago's estimate that 'the total cumulative Soviet economic aid given to Cuba in 1960-79 amounted to $16.7 billion',[32] the net benefit to Cuba would be $7.6 billion. Clearly, this is only a very rough illustrative example since the Banco Nacional and Mesa-Lago estimates are not strictly comparable.

However the costs and benefits may be measured, the point to be stressed is that Soviet aid must be taken into account in estimating the net cost to Cuba of the US embargo. Indeed, the Banco Nacional report tacitly accepted such a conclusion:

Cuba

> The substantially more advantageous economic relations which had been developed with the socialist countries were even further improved...in the second half of the 1970s, and this helped the Cuban people to counteract, in large measure, the enormous harm U.S. policies were inflicting on the nation's economy.[33]

Realisation of the Objectives

The early objective of US economic sanctions (i.e. to overthrow the Castro regime) has clearly not been realised. The later expectation that in the long-run the embargo would somehow create the conditions for the eventual removal or perhaps amelioration of Premier Castro has also floundered.

Basically, after 1961 the internal political institutions and practices of Cuba and its economic organisation and policies were outside the concern of US policy. Washington was prepared to accept Cuban socialism at home but to prevent its export. The basic US policy became containment. But Cuba actively pursued its own policy of involvement (trying to export revolution, fomenting guerrilla activity), without regard to the potential effects of the embargo. The degree of realisation of US objectives was minimal or zero. Ironically, Cuban foreign policy in the mid-1960s was also in sharp contrast with Soviet positions. Despite Moscow's leverage over Havana, the Cubans persisted on the Camino Revolucionario both at home and abroad. If Premier Castro managed, in large measure, to maintain his political and ideological independence from the Soviet Union, what degree of compliance with US aims could Washington have expected? When, after 1968, Cuba desisted temporarily from using the Guevara approach, it was due to the lack of local objective conditions in Latin America and not in response to Soviet pressure.

The major accomplishment of the US economic embargo has consisted of increasing the cost to Cuba of surviving and developing as a socialist country and of pursuing an internationalist commitment. Since the Soviet Union provides Havana with substantial economic aid, the cost is also borne by Moscow. In the absence of any significant modification of Cuban behaviour in favour of the patterns posited by the United States, the embargo at present fulfils a largely punitive function. The question that must be raised is: Who is paying the price? In this connection, the issues debated in a recent article by Thomas O. Bayard and others are quite appropriate:

> The ultimate efficacy of sanctions depends not just on the costs borne by both sides, but also on the Soviet bloc's willingness and ability to depress civilian con-

sumption in pursuit of other goals. This is the subject of much debate and little conclusive analysis.[34]

Factors Affecting Realisation

There are three major factors which have militated against the realisation of the objectives of the US embargo:

1. the presence of the Soviet alternative;
2. the extension of financial credits by Western governments and banks (i.e. the failure of US allies to apply or maintain economic sanctions); and
3. Premier Castro's leadership abilities and domestic political control.

To discuss US shortcomings in the design of objectives and the objectives and the application of sanctions would require additional research and more space.

The most critical factor preventing the realisation of the objectives was the massive levels of Soviet economic and technical aid provided to Cuba since 1960 - the cumulative total probably surpassed US $23 billion in 1982. In the words of Blasier: 'Cuba has received far more comprehensive, sustained, and massive economic assistance from the USSR than any other developing country outside the Soviet Union's Eurasian orbit'.[35] The Banco Nacional report disclosed that in the 1970-81 period the 'average cost of the foreign debt' held by capitalist creditors 'was about fifteen times higher' than that owed to socialist countries.[36] During the legislative debate of the 1983 economic plan, Premier Castro intervened to argue that, in view of the current international financial situation, Cuba's modest growth target was made possible not only due to 'the virtues of socialism', but 'above all because of our excellent economic relations with the socialist camp'.[37] His amendment was incorporated into the plan's preamble by a unanimous vote of the delegates.

The second factor in the US failure to achieve its objectives was the sharp increase in Western trade and financial flows to the island in the late 1970s. The value of Cuba's total trade (exports plus imports) with non-socialist European countries increased from an annual average of 367 million _pesos_ in 1959-75 to 943 million _pesos_ in 1980.[38] In the same period, the value of Cuban exports to Canada increased ninefold. Outstanding Western financial credits and loans to Cuba climbed from under US $300 million in 1969 to US $3.3 billion in 1981, a more than tenfold increase. The loose embargo 'cartel', like all cartel arrangements, could not long survive the economic forces leading individual members to pursue their own self-interest. The US embargo 'cartel', if it can be called that, did not last effectively for more than a few years.

Lastly, US economic sanctions confronted a difficult target - a social revolution led by a powerful charismatic individual who possessed a radical vision and exercised virtually total domestic political control. If Premier Castro practiced revolutionary internationalism against the expressed policy of the Soviet Union, what was the United States to expect? If Premier Castro implemented a Maoist economic model while dependent on Soviet assistance, what could Washington hope to accomplish? There should be no element of surprise in this recent statement by a US State Department official:

> Cuba has proven unwilling to sacrifice its aggressive foreign policy to improve relations with us. It wants better relations but apparently not at the cost of abandoning its position at the forefront of those seeking revolutionary change.[39]

In fact, in the name of an internationalist commitment, Cuba has been willing to forgo far more than potential economic benefits from improved US relations. In a detailed study of Cuba's African policies, I concluded: 'It is incontrovertible that Cuba's involvement in Africa, in both its military dimension and its civilian aspects, has imposed a severe burden on the domestic economy'.[40]

In sum, the availability of substitute markets and credit sources, coupled with a tough and resilient target country, contributed to the embargo's inefficacy.

Unintended Consequences

The key issue is to what extent and in what way US economic sanctions pushed Cuba toward the Soviet Union. In a series of developments full of ironic twists and results, Havana was first pulled and only later pushed toward a close relationship with Moscow.

The decisive break with the United States originated in the nature of the Cuban process as it was being defined by the revolutionary leadership. It was Cuba that broke away from the tight and lengthy embrace of the United States; Washington did not reject the former suitor. Jorge Dominguez has put it very well:

> A new source of legitimacy had arisen: the revolution itself. No aid that the United States could have offered would have been compatible with the revolutionary transformation of Cuba as the leadership had begun to envisage it in the early spring of 1959. The decisive issue became, not United States aid or its condition, but the nature of the revolution....

> There is no evidence that these decisions were taken because of particular United States actions, nor that the United States 'pushed' the revolutionary leadership into them. A small number of revolutionary leaders concluded well ahead of the population that it was impossible to conduct a revolution in Cuba without a major confrontation with the United States.[41]

Clearly, the imposition of the sugar boycott in 1960 and the application of economic sanctions in 1962 made Cuba economically dependent on Soviet sugar markets and financial assistance. In other words, Cuba now became vulnerable to Soviet economic pressure. Although for many years Castro enjoyed considerable independence from both Washington and Moscow in a wide range of policy areas (foreign and domestic), the potential use of economic sanctions now emanated from the Soviet Union.

In 1968 Moscow used its 'oil weapon' against Cuba. According to William M. Leogrande:

> Cuba is highly vulnerable to a conscious policy of politico-economic coercion on the part of the Soviet Union. Most analysts of Cuban-Soviet relations are convinced that the USSR took advantage of this vulnerability in late 1967 and early 1968 by delaying petroleum shipments to Cuba and by moving very slowly in the 1968 annual trade agreement negotiations.[42]

Subsequently, Cuban policy moved closer to Soviet expectations in foreign, political and ideological issues and also in the domestic economic agenda. In a key concern, Cuba retreated from its active support of guerrilla forces in Latin America and instead backed traditional Communist parties. Ironically, only when Cuba came under greater Soviet influence were some of the US objectives realised, at least temporarily. Soviet economic sanctions were effective in producing their intended results because Cuba lacked alternatives. It was the combined effect of Soviet sanctions and US sanctions that induced the desired change in Cuban behaviour.

However, in the period after 1974, a pattern of increased Soviet-Cuban coincidence in pursuing radical foreign policy goals and tactics became well established. In other words, the Cuban proclivities intruded upon the Soviet agenda. Havana helped to radicalise Moscow, and the results can be observed in Angola and Ethiopia, in Central America and the Caribbean. At present, US economic sanctions are largely impotent to realise their objectives because Soviet and Cuban perceptions and interests are quite similar. In addition, the cost to Cuba of US economic sanctions continues to be minimal.

Conclusions

At present, the US policy of containing Cuban support of international revolutionary activities by using economic sanctions appears to be futile. In general terms, Cuba is not harmed and US interests are not advanced by the continued application of Washington's economic sanctions. On the other hand, the lifting or moderation of US economic sanctions would represent a major gamble to Washington in that foreign and domestic political risks are considerable while Havana's reaction is unpredictable. However, in view of the current stalemate affecting the pursuit of US objectives, such a move appears to carry acceptable downside costs. That is, the removal or amelioration of US economic sanctions may be a worthwhile calculated risk designed to provide an incentive for Cuba to reassess its foreign behaviour. At present, Cuba's foreign debt situation may provide a propitious context for such reappraisal to be undertaken. Afterwards, the potential process is fraught with uncertainty and full of promise. The ultimate outcome is likely to depend on the mutual moderation of demands and expectations.

Notes

1. Cole Blasier, 'The Elimination of United States Influence', in Carmelo Mesa-Lago (ed.), Revolutionary Change in Cuba (University of Pittsburgh Press, Pittsburgh, 1971), p. 72.
2. Philip Bonsal, Cuba, Castro and the United States (University of Pittsburgh Press, Pittsburgh, 1971), p. 151.
3. Blasier, 'The Elimination of United States Influence', p. 68.
4. Ibid., pp. 66-8.
5. Lynn D. Bender, The Politics of Hostility: Castro's Revolution and United States Policy (Inter-American Press, Hato Rey, Puerto Rico, 1975), pp. 26-7.
6. Ibid., p. 29.
7. Thomas O. Enders, 'Tasks for U.S. Policy in the Hemisphere', US Department of State, Bureau of Public Affairs, Current Policy No. 282 (3 June 1981), p. 2.
8. Carmelo Mesa-Lago, 'The Economics of U.S.-Cuban Rapprochement' in Cole Blasier and Carmelo Mesa-Lago (eds.), Cuba in the World (University of Pittsburgh Press, Pittsburgh, 1979), p. 214.
9. Bender, The Politics of Hostility, pp. 27-8.
10. US Department of Commerce, United States Commercial Relations with Cuba: A Survey (United States

Government Printing Office, Washington, D.C., 1975), p. 23.

11. Banco Nacional de Cuba, *Economic Report*, August 1982, p. 38.

12. *Financial Times* (London), 23 Mar. 1982.

13. *Wall Street Journal*, 13 Sep. 1982.

14. *Obra Revolucionaria*, no. 30 (1961), p. 115.

15. *Revolucion*, 2 August 1963, p. 5.

16. Alban Lataste, '1964: ano de la economia', *Cuba Socialista* 4 (February 1964), p. 14.

17. *Revolucion*, 2 November 1964, p. 6.

18. *Economia y Desarrollo* (January-March 1970), p. 40.

19. *Economia y Desarrollo* 20 (November-December 1973), p. 56.

20. *Report of the Central Committee of the Cuban Communist Party to the First Congress* (Department of Revolutionary Orientation of the Central Committee of the Communist Party of Cuba, Havana, 1977), p. 147.
For a full treatment of the 'idealistic mistakes', see Carmelo Mesa-Lago, 'Conversion of the Cuban Economy to Soviet Orthodoxy', *Journal of Economic Issues* 8 (March 1974); and Sergio Roca, 'Cuban Economic Policy in the 1970's: The Trodden Paths', *Studies in Comparative International Development* 12 (Spring 1977).

21. Maryanna Craig Boynton, 'Effects of Embargo and Boycott: The Cuban Case', unpublished Ph.D. thesis, University of California at Riverside, 1972. See pp. 83, 123-4 and 149-51.

22. Ibid., p. 151.

23. Eric N. Baklanoff, 'International Economic Relations', in Mesa-Lago (ed.), *Revolutionary Change*, pp. 262-3.

24. Carmelo Mesa-Lago, 'Present and Future of the Revolution', in Ibid., p. 505.

25. Jorge I. Dominguez, *Cuba: Order and Revolution* (Harvard University Press, Cambridge, 1978), pp. 147-8.

26. Julio Le Riverend, *Economic History of Cuba* (Book Institute, Havana, 1967), p. 274.

27. Panorama Economico Latino Americano, September 1969, p. 27. Currently, Rodriguez is a member of the Party's Politburo and Vice-President of the Council of State and Council of Ministers.

28. *Economia y Desarrollo* 1 (January-March 1970), p. 32.

29. *Granma*, 23 Dec. 1975, p. 2.

30. *Granma*, 18 Dec. 1980, p. 2.

31. Banco Nacional de Cuba, *Economic Report*, p. 12.

32. Carmelo Mesa-Lago, 'The Economy: Caution, Frugality and Resilient Ideology', in Jorge Dominguez (ed.), *Cuba: Internal and International Affairs* (Sage Pub-

lications, Beverly Hills, California, 1982), p. 150.

33. Banco Nacional de Cuba, Economic Report, p. 14.

34. Thomas O. Bayard, Joseph Pelzman and Jorge Perez-Lopez, 'A Primer on Economic Sanctions', The World Economy, 1983.

35. Cole Blasier, 'Comecon in Cuban Development', in Blasier and Mesa-Lago (eds.), Cuba in the World, p. 225. For an analysis questioning the extent and utility of Soviet assistance to the island, see Andrew Zimbalist, 'Soviet Aid, U.S. Blockade and the Cuban Economy', The ACES Bulletin 24 (Winter 1983), pp. 137-45.

36. Banco Nacional de Cuba, Economic Report, p. 46.

37. Granma Weekly Review, 9 Jan. 1983, p. 3.

38. Comite Estatal de Estadisticos, Anuario Estadistico de Cuba 1980, pp. 168-70.

39. Myles R. Frechette, 'Cuban-Soviet Impact on the Western Hemisphere', US Department of State, Bureau of Public Affairs, Current Policy No. 167 (17 April 1980), p. 3.

40. Sergio Roca, 'Economic Aspects of Cuban Involvement in Africa', Cuban Studies/Estudios Cubanos 10 (July 1980), p. 70. See pp. 70-5 for examples of domestic opportunity costs.

41. Dominguez, Cuba: Order and Revolution, p. 145.

42. William M. Leogrande, 'Cuban Dependency: A Comparison of Pre-Revolutionary and Post-Revolutionary International Economic Relations', Cuban Studies/Estudios Cubanos 9 (July 1979), p. 26. See also Blasier, 'Comecon in Cuban Development', p. 246-9.

Chapter Six

POST-AFGHANISTAN SANCTIONS

Peggy L. Falkenheim

In recent years, East-West economic relations have become a focus of sharp debate within the Western Alliance. The United States has been pressuring its allies to restrict economic relations with the Soviet Union in order to influence Soviet foreign policy and to deny the Soviet Union technology with military applications. Washington's allies have not always been willing to give in to US pressure because they have disagreed with US assumptions about the ways in which East-West trade affects political relations between the two blocs.

These differences of opinion among Western leaders have been echoed by differences of opinion among foreign policy analysts. They have disagreed about the extent to which Soviet foreign policy can be influenced by East-West economic relations and about the best means to do this. This chapter is a case study relating to one aspect of that debate. The chapter will focus on the post-Afghanistan sanctions in order to evaluate the utility of economic sanctions as a means of influencing Soviet foreign policy behaviour. It will begin with a description of the sanctions and motivations for them and then evaluate how successful they have been in achieving their objectives.

Impositions of the Sanctions

On 27 December 1979 Soviet troops marched into Afghanistan and staged a coup in which the Marxist President Hafizullah Amin was killed and replaced by Babrak Karmal, who had been serving as Kabul's ambassador to Czechoslovakia. Mr Karmal was flown in from Eastern Europe in a Soviet plane and arrived in Kabul after the takeover was completed.

By means of the invasion, the Soviet Union replaced a leader whose loyalty to Moscow was doubtful and whose radical policies were considered responsible for fuelling resistance against the Marxist regime created by the April

1978 coup in Afghanistan. A previous attempt in September 1979 to stage a coup against President Amin had failed when the Afghanistan President succeeded instead in removing from power and then executing the more moderate Prime Minister Nur Mohammad Taraki, who had just returned from Moscow. After the failure of this coup attempt, President Amin adopted more moderate policies, but this change failed to stem the growing rebellion threatening the Marxist regime in Kabul.

In light of this history, the invasion was interpreted by some as a largely defensive reaction by Moscow designed to prevent the overthrow of a Marxist regime and its replacement by an anti-Soviet government in a country bordering the Soviet Union in which the Soviet Union traditionally has maintained a strong interest. From this perspective, Soviet concern about developments in Kabul was increased by fear that the growing strength of Islamic fundamentalism, first in Iran and then in Afghanistan, threatened to influence the Moslem population of Soviet Central Asia. Other analysts stressed the offensive aspects of the Afghanistan invasion, noting that it was the first time since World War II that the Soviet Union, using its own troops and not proxies, had invaded territory not assigned to its sphere of influence by the post-war settlement.

This second interpretation was shared by US President Jimmy Carter who said that Moscow's action 'could pose the most serious threat to world peace since the Second World War'.[1] Other members of his Administration felt that although the invasion may have had defensive as well as offensive motivations, its effect was to increase the Soviet threat to Western oil supplies and oil routes in the Persian Gulf. They were concerned that the invasion had put Soviet troops in a favourable position to take advantage of ethnic rivalries and instability in Iran and Pakistan, which might make it possible to station Soviet troops near the Persian Gulf bordering the oil lifeline upon which so many of Washington's allies depended. Their anxiety about Western security interests in this broader region was heightened by several recent setbacks, especially the Soviet- and Cuban backed Ethiopian victory over Somalia in Ogaden, the emergence of a Marxist regime - the People's Democratic Republic of Yemen - on the Arabian peninsula, and the overthrow of the Shah and taking of US hostages in Iran. These concerns were shared not only by President Carter's National Security Adviser, Zbigniew Brzezinski, and others who had been advocating the adoption of a tougher policy toward the Soviet Union, but also by officials such as Secretary of State Cyrus Vance and his Special Adviser for Soviet Affairs, Marshall Shulman, who up until then had advocated a more moderate Soviet policy.

The Carter Administration discussed various options

for dealing with this perceived Soviet threat, ranging from military intervention to doing nothing. While military intervention seemed too extreme, doing nothing also was not considered a viable option. Members of the Carter Administration were convinced of the need to make the Soviet Union pay a tangible price for its intervention in the hope that this would deter it from future acts of aggression.[2]

Domestic political considerations also influenced the decision, but their effects probably were contradictory. The Afghanistan invasion occurred at the beginning of the primary campaign for the 1980 presidential election. President Carter's popularity was low, and public opinion polls revealed a lack of confidence in his leadership ability. His popular image had not been helped by his handling of the Iranian situation which led to the seizure of hostages at the US embassy in Teheran. It may have seemed that a failure to adopt a firm response would undermine even further general public confidence in President Carter's leadership. His reputation could have been damaged, particularly among those groups, such as the International Longshoremen's Association, whose subsequent actions showed that they were determined to go even further than the government in imposing sanctions on the Soviet Union. These factors worked in favour of imposing an embargo. However, President Carter was aware that he risked losing electoral support by adopting sanctions which hurt the economic interests of important electoral groups. The President's domestic advisers counselled him against imposing a grain embargo because they were afraid that it would hurt his electoral chances in farm states.[3]

Faced by these contradictory pressures, the Carter Administration adopted a series of economic sanctions and other measures which were designed to punish the Soviet Union while at the same time limiting the damage to the economic interests of important domestic groups. President Carter warned Moscow that the United States would react with force if Soviet troops approached the Persian Gulf. He advocated 'collective efforts to meet this new threat to security in the Persian Gulf and in Southwest Asia'. He offered to resume US military and economic assistance to Pakistan and authorised the sale to China of military-related technology and goods, although not of offensive weapons. He proposed resuming draft registration but not the draft itself.[4] In addition, the US Senate was asked to postpone consideration of the SALT II agreement which was scheduled to begin in late January.

The US government also restricted political and economic relations with the Soviet Union. The opening of new US and Soviet consular facilities was delayed indefinitely, and joint US-Soviet commission meetings on agriculture, commerce and health were cancelled. Washington announced that it would not negotiate new scientific and cultural agreements with the Soviet Union. A partial rather than a full embargo was imposed on grain exports to the Soviet Union, and restrictions were placed on other products related to the Soviet feedgrain-livestock complex, including seeds, soybeans, meat, poultry, dairy products and some animal fats. The reason given for not imposing a full embargo was the need to honour commitments made to Moscow in the 1976 Soviet-American Long-Term Grain Agreement. However, this decision may well have been influenced by a desire to limit the negative impact on US farmers which could hurt President Carter's re-election prospects. Stricter limitations were placed on the export of high technology and other strategic goods to the Soviet Union, but the Commerce Department lobbied successfully to exempt non-strategic or easily replaceable items. Subsequently, the United States organised a boycott of the summer Olympic games in Moscow.

Support for the Sanctions

Washington put pressure on other countries, particularly its allies, to support the sanctions. This pressure was only partially successful. Although leaders of US allies were annoyed by President Carter's failure to consult them in advance, they realised that an open refusal to support Washington could send the wrong signal to Moscow. However, for various reasons, they were reluctant to give Washington their full support. At least some allied leaders did not fully share President Carter's interpretation of the significance of the Afghanistan invasion. West German Chancellor Helmut Schmidt, for example, was heard to remark that Berlin, not Afghanistan, represented the most serious crisis since World War II.[5] Many of them strongly opposed suspending high-level political relations at a time of crisis when they felt it was more important than ever to continue a political dialogue. In addition, most of them did not believe that economic sanctions could be used effectively to influence Soviet foreign policy. Those who believed in using economic relations as a political tool were far more inclined to use them as a carrot rather than as a stick. At home, many of these leaders, such as President Carter, faced contradictory political pressures. For example, the Canadian government of Progressive Conservative Joe Clark was in the middle of an election campaign at the time of the Afghanistan invasion. The Clark Cabinet included ministers from Western ridings with significant numbers of ethnic constituents who could be expected to support a strong response to the Soviet Union.[6] On the other hand, the Canadian government was aware that the Soviet market was very important to Western farmers, since one out of every ten bushels of wheat produced in Canada was exported to the Soviet Union.[7] For these reasons, Washington's allies all gave some support to the sanctions, although in most cases their support was carefully limited to protect the interests of important domestic groups. Even this limited support quickly eroded when it became clear that the sanctions were hurting the initiating countries as much as the Soviet Union.

Non-economic Sanctions

Washington's call for a boycott of the Summer 1980 Olympics received the highest level of external support. On 20 January 1980 President Carter proposed that if Soviet troops were not withdrawn from Afghanistan in one month's time, then the US Olympic team should lead an international effort to have the Summer 1980 Olympics postponed or transferred from Moscow to another city. Failing that, US and other teams should boycott the games. President Carter chose the 20 February deadline in order to allow sufficient time for arrangements to be made to move the games to another site. Moving the games proved to be impossible because of opposition from the International Olympic Committee, so a boycott of the games was left as the only option. On 12 April 1980 the House of Delegates of the US Olympic Committee voted in favour of a boycott. In late March 1980 the US government also prohibited the export of goods for use in the Moscow Olympics and barred the National Broadcasting Company, which held the US television rights to the games, from making further payments to the Soviet Union.[8]

The Carter Administration argued that the boycott would deprive Moscow of the propaganda benefits it hoped to derive from the games and make the Soviet people aware of the negative effects of the Afghanistan invasion. President Carter himself, not surprisingly, also defended the boycott in moralistic terms, maintaining that it would be as wrong for US athletes to participate in the Moscow Olympics as it was for foreign athletes to attend the 1936 Berlin games while Adolph Hitler was in power.[9]

A significant number of foreign governments opposed Washington's call for a boycott. Although the boycott was a contentious issue in many of these countries, athletes and their supporters did not have the electoral clout wielded by corporations and farmers' associations. Moreover, in many countries, the boycott had a symbolic appeal which won it popular support. In Canada, for example, although athletes protested against the boycott, it was supported by other groups, particularly by those with a strongly anti-Soviet orientation. When Prime Minister Clark announced the government's decision to an audience of Ukrainian

Canadians, he received a standing ovation.[10] Although a few national Olympic committees sent teams to Moscow in defiance of their governments, most were forced to comply by withdrawal of governmental and private funds and by other forms of pressure. Altogether 55 teams stayed away from the games, among them teams from the Federal Republic of Germany, Canada, Japan and China.

The Olympic boycott made the Moscow games less of a propaganda success than the Soviet Union had anticipated. The number of athletes participating in the games was reduced from 10,000 to 6,000 and the quality of competition was affected by the absence of athletes from the United States, the Federal Republic of Germany and Japan which had placed third, fourth and fifth respectively in the number of gold medals won at the Montreal Olympics. International news agencies either cancelled or radically reduced their coverage of the games.[11] The boycott also cost the Soviet Union hard currency earnings from Western tourists and the loss of payments for broadcasting rights.

However, the fact that the games took place and were attended by 81 teams deprived the boycott of much of its effect. Moreover, the initiating countries paid a price for the boycott not only in lost opportunities for their athletes, but also in lost revenue from television advertising, sales of Olympic souvenirs, travel agents' commissions, etc. Furthermore, the 1980 boycott may have provided a strong incentive for Moscow's decision to lead an East bloc boycott of the 1984 Los Angeles Olympics.

There was less support for Washington's call for a suspension of high-level political and other contacts with the Soviet Union. The Soviet intervention in Afghanistan was widely condemned not only by the United States and its allies, but also by China, Islamic countries and even members of the non-aligned movement. Some of these countries, for example China and Japan, followed Washington's lead by suspending or reducing ties with the Soviet Union. However, other countries, including some US allies, refused to support Washington, arguing that it was particularly important to maintain high-level political and other ties at a time of heightened tension. For example, both France and the Federal Republic of Germany adopted this view and sent high-level delegations to Eastern Europe shortly after the Afghanistan invasion. In May 1980 French President Valery Giscard d'Estaing went to Warsaw. In June and July West German Chancellor Helmut Schmidt visited the Soviet Union.

In Canada, although the incumbent Clark government supported Washington's call for a suspension of high-level official contacts and other ties, this policy was sharply opposed by both Pierre Trudeau and Ed Broadbent, leaders of the Opposition Liberal and New Democratic parties. After the Liberal party regained power, it decided to reverse this policy but found this decision hard to implement. Implementation of the change was delayed by the adverse reaction to the imposition of martial law in Poland and by concern that it would send the wrong signal to Moscow. When Canada decided to hold discussions with the Soviet Union on the resumption of cultural and academic exchanges, External Affairs Minister Allan MacEachen defended this decision by telling reporters that 'we have not resumed full exchanges with the Soviet Union. It's not business as usual'.[12]

The suspension of political, cultural and economic ties imposed costs on both sides by decreasing the possibility of reaching agreement on other issues and by increasing the danger of misunderstanding and miscalculation.

Impact of the Partial Grain Embargo

Limited support also reduced the impact of the partial grain embargo. This embargo was aimed at hurting the Soviet Union in an area that was considered both economically vulnerable and politically sensitive to the country. Although the Soviet Union produced enough grain to feed its population, it was partially dependent on foreign grain for animal feed. This dependence increased substantially during poor harvest years. In one such year, 1975, sharp limits were placed on US grain exports to the Soviet Union for economic reasons in order to avert a significant increase in the price of grain on the US domestic market. As a consequence, Soviet farmers did not have enough animal feed, which led to substantial distress slaughter of their livestock herds. This action set back by several years efforts to expand livestock herds which were intensified in the early 1970s as a means of increasing the quantities of milk and meat available to Soviet workers. Soviet President Leonid Brezhnev had personally endorsed these efforts, which were considered important because greater food supplies could serve as an incentive for increased labour productivity. Their importance to the Soviet leadership was reflected by its willingness to use large quantities of scarce hard currency to pay for grain imports at a time when concern about the growing Soviet foreign debt had led to some restrictions on non-agricultural imports.

At the time of the Afghanistan invasion, Soviet livestock herds were just recovering to the levels reached before the 1975 distress slaughter. Since the invasion took place after a poor harvest, it was expected that the partial grain embargo would reduce Soviet milk and meat production and might even trigger another distress slaughter.[13]

The partial grain embargo had some limited impact on Soviet agriculture, but less than anticipated. During the year after imposition of the embargo, Soviet meat and milk production declined by 3 per cent and slaughter weights of Soviet livestock also were down. Per capita meat consumption declined by 2 kilos despite a record level of imports. In June 1980 there were reports of work stoppages at two automobile plants caused reportedly by shortages of meat and dairy products. It was reported that the food situation was even worse the following year.[14] However, on the positive side, the Soviet Union was able to avoid another distress slaughter of livestock. Livestock herds even increased slightly during the 16-month embargo although at a slower rate than previously. Moreover, the embargo was only one of several factors and not the most important one responsible for the shortfall in feedgrain availability causing the decline in meat and milk production. This shortfall was caused mainly by poor weather and by systemic problems plaguing Soviet agriculture, not by the embargo. According to one estimate, the embargo caused only a 0.16 per cent decline in beef production, a 0.10 per cent decline in pork production, a 0.64 per cent decrease in poultry production and a 0.73 per cent decline in milk production in its first year.[15]

The partial grain embargo had only a small impact on Soviet agricultural production because it decreased by only a small percentage the total amount of feedgrain available for Soviet livestock. According to various estimates, the embargo caused only a 3 to 6.5 million metric ton decrease in Soviet grain imports in the 1979-80 crop-year. This represented a reduction of only approximately 3 to 5 per cent [in feedgrain available during this period]. The Soviet Union was able to compensate for some of this shortfall by drawing down grain reserves and by increasing use of non-grain feed sources.

The embargo's impact was so small because the United States and its allies restricted but did not eliminate grain exports to the Soviet Union, and other nations took advantage of these restrictions to expand Soviet sales. From the beginning, the embargo's impact was limited by Washington's decision to honour the 1976 agreement in which it had promised to sell the Soviet Union 6 to 8 million metric tons of grain a year for five years. Although the embargo led to the cancellation of contracts for exporting 17 million metric tons of US grain to the Soviet Union, a record 15.2 million metric tons of US grain were exported to the Soviet Union in the 1 July 1979 to 30 June 1980 US crop-year. These shipments included 7.2 million metric tons exported before 1 October 1979, the beginning of the year specified in the US-Soviet agreement, and 8 million metric tons exported between the beginning of October and the end of June. An additional 8 million metric tons of grain were sold to the Soviet Union early in the next agreement year (1 October 1980 to 30 September 1981) at a time when the Soviet Union was suffering the effects of a second poor harvest.

Washington's allies also continued to export substantial quantities of grain to the Soviet Union despite their pledges to support the embargo. At a meeting of grain exporting countries convened in Washington, D.C., shortly after President Carter's announcement of the sanctions, Canada, the European Economic Community (EEC) and Australia promised to support the embargo by not selling to the Soviet Union more than their 'normal and traditional' level of grain.[16] However, the meaning of these pledges was ambiguous because grain sales in previous years had fluctuated so widely. Although some restrictions were placed on grain sales to the Soviet Union, substantial amounts still were exported. For example, the Clark government set a limit of 3.8 million metric tons on Canadian grain exports to the Soviet Union in the 1979-80 crop-year. Although this figure was 600,000 metric tons less than Canada had sold to the Soviet Union in 1976, a previous boom year, it was higher than the average level of Canadian sales during the previous decade.[17] The EEC restricted grain sales to the Soviet Union after the embargo, but Moscow still was able to purchase 800,000 metric tons of EEC grain in 1979-80, four times the previous year's level. In addition, European crushers sold 1 million metric tons of soybean meal to the Soviet Union during the embargo, made largely from US soybeans bought at distress prices. In 1979-80 Australia exported a record quantity of grain to the Soviet Union. Although most of the 4.3 million metric tons of Australian sales to the Soviet Union was based on contracts signed before the embargo, some of this amount was based on sales made by state marketing boards after the federal government had announced its support for the embargo.

Other countries took advantage of the embargo to increase grain sales to the Soviet Union. Most important among them was Argentina, which made clear its opposition to the embargo at the January meeting of grain exporting countries. Argentina's refusal to support the United States was not surprising given the strains created by President Carter's human rights and nuclear non-proliferation policies and Washington's failure to consult other countries before announcing the embargo. In the 1979-80 crop-year, Argentina exported 7.6 million metric tons of grain to the Soviet Union, about four times more than its sales the previous year. In July 1980 Buenos Aires concluded a grain agreement with the Soviet Union in which it promised to sell a minimum of 4.5 million metric tons of corn, sorghum and soybeans annually for the next five years. Brazil, too, increased grain sales to the Soviet Union in 1979-80, and the following year signed a five-year trade accord with Moscow providing for an exchange of Soviet oil for Brazilian soybeans, soya oil and corn. Another 4.7 million metric tons of grain were sold to the Soviet Union in 1979-80 by several small exporters.[18]

When it became clear that the embargo was not working, even the limited, initial support by the United States and its allies quickly eroded. In July 1980 the Canadian government announced that in the 1980-81 Canadian crop-year starting on 1 August, the limit on Canadian grain sales would be raised from 3.8 to 5 million metric tons. This announcement was made by Senator Hazen Argue, Minister of State for the Canadian Wheat Board in the new Liberal Cabinet elected the previous February. Senator Argue said that this new, higher limit more accurately reflected the 'annual and traditional' level of Canadian grain sales to the Soviet Union during the previous decade. In November 1980 Ottawa withdrew its support from the embargo. This decision was made after Jimmy Carter lost the US presidential election to Ronald Reagan who had made lifting the embargo one of his campaign pledges. Another motivating factor was Canadian anger over the US-China grain agreement of October 1980 in which Beijing promised to buy 8 to 9 million metric tons of US grain annually for four years starting in January 1981.[19] This agreement was seen in Canada as a violation of Washington's promise at the time of the embargo that US farmers would not try to expand sales in their allies' traditional export markets.

Washington's decision to lift the embargo was delayed for four months after President Reagan's accession to power because of concern, particularly of Secretary of State Alexander Haig, that ending the embargo would send the wrong signal to Moscow at a time when the United States was trying to deter a Soviet invasion of Poland. The decision to end the embargo was finally made in April 1981 in response to strong domestic pressure. The timing of the decision was influenced by President Reagan's desire to curry favour with senators and representatives from agricultural districts, whose support he needed to pass an important farm bill. President Reagan tried to mitigate the adverse foreign policy effect of this decision by stressing in the announcement that 'the United States...remains opposed to the Soviet occupation of Afghanistan and other aggressive acts around the world and will react strongly to acts of aggression wherever they take place'.[20] A few months later, the Reagan Administration agreed to extend for an additional year the expiring five-year US-Soviet grain agreement. The United States previously had agreed to allow the Soviet Union to buy an additional 6 million metric tons above the 8 million metric ton limit in the 1980-81 crop-year.[21] In 1981-82, Washington authorised Moscow to buy 23 million metric tons. In 1982-83 the limit was raised to 25 million metric tons, even though the Soviet Union had bought only 13.9 million metric tons of US grain in the previous crop-year.[22]

The decision to lift the embargo was made largely in response to farmers' groups in the United States, Canada and their allies, who were convinced that the embargo not only was ineffective but also was hurting them more than the Soviet Union. Washington and Ottawa had adopted price supports and other measures to counteract the embargo's effects on agricultural prices and to compensate farmers for any losses. These measures, which cost US and Canadian taxpayers US $2.2 billion and CDN $81 million respectively, clearly had some positive effect. Farm prices, which declined precipitously after President Carter's announcement of the embargo, soon began to rise again thanks in part to these measures. After a severe midsummer drought, farm prices increased rapidly, and by the fall of 1980 even surpassed their pre-embargo level. However, US and Canadian farmers' groups were convinced that prices would have been even higher without the embargo, which depressed prices by putting record amounts of grain in storage overhanging the market. They maintained that government payments did not provide full compensation for their losses. For example, US farmers' associations estimated that the embargo resulted in billions of dollars of losses to the farm sector and related sectors such as farm equipment manufacturers, food processing industries, transportation workers and the like.[23] These claims are hard to evaluate since it is difficult to separate the embargo's effects from the influence of high interest rates, inflation, transportation problems, the world-wide economic recession and other factors affecting prices. Overall, the evidence suggests that the farmers' claims were exaggerated because they were based on incorrect assumptions regarding the net decrease in US grain exports caused by the embargo. Nevertheless, the embargo clearly had some significant negative impact on prices, since it stimulated increased grain and soybean production by Argentina, Brazil and other countries by providing them with a long-term guaranteed export market.

In the long run, the embargo has imposed uneven costs on the initiating countries. The Soviet Union has taken steps to reduce reliance on US grain and to diversify its grain trading partners. The Soviet Union has signed long-term grain agreements not only with Argentina and Brazil but also with Canada, Australia and other countries. For example, in May 1981 Ottawa concluded a grain agreement with the Soviet Union in which Moscow agreed to buy a minimum of 25 million metric tons of Canadian grain over the next five years.[24] In August of the following year, the Canadian government established a 1 billion dollar line of credit for Soviet grain purchases in order to promote exports in a bumper crop year. This line of credit was at the same preferred rate of interest (0.25 per cent below prime) available to the Canadian Wheat Board.[25]

As a consequence of these Soviet trade diversification efforts, US farmers' share of the Soviet market has significantly decreased. In the eight years before the embargo, between 55 and 75 per cent of Soviet grain imports came from the United States, which was Moscow's preferred supplier, because it could be relied on to provide large quantities of grain in poor harvest years and to meet its delivery schedule. Since 1980 one-third or less of Soviet grain imports have come from the United States. Canada and Argentina have been the main beneficiaries of this shift in Soviet grain buying patterns. United States farmers have tried to compensate for their reduced share of the Soviet market by increasing exports to China and other countries. However, in the long run, they may not prove to be as reliable a market for US grain as the Soviet Union.

In an effort to regain its share of the Soviet market, the United States in August 1983 concluded a long-term grain agreement with the Soviet Union. Negotiation of this agreement was delayed for more than two years after the lifting of the grain embargo because of US concern about the situation in Poland, which led to the imposition of martial law in that country. This new five-year US-Soviet agreement sets higher minimum and maximum levels than the previous one. Under its terms, the Soviet Union has agreed to buy a minimum of 9 million metric tons of corn and wheat a year, and may buy up to a maximum of 12 million metric tons. The Soviet Union can reduce the minimum for corn and wheat to 8 million metric tons by buying 500,000 tons of soybeans or soybean meal in any year. If Moscow wants to buy more than the maximum, it must obtain Washington's permission. So far, it has had no trouble in doing so.[26]

In order to encourage Soviet purchases by demonstrating that the United States intends to be a reliable supplier, the US government has passed legislation that would make it extraordinarily difficult to impose a future grain embargo. The Agriculture and Food Act passed in December 1981 contains a clause ensuring that farmers would receive very generous compensation if the United States should impose another embargo for economic or national security reasons, unless the embargo covered all US exports. An amendment to the Futures Trading Act makes it mandatory to honour export commitments concluded before an embargo if they call for delivery within 270 days after its imposition.[27]

These measures so far have not restored to US farmers their former share of the Soviet market. In absolute terms, US grain exports to the Soviet Union have reached 15.5 million metric tons, exceeding the level of the peak year before the embargo. In the current 1984-85 crop-year, some analysts are predicting that the Soviet Union will import a record 19 to 21 million metric tons of US grain.[28] However, even if this prediction is correct, this amount still will be significantly lower than the 27.5 million metric tons that the Soviet Union had contracted to buy from the United States in 1979-80 before the embargo was imposed. Moreover, US grain still would comprise only approximately 40 per cent of anticipated total Soviet grain imports, a much smaller proportion than in peak years before the embargo. This is so because total Soviet grain imports have increased significantly in the 1980s. The Soviet Union has experienced six poor harvests in a row, which have undermined increased Soviet efforts to become more self-sufficient.

Impact of the Superphosphate Embargo

One and a half months after the announcement of the grain embargo, the Carter Administration imposed an embargo on superphosphate exports to the Soviet Union. This embargo was intended to delay Soviet liquid fertilizer production, making it harder for the Soviet Union to expand its own grain production to substitute for embargoed imports. It was imposed largely in response to pressure from US farmers' organisations which argued that it was unfair for Washington to ask them to limit grain sales to the Soviet Union if it did not at the same time take steps to restrict Soviet fertilizer production.

The superphosphate embargo caused some inconvenience to the Soviet Union by forcing it to replace US superphosphates by Mexican and Moroccan phosphate rock, which requires processing and is highly corrosive. Since the Soviet Union was able to replace only a little over half of the embargoed superphosphate in 1980, the embargo impeded the expansion of Soviet liquid fertilizer production. However, the embargo was lifted in April 1981 before it could have any significant impact on Soviet agriculture.

The embargo's impact on the US economy was mixed. It caused a price decline which hurt superphosphate producers, particularly Occidental Petroleum, which in 1978 had begun a US $20 billion, 20-year exchange of US superphosphates for Soviet ammonia. However, US farmers benefited from a reduction in fertilizer prices caused by the embargo.[29]

High Technology Sanctions

In addition to the grain and superphosphate embargoes, the United States also imposed tighter restrictions on the export of high technology and other strategic items to the Soviet Union. In January 1980, pending the completion of a policy review, Washington temporarily suspended all licences for the export to the Soviet Union of high technology goods and other products that required validated licences. Several applications were denied for licences to export high technology products such as telecommunications technology and seismic data processing equipment. The US government revoked the licence for the export of spare parts for an IBM computer at the Kama River Truck Plant, since trucks from that plant were being used by Soviet troops in Afghanistan. Ingersoll-Rand was forced by the government to renege on its contract to export equipment and a computer for a second truck engine assembly line to be built at this plant.

When the policy review was completed in March, it was decided that new, more restrictive criteria would be applied for goods requiring validated licences in order to deny the Soviet Union any technology with potential military applications. In particular, stricter controls were placed on exports of computers, computer software, oil and gas production equipment and process control technology in industries with military relevance. By September, after completion of a case-by-case review of validated licences, only 281 of the 476 suspended licences were reinstated.

Besides tightening unilateral controls on high technology exports, the United States announced that it would adopt a no-exceptions policy in the Coordinating Committee (CoCom), which was established by the United States and its allies after the Second World War to control exports to the Soviet Union and other Communist countries. This was done through the establishment of agreed-on lists of items restricted for export to particular countries. If a CoCom member wished to sell the Soviet Union an item on its restricted list, it could do so only by requesting an exception that required the unanimous approval of the other members. In the late 1970s, the United States had made approximately half of the requests for exceptions.[30]

In the case of high technology controls, the Afghanistan invasion provided a pretext for the US government to take steps which were being advocated for other reasons. Even before the invasion, there was growing pressure within the US government to impose tighter restrictions on high technology exports to the Soviet Union. Support for this measure increased after the 1976 Bucy Report highlighted the need for greater control over 'criticial technologies' with potential military application.

These stricter controls could not be effective without the support of Washington's allies, since only about 10 per cent of Soviet high technology imports in the late 1970s came from the United States.[31] Therefore, Washington proposed to its allies in CoCom that they adopt more stringent restrictions on the export of computers and process control technology to the Soviet Union and follow the United States lead by subscribing to a no-exceptions policy. The US government also wanted turnkey plants worth more than US $100 million to be subject to special scrutiny. In addition, Washington pressed its allies not to extend subsidised credits to the Soviet Union.

Most US allies did not fully share US leaders' convictions about the need for tighter controls on high technology. Although Washington's allies agreed that it was necessary to prohibit exports to the Soviet Union of products or technology with direct military applications, they were less convinced of the need to limit export of civilian technology with potential military applications. In general, they doubted that Western high technology had made a substantial contribution to Soviet military development because they believed that barriers to diffusion of new technology in the Soviet Union were very strong.[32] There also were economic reasons for the reluctance of some US allies to support fully Washington's call for tighter controls on high technology exports. Non-agricultural trade with the Soviet Union was far more important to Western Europe and Japan than it was to the United States and Canada. Whereas machinery and equipment constituted only 14 per cent of US exports to the Soviet Union in 1979, it comprised 74 and 84 per cent respectively of Soviet imports from Western Europe and Japan. Although overall trade with the Soviet Union still constituted a very small proportion of Western Europe's or Japan's total trade, its significance for certain regions, industries and firms was much greater. For example, significant numbers of jobs in Le Havre, France, Glasgow, Scotland, and Dusseldorf, Federal Republic of Germany, were said to be dependent on trade with the Soviet Union. Soviet sales also were important to firms such as the FRG steel company Mannesman, which sold one-quarter of its pipe to the Soviet Union in the 1970s and made 7 per cent of its profits from these sales. These localities, firms and industries constituted an important lobby in Western Europe against restricting exports to the Soviet Union.[33] Moreover, some Western European countries for example, the Federal Republic of Germany carried out trade with the Soviet Union on the basis of long-term agreements. They were unwilling to break contracts concluded under these agreements out of fear that it might be difficult to resume trade in the future. The timing of the post-Afghanistan sanctions also increased resistance in some countries whose companies were eager to sign contracts for exports to be delivered under the Soviet Union's 11th Five Year Plan starting in 1981. United States allies also were annoyed by Washington's efforts to use the post-Afghanistan sanctions as a pretext for strengthening new CoCom restrictions on computers which had just been hammered out and agreed upon after long deliberations.

For all these reasons, the United States received only limited and uneven support from its allies for its high technology sanctions. Conservative governments in the United Kingdom and Canada promised to impose tighter restrictions on high technology exports and not to renew general lines of subsidised credits to the Soviet Union. However, in both countries, it was made clear that requests for subsidised credits would be considered on a case-by-case basis.[34] Japan promised to support the US sanctions by not concluding new joint development projects with the Soviet Union and by not extending official credits for new projects. However, Tokyo pressed Washington to exempt the Sakhalin offshore oil and gas development project from the sanctions' sphere of application. This pressure was successful. In the early spring of 1980, Washington approved 15 licences for oil-drilling equipment needed for this project. Not long after the Afghanistan invasion, Japan's official Export-Import Bank approved a large credit for the third Soviet-Japanese forestry development project, maintaining that the ban on official credits for new projects did not apply in this case because it was really phase three of an ongoing project.[35] The Federal Republic of Germany, France and Italy made it clear that they intended to continue normal trade relations with the Soviet Union but pledged not to take advantage of the US sanctions for their commercial benefit. These pledges were not always kept. There were several cases when Washington's Western European allies made important sales after the United States had refused to approve a licence for a particular contract. For example, after Armco and a Japanese company Nippon Steel were denied permission to use US technology in a steel plant at Novolipetsk, the French company Creusot-Loire signed a contract to build a steel plant at the same site. Creusot-Loire denied that it had taken advantage of the sanctions to make the sale, arguing that its contract was significantly different from the original because it had agreed only to build a cold rolling mill and not to supply steel making equipment. A contract to build an aluminum plant at Sayansk was signed by the Klockner group of the Federal Republic of Germany, which previously had formed part of a co-operative venture with Alcoa Company of the United States. Klockner officials maintained that the new contract differed from the old one because it was not based on Alcoa technology. The Italian company Fiat agreed to sell the Soviet Union the second truck engine assembly line needed for its Kama Plant. The Federal Republic of Germany and French firms took over a contract for a sour gas treatment complex at Astrakhan, which originally was supposed to go to a Canadian firm.[36]

In the period immediately after Afghanistan, the Federal Republic of Germany and France concluded some important long-term economic agreements with the Soviet Union. In the winter and spring of 1980, FRG companies and banks sent representatives to the Soviet Union to discuss the Yamal gas pipeline project which has since become such an object of controversy. When FRG Chancellor Schmidt visited Moscow in late June and early July, he signed a communique which contained a clause approving the pipeline. Also signed during his visit was a long-term co-operation agreement which provided for joint oil and gas exploration projects and joint exploitation of raw materials. In February 1980 Paris signed a five-year accord with Moscow promising to extend export credits at subsidised rates. In November the French state gas company announced that it would soon sign a contract for the import of 24 to 30 billion cubic feet of Soviet natural gas a year starting in 1985.[37]

Given this limited support by US allies, the high technology sanctions had only a small impact on the Soviet economy. They impeded or delayed Soviet access to computers and other high technology products and caused some delays in planning and construction schedules.[38] However, no major Soviet projects were blocked by the sanctions, since in most cases the Soviet Union was able to find alternative Western suppliers or to use Eastern European or domestic technology.

The sanctions caused some marginal losses to the United States and to countries such as Canada and Japan which supported it. Their corporations and workers suffered when foreign firms took over contracts they had concluded or were about to finalise. In the first nine months of 1980, US high technology exports to the Soviet Union, instead of rising as expected, dropped by 52 per cent in comparison with the same period in the previous year. The US share of Soviet orders for Western equipment declined from somewhere in the range of 12 to 20 per cent in the late 1970s to just a little over 5 per cent in 1980. Canadian equipment sales to the Soviet Union also declined, dropping from CDN $78 million in 1979 to CDN $16 million in 1981.[39] Besides these short-term effects, the sanctions also have had a longer-term impact on these countries' trade with the Soviet Union by undermining the climate of business confidence needed to support economic relations. United States firms have become reluctant to invest the time and money needed to build up a market in the Soviet Union or cannot obtain the backing needed to do so. For example, although Ingersoll-Rand received partial compensation for its loss of the US $8 million Kama contract, its political risk insurance policy was cancelled. The company then decided not to pursue other potential contracts with the Soviet

Union and the Democratic Republic of Germany worth US $60 million. This decision resulted in layoffs for several hundred workers and contractors.[40] On the Soviet side, foreign trade officials now are more inclined to purchase goods or technology from Western Europe or Japan, rather than from the United States.

Evaluation of the Sanctions

The sanctions were imposed to punish the Soviet Union for its invasion of Afghanistan in order to moderate future Soviet foreign policy behaviour. To what extent did they further these objectives? The sanctions succeeded in inflicting some costs on the Soviet Union. In the economic sphere, these costs were quite limited. The partial grain embargo impeded Soviet efforts to improve the population's diet by marginally reducing milk and meat production and per capita consumption. The high technology restrictions delayed some projects and inconvenienced Soviet planners. In the political and military spheres, the costs were significantly greater. The Afghanistan invasion acted as a spur to US rearmament and military co-operation with China, Pakistan and other countries. It strained Soviet relations with a large number of countries, some of which reduced or suspended contacts with the Soviet Union. A significant number of these countries boycotted the Summer 1980 Olympics in Moscow, making the games less of a propaganda success than anticipated.

Although the Soviet Union was forced to pay a concrete price for its aggression, it is difficult to demonstrate that this punishment had a salutary effect on Soviet foreign policy behaviour. The sanctions clearly have not produced any concessions in Afghanistan but this was not their main objective. Their primary objective was to deter future Soviet acts of aggression. The only instance when it is possible to argue that they might have had this kind of effect is Poland, but this argument is not very compelling. There is evidence that on two occasions, in December 1980 and again in March 1981, Soviet troops were mobilised to invade Poland in order to suppress the threat to Communist Party rule posed by Solidarity and its supporters. On both occasions, Soviet troops were withdrawn amid signs of differences of opinion in the Soviet leadership. Subsequently, martial law was imposed in Poland to deal with this internal threat. Clearly, a threat of economic sanctions by the United States and its allies lent support to those Soviet leaders who were opposed to military intervention. However, the decision not to intervene was influenced by a number of other equally important or more important considerations, in particular, by US warnings to Poland which deprived the Soviet Union of the advantage of surprise, by evidence that an invasion would likely be met by armed Polish resistance, and by indications of discipline problems among Soviet reservists mobilised for the intervention and of deficiencies in Soviet military preparedness.[41] Moreover, even if one could show that the threat of new sanctions had a significant influence on Soviet policy toward Poland, it would still be difficult to gauge the impact of the post-Afghanistan sanctions on this decision. Former National Security Adviser Zbigniew Brzezinski has argued that the post-Afghanistan sanctions 'must have contributed to the greater credibility of our response to the Polish challenge'.[42] However, it is possible that the Soviet leaders took the threat seriously not because of but in spite of their experience with the post-Afghanistan sanctions. They may have realised that Western European leaders considered Poland more important than Afghanistan, making it more likely that they would support the United States.

Although there have not been other cases of direct Soviet military intervention since Afghanistan, this fact can hardly be taken as proof that the sanctions are working. Since the Second World War, instances of direct intervention by Soviet troops have been the exception, rather than the norm. Usually, the Soviet Union has tried to exert influence by aiding one side in an internal power struggle and/or by intervening through proxies. It has used its own troops to intervene only when it has concluded that important interests are threatened and the chances of success are high. The post-Afghanistan period has not seen any moderation of this policy. The Soviet Union has continued its efforts to exert influence through aid or proxies in a number of Third World areas, including the Middle East and the Horn of Africa, and has stepped up such efforts in Central America where Soviet leaders have perceived new opportunities. Although in two cases, Grenada and El Salvador, the Soviet Union did not send in troops to protect its allies when they were being threatened, this reluctance is attributable not to the post-Afghanistan sanctions but to an understandable unwillingness to challenge superior US regional power in Washington's back yard. In other areas, Soviet behaviour is hardly less belligerent than before Afghanistan. This period has witnessed the continued buildup and deployment of Soviet arms including intermediate range missiles in Europe and submarines in the territorial waters of neutral Sweden, the shooting down of an unarmed civilian airliner over Soviet territory, and Moscow's walkout from arms control negotiations with Washington. Soviet leaders have adopted tough policies toward internal dissidents and Jewish emigration which fly in the face of long-standing and oft-expressed Western objections.

The sanctions did not have a greater impact on Soviet

foreign policy in part because they were based on certain misconceptions about the Soviet economy and about Soviet attitudes and perceptions. Even if the sanctions had commanded greater support, their impact on the Soviet economy still would have been limited. The Soviet economy is largely self-sufficient. Western machinery and equipment are important to certain branches of Soviet industry where they help to overcome critical bottlenecks and to speed up production. However, their overall impact is limited because they constitute such a tiny percentage of the Soviet Union's total stock and because the Soviet Union still has difficulty absorbing and diffusing advanced technology. Western grain imports help the Soviet Union to increase milk and meat production and to avoid the distress slaughter of livestock in poor harvest years. Their importance is recognised by Soviet leaders who have shown an inclination to use scarce hard currency to pay for grain imports to compensate for poor harvests. In the highly unlikely event that the West could control all foreign sources of grain, this would give it some leverage over Soviet policy. However, even then, its leverage would be limited because foreign grain is used mainly for livestock feed, not to feed the Soviet population. Without it, Soviet citizens would not starve and their diets would still be ample in calories although somewhat deficient in protein. This point was made in a Tass commentary which had the following to say about the likely effects of the grain embargo:

> Even if one cannot rule out the possibility that a tear may roll, unbidden, from the wistful eye of a ruminating cow in Russia as a result of Washington's grain decision, the Soviet people will not shed tears....The fact is that the Soviet Union today is not the poor czarist Russia where a piece of bread was frequently a coveted dream for the masses. Today, the USSR is a mighty industrial power with a developed agriculture.[43]

The last sentence of the Tass commentary is strikingly similar to the conclusions of a recent CIA study of the Soviet economy.[44]

The sanctions' effect also was limited by their delayed impact on the Soviet economy. The effects of a reduction in feed grain supplies and of high technology restrictions are more likely to be felt in future years than in the year in which they are implemented. However, the sanctions' negative impact on employment and income in the initiating countries is immediate, rather than delayed, which makes it difficult politically to sustain them for long enough to be effective.

Supporters of the sanctions failed to give adequate

consideration to certain important Soviet attitudes and perceptions. It has been observed that economic sanctions often increase the spirit of resistance in target countries rather than inducing them to make concessions. This is likely to be particularly true of the Soviet Union. One major Soviet objective since the Cuban Missile Crisis has been to increase Soviet military power in order to deal with the United States on a basis of equality, not inferiority. Soviet leaders are determined to avoid the humiliation of being forced to give in to public pressure. This attitude was reflected in Moscow's reaction to past attempts to use economic sanctions to influence Soviet behaviour. For example, when the US Congress in 1974 tried to use economic pressure to influence Soviet emigration policy. Moscow reacted by renouncing the 1972 US-Soviet Trade Agreement granting the Soviet Union most-favoured-nation status. It is instructive to note that this response was made at a time when East-West economic relations were considered more important by Soviet leaders than they are today.

Soviet leaders' determination to resist external pressure was also reflected in Soviet statements after the Afghanistan invasion. For example, a book written by a Soviet foreign trade official, V. Malkevich, had the following to say about the sanctions:

> It would be useful to recall, as well, that no one has yet succeeded in influencing the home or foreign policy of the USSR by means of economic blackmail, discrimination, or diktat. If it ever had any effect, moreover, it has been simply the opposite of the one counted on: tension between countries always forces each of them to harden its position.[45]

A similar theme appeared in Premier Brezhnev's initial comments on the sanctions.

Soviet leaders may see no reason why they should make concessions to the West in order to promote East-West trade. They are far more ambivalent about its benefits to their country than some supporters of the sanctions realised. Soviet writings stress that East-West trade provides important benefits for Western countries which want access to the Soviet market and to Soviet raw materials. Sanctions inflict costs on Western countries which create pressure for their removal. These points are made in the following passages from Malkevich's book:

> The notorious 'linkage', i.e. the artificial tying together of quite unconnected economic, political, and military problems, is not an original invention of the present Washington Administration. It is rather evi-

> dence of a lack of understanding of the essence of international exchange: trade, economic, scientific, and technical cooperation are neither charity, nor a gift. They are a mutually advantageous affair. Countries enter into economic relations with one another because they see something in it for themselves, and not because they like each other, or want to do their partners a favour. It is just the same with breaking off trade and economic relations: it is not punishment of one of the parties for bad behaviour, but deliberate (or unconscious) loss of certain advantages of economic intercourse for both.[46]

Malkevich's stress on the mutual advantages of East-West trade is instructive since sanctions are not likely to be effective unless the target perceives that it derives one-sided advantage from the activity being embargoed.

The sanctions not only had very limited success, they also had some unintended consequences with negative implications for the initiating countries. Rather than moderating Soviet foreign policy behaviour, the post-Afghanistan sanctions may instead have encouraged Soviet leaders to adopt a tougher and more bellicose policy by increasing their sense of perceived threat and by persuading them that they had little left to lose in their relationship with the United States. In addition, lack of support for the sanctions may have reinforced Moscow's long-standing belief that it could manipulate differences among Western allies to its own advantage. In the period since Afghanistan, Soviet voices stressing the importance of Moscow's relations with the United States have been relatively muted, while Soviet policy has been directed increasingly toward courting US allies in Western Europe.

The sanctions have served as a divisive force in the Western Alliance by increasing resentment of and disillusionment with US leadership. In the post-Afghanistan period, the United States and its allies have been much farther apart than before on the question of what is appropriate Soviet policy. While US leaders have become thoroughly disillusioned with detente, Western European leaders still cling to the idea that detente is possible and that East-West trade and political ties should be continued to support it.

In the economic sphere, the sanctions have strengthened the hand of those in the Soviet Union who argue against spending scarce hard currency to import Western goods which the Soviet Union should be able to produce for itself. The following statement by Premier Brezhnev at the 26th Party Congress in March 1981 is typical of the arguments that have been heard with increasing frequency in recent years: 'We must look into the reasons that we sometimes lose our priority and spend large sums of money to purchase from foreign countries equipment and technologies that we are fully capable of producing ourselves, and often of a higher quality too'.[47] In areas where the Soviet Union still needs Western imports, it now is more likely to turn to Western Europe, Canada or Japan than to the United States. This not only reduces US economic benefits from trade with the Soviet Union but also decreases future US opportunities to exert leverage. United States potential leverage also has been circumscribed by the passage of laws making it almost impossible to impose another grain embargo. Without a grain embargo, it would be difficult to impose sanctions on non-agricultural exports.

Lessons for the Future

What lessons for the future should be derived from the West's experience with the post-Afghanistan sanctions? One lesson is that it often is harder to reverse sanctions than to impose them. If sanctions are imposed in order to send a message of disapproval, then there is a danger that lifting the sanctions will send the wrong signal.

Another lesson is that it is important for a government considering sanctions to consult more widely both within its own country and with allies before imposing them. Such consultation should allow the government to appraise more realistically the sanctions' prospects for success and to increase support for them if a decision is made to go ahead. Some have argued that the Carter Administration would not have been able to avoid sanctions even if it had had a more realistic idea of their likely impact. According to those who make this argument, sanctions are imposed largely in response to domestic pressure and serve an important symbolic function by making it appear that the government is doing something even when it has little power to affect the external situation. This function has been called a 'Sunni rain dance'[48] because it makes the participants feel better without accomplishing anything. Proponents of this view argue that sanctions serve an important function by reducing pressure for military intervention. One flaw in this argument is that it underestimates governments' capacity to shape popular perceptions of foreign policy situations and of the appropriate ways to respond to them. If the Carter Administration had not depicted the Afghanistan situation in such apocalyptic terms, it would have been under less pressure to adopt sanctions. Proponents of this argument also ignore the possibility that sanctions may be not only ineffective but also counterproductive by encouraging the very foreign policy behaviour they were designed to prevent.

Notes

1. Transcript of State of the Union Address, Facts on File, 25 January 1980, p. 42.
2. Zbigniew Brzezinski, Power and Principle: Memoirs of a National Security Adviser (Farrar Straus Grioux, New York, 1983), pp. 430-7; Jimmy Carter, Keeping Faith: Memoirs of a President (Bantam Books, Toronto, 1982), pp. 471-2.
3. Brzezinski, Power and Principle, pp. 431, 433.
4. 'Transcript of State of the Union Address', p. 42.
5. John P. Hardt and Kate S. Tomlinson, 'Soviet Economic Policies in Western Europe', paper presented at the University of Washington, 11 October 1982 (mimeo.), p. 39.
6. Carl H. McMillan, 'Canada and the Soviet Union'. Paper presented to a Session on Canadian and American Policy toward the Soviet Union, Fletcher School of Law and Diplomacy, Tufts University, 15 February 1983 (mimeo.), p. 16.
7. M. M. Kostecki, 'Canada's Grain Trade with the Soviet Union and China', Canadian Journal of Agricultural Economics (30 July 1982), pp. 223-6.
8. Office of the Senior Specialists, Congressional Research Service, Library of Congress, An Assessment of the Afghanistan Sanctions: Implications for Trade and Diplomacy in the 1980's: Report Prepared for the Subcommittee on Europe and the Middle East of the Committee on Foreign Affairs, U.S. House of Representatives (United States Government Printing Office, Washington, D.C., 1981), hereinafter referred to as: Assessment, pp. 79-85, 89-90; New York Times, 6 Jan. 1980.
9. Carter, Keeping Faith, p. 481.
10. Globe and Mail, 28 Jan. 1980.
11. New York Times, 7 and 20 July 1980; Assessment, pp. 85-8, 92.
12. Globe and Mail, 20 Nov. 1982, pp. 1, 2.
13. See Chapter 10 in this volume.
14. Anton F. Malish, 'The Food Program: A New Policy or More Rhetoric?', in Soviet Economy in the 1980's: Problems and Prospects Part 2: Selected Papers Submitted to the Joint Economic Committee, Congress of the United States, December 31, 1982 (United States Government Printing Office, Washington, D.C., 1982), p. 45; John C. Roney, 'Grain Embargo as Diplomatic Lever: A Case Study of the U.S.-Soviet Embargo of 1980-81', in ibid., p. 134.
15. Allan P. Mustard, 'Impact of the U.S. Grain Embargo on World Grain Trading Patterns and Soviet Livestock Output', unpublished thesis, Master College of the University of Illinois at Urbana-Champaign, 1982, p. 115, cited in footnote 21, Chapter 10 in this volume.

16. Roney, 'Grain Embargo as Diplomatic Lever', p. 133.
17. Financial Post, 19 Jan. 1980.
18. New York Times, 4 May 1981; Mainichi Daily News, 13 July 1981. See Chapter 10 in this volume.
19. Halifax Chronicle Herald, 25 Oct. 1980.
20. New York Times, 25 Apr. 1981.
21. New York Times, 16 June 1981.
22 New York Times, 21 Oct. 1982; Mainichi Daily News, 3 Nov. 1982.
23. U.S. Congress Senate Committee on Agriculture, Nutrition and Forestry, Subcommittee on Foreign Agricultural Policy, The Evaluation of the Economic Impact of Previous Agricultural Embargoes on Both the United States and the Embargoed Countries: Hearings before the Subcommittee on Foreign Agricultural Policy, 9th Congress, 2nd session, February 3-5, 1982 (United States Government Printing Office, Washington, D.C., 1982), pp. 103-8; Office of Technology Assessment, Congress of the United States, Technology and East-West Trade: An Update (Congress of the United States, Office of Technology Assessment, Washington, D.C., May 1983), p. 54.
24. New York Times, 27 May 1981.
25. Globe and Mail, 30 Aug. 1982.
26. Mainichi Daily News, 30 July 1983, p. 6.
27. Roney, 'Grain Embargo as Diplomatic Lever', p. 139; Technology and East-West Trade: An Update, p. 44.
28. Globe and Mail, 14 Aug. 1984.
29. Assessment, pp. 53-64.
30. Jack Brougher, '1979-82: The United States Uses Trade to Penalize Soviet Aggression and Seeks to Reorder Western Policy', in Soviet Economy in the 1980's: Problems and Prospects Part 2, pp. 427-9.
31. Thane Gustafson, Selling the Russians the Rope: Soviet Technology Policy and U.S. Export Control (Rand Corporation, Santa Monica, California, R-2649 ARPA), p. 67.
32. Brougher, '1979-82: The United States Uses Trade to Penalize Soviet Aggression', p. 429; Stephen Woolcock, Western Policies on East-West Trade, Chatham House Papers No. 15 (Routledge & Kegan, Boston, 1982), pp. 43-4.
33. John P. Hardt and Donna L. Gold, 'Changes in East-West Trade: The Political Context', paper presented to a Conference on the Future of East-West Economic Relations in a Changing World Economy, 13-15 June 1984, Canadian Institute of International Affairs, Toronto (mimeo.), p. 2.
34. Financial Post, 26 Jan. 1980; William H. Cooper, 'Soviet-Western Trade', in Soviet Economy in the 1980's: Problems and Prospects Part 2, p. 459.
35. Peggy L. Falkenheim, 'Changing Japanese

Perceptions of the Soviet Threat: The Impact of the Afghanistan Invasion', in *Forum on the Pacific Basin: Growth, Security and Community* (Foreign Policy Research Institute, Philadephia, 1981), pp. 119-30.

36. *New York Times*, 15 Oct. 1980; *Technology and East-West Trade: An Update*, pp. 33-4; McMillan, 'Canada and the Soviet Union', pp. 20-1; Woolcock, *Western Policies on East-West Trade*, p. 44.

37. *New York Times*, 18 Jan., 31 May, 30 June, 5 July and 24 Nov. 1980.

38. Homer E. Moyer, Jr., General Counsel, U.S. Department of Commerce, Statement before Senate Committee on Banking, Housing and Urban Affairs, 20 August 1980, cited in Brougher, '1979-82: The United States Uses Trade to Penalize Soviet Aggression', p. 432.

39. Brougher, '1979-82: The United States Uses Trade to Penalize Soviet Aggression', p. 431; McMillan, 'Canada and the Soviet Union', pp. 20-1.

40. *Technology and East-West Trade: An Update*, pp. 33-4.

41. Richard D. Anderson, Jr., 'Soviet Decision-Making and Poland', *Problems of Communism* 31:2 (March-April 1981), pp. 22-36; Brzezinski, *Power and Principle*, pp. 463-8.

42. Ibid., p. 468.

43. *New York Times*, 10 Jan. 1980.

44. Statement by the Honourable Henry Rowen, Chairman, National Intelligence Council, Central Intelligence Agency, before the Joint Economic Committee, Subcommittee on International Trade, Finance and Security Economics, 'Central Intelligence Agency Briefing on the Soviet Economy', 1 December 1982 (mimeo.).

45. V. Malkevich, *East-West Economic Cooperation and Technological Exchange* (Academy of Sciences, Moscow, 1981), p. 15.

46. Ibid., pp. 13-14.

47. *Pravda and Izvestia*, 24 Feb. 1981, translated in *Current Digest of the Soviet Press*, 33:8 (25 March 1981), p. 18.

48. *Economic Relations with the Soviet Union: Hearings before the Subcommittee on International Economic Policy of the Committee on Foreign Relations, U.S. Senate, 97th Congress, 2nd session* (United States Government Printing Office, Washington, D.C., 1982), p. 110.

Chapter Seven

ECONOMIC SANCTIONS IN THE POLISH CRISIS

Paul Marantz

There was growing alarm in Western capitals over the possibility of Soviet military intervention in Poland as the Polish crisis deepened in the latter part of 1980, and Soviet troops engaged in threatening manoeuvres along that country's borders. Reflecting upon the sad lessons of Afghanistan, it was recognised that previous Western policy had suffered from two fatal defects: (1) the failure to warn the Soviet Union unambiguously <u>prior</u> to the December 1979 invasion just how serious the consequences of armed intervention would be; and (2) the absence of a co-ordinated joint policy once the invasion had occurred. To avoid a repetition of this situation, the NATO ministers, in their communique of 12 December 1980, issued a stern warning to the Soviet Union: 'Any intervention [in Poland] would fundamentally alter the entire international situation. The allies would be compelled to react in the manner which the gravity of this development would require'.[1] Moscow was informed that should its troops be sent into Poland, the West would retaliate with a broad range of economic sanctions.[2] Although little is known about Kremlin decision-making during the Polish crisis, it may well be that Soviet concern about the effect of an invasion on East-West economic relations was one of the factors that caused the Soviet leadership to temporise for so long and ultimately to choose a more indirect and less provocative means of crushing Solidarity.

If there was a measure of Western unity in warning the Soviet Union not to use its army in Poland, this quickly evaporated once martial law was proclaimed on 13 December 1981. Many Europeans argued that the fact that the Polish government was carrying out the crackdown and Soviet troops were not being employed created a situation fundamentally different from that envisaged in the NATO communique of December 1980. Disputing this view, the US government contended that Moscow was calling the shots in Poland, and the use of Polish forces rather than the Soviet military made no difference whatsoever.[3] The Reagan Administration, which had come into office openly proclaiming its deep mistrust of the Kremlin's intentions, quickly imposed sanctions against Poland and the Soviet Union. European governments, with much less enthusiasm and largely as a result of US pressure, imposed much weaker economic penalties.

It is instructive to look at the factors and thinking that produced these differing responses and the effect they had on the Polish crisis. In so doing, this chapter is divided into four major sections: an examination of the reasons why the West imposed sanctions; an outline of the nature of these sanctions; a discussion of their effect upon Poland and the Soviet Union; and an analysis of why the sanctions failed.

Reasons for the Sanctions

The US decision to impose sanctions upon Poland and the Soviet Union and to pressure its NATO allies to follow suit was based upon a wide range of considerations, many of which went far beyond the Polish issue. These considerations can best be understood by distinguishing three broad categories of motivating factors: (1) those specifically related to Poland; (2) those based upon broader policy objectives concerning the nature and direction of East-West relations; and (3) those derived from US domestic politics and the internal political standing of the Reagan Administration. After discussing each of these, we will then turn to an examination of the European response.

In regard to Poland itself, it was the hope of the Reagan Administration that the imposition of sanctions would have some effect in inducing the Soviet and Polish authorities to lessen the severity of martial law and to shorten its duration. It appears that the United States misjudged the reaction of its European allies and was overly optimistic in expecting that its NATO partners would join together in forging a joint policy of sanctions which, together with the actions taken by the United States, would impose sufficient costs upon the Soviet Union to have a significant impact on the situation in Poland. Even though US policy-makers recognised that they could not be certain that sanctions would succeed, it was their belief, as expressed by an editorial in the *New York Times*, that 'as long as the economic weapon may have some effect, it would be irresponsible not to employ it'.[4]

There was also an important moral component to US thinking in Poland. It was felt that inaction would be tantamount to complicity in Polish repression and that it was incumbent upon the United States to provide moral support for the courageous people who were sacrificing so much in their brave struggle against Soviet tyranny. Above and beyond any hopes of actually influencing events in Poland, the Reagan Administration felt that it could not abandon the Polish people, and it had to demonstrate disapproval of Soviet repression. When the Polish authorities went ahead with the formal banning of Solidarity in October 1982, the United States responded by terminating the most-favoured-nation tariff status that Polish goods had enjoyed since 1960. In explaining this action, US officials openly acknowledged that this was largely a symbolic act whose economic impact would not be all that great, since the value of Polish goods entering the United States which would be affected was already quite low. However, it was stated that this was one of the few concrete steps available to the United States for demonstrating its indignation over the dissolution of Solidarity.[5]

A second set of considerations, which was probably of greater significance in shaping the sanctions policy of the Reagan Administration, was its perspective on the general state of East-West relations. President Reagan came into office convinced that the United States had to take a tougher stand vis-a-vis the Soviet Union. He advocated a massive build-up of US military forces, not just so that the United States would have the means of standing up to the Soviet Union, but as an unmistakable signal that the post-Vietnam malaise was over and the United States was once again an international force with which to be contended. Unlike most Europeans, the Reagan Administration saw Poland as an integral part of the broader East-West confrontation: yesterday Afghanistan, today Poland, and tomorrow - if the West did not stand firm - the Persian Gulf, the Middle East or Central America. In its view, a line had to be clearly drawn.

This predilection for firm action was reinforced by Washington's perception that the growing economic crisis of the Soviet bloc made this an especially auspicious moment to lean on the Soviets. The unprecedented decline in growth rates throughout Eastern Europe was thought to mean that the Soviet Union was vulnerable to economic pressure as never before. It was President Reagan's view that at the very least, the West should reverse its short-sighted generosity and stop subsidising its ruthless adversary through billions of dollars in loans and the eager pursuit of trade on terms highly favourable to the Communist world. President Reagan argued that Western credits and trade had enabled the stumbling Soviet economy to continue to strengthen its military might at a rapid pace, to obtain easy access to militarily relevant technology and to override domestic pressures for economic reform and the re-allocation of more resources to the civilian sector.[6] The Polish crisis was seen as a golden opportunity to reverse the economic detente of the 1970s.

In the eyes of the Reagan Administration, Western myopia was epitomised by the European decision to go ahead with the massive pipeline that would deliver huge quantities of Soviet natural gas from the Urengoy gas field to Western Europe. Billions of dollars in credits were to be advanced to the Soviet Union to complete a project which, in Washington's view, would only serve to strengthen the Soviet economy by generating many billions of dollars in hard currency earnings and to weaken NATO by making the countries of Western Europe dependent upon Soviet benevolence for their future energy needs. Since mid-1981 Washington had been trying, without any success, to get the countries of Western Europe to reconsider this project. The Polish crisis enabled the White House to prohibit US companies from supplying pipelaying equipment and compressor stations needed for this project.

It was hoped that this action would delay the completion of the pipeline for approximately one to three years and would significantly increase its cost. This in turn might well cause the Europeans to reconsider the whole project. Failing this, it would at least impose an increased burden upon the Soviet economy.[7] In the absence of the Polish crisis, unilateral US moves to delay the pipeline would have been impossible because of the damage they would have done to relations with Western Europe. Hence the imposition of martial law provided the rationale for a policy which already had strong support inside the Reagan Administration, especially within the Department of Defense.[8]

The third set of factors conditioning US policy relates to domestic political considerations. There was wide-spread support throughout the United States for Solidarity's bold efforts to liberalise Polish society, and the imposition of martial law met with angry disapproval. Influential senators, such as Jesse Helms and Daniel Patrick Moynihan, called for a strong US response, as did Lane Kirkland, the president of the powerful AFL-CIO trade union.[9] Even prior to this, there was growing dissatisfaction with President Reagan's first year in office among many of his conservative supporters who were unhappy with his decision to lift the post-Afghanistan grain embargo, to adhere to the provisions of the unratified SALT treaty and to enter into new arms negotiations with the Soviet Union. The application of sanctions enabled President Reagan to satisfy these constituencies as well as to defuse pressure for actions that even he regarded as too stringent (such as a new grain embargo, a formal declaration that Poland was in default of its loan obligations, or a US withdrawal from arms control negotiations and the Conference on Security and Co-operation in Europe). Economic sanctions were a happy middle path which avoided the perils of inaction as well as the dangers of a full-blown East-West confrontation.

Finally, account must also be taken of the role of bureaucratic politics. Throughout the first half of 1982, there was a sharp struggle between the Department of State headed by Alexander Haig and the Department of Defense led by Caspar Weinberger. In June 1982 Secretary of State Haig lost out and the result was the controversial policy which the State Department had strenuously resisted, namely the broadening of pipeline sanctions to include not just equipment manufactured in the United States (the December 1981 embargo), but also components produced in Western Europe by US subsidiaries or by wholly-owned European firms utilising US licences.[10] Mr Haig's terminal weakness opened the door to these sanctions just as the mediating skills of his successor, George Shultz (combined with the furious European reaction), contributed to their revocation five months later.

Almost three months after the United States initiated sanctions against Poland and the Soviet Union, the members of the European Economic Community (EEC) reluctantly and half-heartedly agreed to impose a much milder set of economic penalties upon the Soviet Union. Although portrayed as an attempt to influence Polish events, it is clear that by far the most important reason for instituting this economic slap on the wrist was the need to appease the United States and to preserve at least a semblance of Alliance harmony. A second factor was the demand for action put forth by various groups within Western Europe and the attempt to satisfy or defuse this demand in a way that would undercut any pressure for stronger action.

In agreeing to sanctions, the Western Europeans were careful to protect two concerns of primary importance: (1) that the volume of East-West trade, and above all the gas pipeline, not be significantly affected (this was especially important to the Federal Republic of Germany); and (2) that their governments preserve their full independence of action and not appear to their own people as meekly bowing to US dictates (a major concern of the French). Thus, while the members of NATO formally agreed not to undermine the effect of US sanctions, they also stated in their communique of 11 January 1982 that each nation would act in accord with 'its own situation and laws'.[11] In the final analysis, this meant that UK, French and Italian companies were ordered by their respective governments to defy the US embargo and supply the equipment that was needed for the pipeline to proceed.[12]

United States and Western European perspectives on East-West trade were clearly far apart. The governments of Western Europe continued to place a higher value than the United States on trade with the Soviet bloc as a means of moderating political conflict. In addition, it has been their belief that sanctions would prove ineffective and would hurt Western economies more than they would harm the Soviet Union. It was also feared that sanctions would only stiffen the resolve of the Soviet government and undercut pressures for economic reform emerging within the Soviet Union.[13] The unwillingness of the Europeans to impose stronger sanctions meant that the Soviet Union was made to pay only a minor economic penalty for its actions in Poland, a penalty which indeed was insufficient to alter Soviet conduct.

The Nature of the Sanctions

The United States initiated four separate sets of sanctions. These were imposed over a ten-month period from December 1981 to October 1982, and some were aimed at Poland while others were targeted at the Soviet Union.

On 23 December 1981 the United States imposed sanctions against Poland. The major steps taken were: an end to further governmental credits for the purchase of food and other commodities; cancellation of any further export credit insurance from the Export-Import Bank; suspension of Poland's civil aviation privileges in the United States (such as landing rights at US airports); withdrawal of permission for the Polish fleet to fish in US territorial waters; and increased restrictions on the granting of export licences for high technology products.[14]

On 29 December 1981 the Reagan Administration directed a series of measures against the Soviet Union, the country considered the main culprit responsible for the imposition of martial law. Export licences were cancelled for equipment that could be used on the Soviet gas pipeline (e.g. pipe-laying machines and turbine technology); restrictions were tightened on the export of high technology items (such as computers and electronic instruments), including equipment that could be used in locating or extracting petroleum products; negotiations were postponed on a new long-term grain agreement to replace the previous five-year agreement which had expired on 1 October 1981; negotiations on a maritime accord were suspended and the access of Soviet ships to US ports was restricted; the US landing rights of the Soviet airline Aeroflot were withdrawn; the Soviet Purchasing Commission, which had accounted for approximately one-third of Soviet orders for non-farm products, was closed; and the conclusion of any agreements in the areas of energy, science, technology and culture was to be held in abeyance pending a policy review.[15]

On 18 June 1982 Washington announced its intention to extend the ban on the export of equipment for the pipeline so that it would affect not just goods manufactured within the United States, but also equipment made by foreign subsidiaries of US companies or made by foreign companies using US licences. By this time it had become clear that the ban on US exports of pipeline equipment was having little effect since the Soviet Union could buy whatever it needed in Europe or Japan. The Reagan Administration decided upon this unilateral action after it was unable to gain allied agreement at the Versailles Economic Summit on joint measures aimed at restricting trade and the granting of credits to the Soviet bloc.[16]

In October 1982 the United States suspended most-favoured-nation tariff status for Polish goods. This action was taken in retaliation for Poland's formal outlawing of Solidarity.[17]

In contrast to the energetic US use of economic weapons, the European response was much more muted. After some hesitation, the nations of the EEC agreed to a partial restriction of their trade with the Soviet Union. However, rather than limit their exports, which would directly affect employment in their own industries, they curtailed imports from the Soviet Union. Original proposals called for a 50 per cent reduction in EEC imports of approximately 100 different products.[18] However, various EEC member nations objected to restrictions on one item or another, and the final list affected only 58 products whose purchase was to be reduced by 25 per cent.[19] In the end, cars, diamonds and furs were removed from the restricted list, and the EEC was left the least common denominator composed of such crucial items as upright pianos, caviar, alarm clocks, pearls and picture tubes for black-and-white televisions. The truly significant commodities such as oil, natural gas and raw materials were never even considered for restriction. Thus, it has been estimated that the measures adopted would affect no more than 1.5 per cent of the US $10 billion in goods that the nations of the EEC import annually from the Soviet Union.[20]

Aside from this ineffectual economic move against the Soviet Union, the members of the EEC also agreed not to provide any new governmental loans to Poland.[21] However, economic conditions alone in all probabililty would have dictated this step given the disastrous condition of the Polish economy by early 1982. Moreover, both European and US banks (as opposed to the governments) continued to negotiate with Poland over the rescheduling of its loans, and when an agreement was finally reached in November 1982, the terms were quite favourable to Poland.[22]

Finally, some nations instituted independent measures of their own. The United Kingdom restricted the movements of Polish and Soviet diplomats, cut back on various technical exchanges and announced its intention to restrict Soviet fishing in UK waters.[23] Japan moved even more gingerly, simply restricting credits to Poland and postponing consultations with the Soviet Union over trade and scientific exchanges.[24] These actions were largely symbolic in nature. They were meant to show official displeasure with Moscow rather than seriously harm the Soviet economy.

The Effect of the Sanctions

It is clear that the economic and political consequences of Western sanctions were relatively minimal. Sanctions did not impose a significant economic cost on either Poland or the Soviet Union, and they did not have a noticeable effect on the political behaviour of either country.

By December 1981, when the United States applied sanctions, the Polish economy was already declining precipitously. National income dropped approximately 13 per cent in 1981 and 7.5 per cent in 1982.[25] In this context, the economic penalties imposed by the United States were a definite irritant, but not really of major consequence. For example, the withdrawal of most-favoured-nation tariff status affected only Poland's non-agricultural exports to the United States. In 1980 these amounted to approximately US $250 million, which was less than 3 per cent of the approximately US $10 billion in goods and services that Poland exported to non-Communist countries.[26] Other measures taken by the United States also had a minimal impact. The Polish national airline had to cancel its six weekly flights to New York City; Poland lost US export insurance worth approximately US $25 million a year; and the Polish fishing fleet, which may have obtained as much as one-third of its catch off the United States coast (an estimated 230,000 tons), would have to fish elsewhere in less abundant waters.[27]

Somewhat more significant was the US suspension of further credits. The Polish government received almost US $800 million in US government credits and food assistance in 1981, and it was requesting a similar amount for 1982.[28] At the time that sanctions were imposed and further loans ended, it appears that the US government was about to announce the granting of US $100 million in credits for the purchase of food.[29] In absolute terms this was not a insignificant sum of money, but in the context of the Polish economy, with a Gross National Product of US $100 billion and a hard currency debt of US $23 to $29 billion (depending on whose figures and what method of calculation are used), this was still not a truly decisive figure.[30]

This is especially so since the Soviet Union had already committed itself to expending billions of dollars in subsidies and credits to keep Poland afloat, and the imposition of sanctions only increased Moscow's stake in continuing to shoulder this burden.[31] It is significant that Polish economic performance in 1982 (that is after US sanctions were imposed), was less dismal than in 1981.[32] The impact of US sanctions on the Polish economy was minor compared to the self-inflicted damage caused by the Polish government in 1979-82.

If anything, Western sanctions were even less consequential for the Soviet Union. Many of the consumer goods and luxuries, whose importation the EEC nations limited in March 1982, could simply be sold to other nations. Some of them were even likely to find their way eventually into European markets through various intermediaries.[33] United States restrictions on such things as the landing of Aeroflot, the access of Soviet ships to US ports and the operation of the Soviet Purchasing Commission were also of marginal economic significance.

In contrast, had the United States succeeded in blocking the natural gas pipeline to Western Europe, this would have had a major impact on Soviet economic fortunes. It is estimated that the pipeline will bring the Soviet Union approximately US $4 billion per year in hard currency earnings.[34] This is a large sum both in absolute and relative terms considering that total Soviet hard currency earnings currently run at about US $20 billion per year (excluding earnings from the sale of gold and arms).[35] Income from the export of natural gas will be especially important for the Soviet Union as its dwindling supply of oil causes foreign exchange earnings from this source to drop by the end of the decade.

However, all of this is rather hypothetical since the United States was unable to block or even significantly delay the completion of the 3,700-mile pipeline. When the US government denied Caterpillar Tractor Company a licence to sell pipelaying vehicles to the Soviet Union, Moscow simply turned to a Japanese company which was able to provide virtually identical equipment.[36] United States efforts to prevent the Soviet Union from purchasing the turbines needed to power the pipeline were equally futile. The governments of the United Kingdom, France and Italy made it clear that they would order domestic producers to defy US attempts to extend sanctions to foreign subsidiaries and licensees.

If anything, Moscow was probably sorry to see US Secretary of State George Shultz succeed in negotiating a face-saving compromise that enabled the United States to abandon its ill-fated attempt to stop the pipeline. From the Soviet perspective, the minor economic inconvenience caused by having to shift to European suppliers was far outweighed by political benefits resulting from the deep cleavage in the Western Alliance that was provoked by US attempts to limit the activities of European companies.

Given the marginal economic significance of the sanctions imposed on Poland and the Soviet Union, it is not surprising that the political gains for the West were equally inconsequential. In January 1982 a NATO communique pointed to three steps that would constitute a significant improvement in the Polish situation: the lifting of martial law; the freeing of political detainees; and the Polish government's willingness to enter into a genuine dialogue with the Church and Solidarity.[37] Using these three conditions as a benchmark, it is apparent that even now, little has been gained from Western economic pressure. While many detainees (including Lech Walesa) have been released, others still languish in prison. In December 1982 Warsaw declared that martial law was 'suspended', but the new civil laws enacted to replace it - and the resulting political climate - are even more repressive than those existing previously. Solidarity has been formally dissolved, and the Polish people, no less than the Church to which they look for moral leadership, have been driven into sullen opposition.

The West clearly has not succeeded in reversing the effects of martial law. Yet in a strict sense it cannot be said that the West has failed, since the West never really tried to bring its full economic weight to bear. 'Non-sanctions' (i.e. sanctions of only marginal economic significance) were bound to produce a resounding 'non-effect'.

Why Sanctions Failed

Given the formidable obstacles to the effective utilisation of sanctions against Poland and the Soviet Union, it is scarcely surprising that they have been so ineffective. We can identify no less than ten significant factors that have undercut and weakened Western efforts to use economic pressure as a means of punishing the Soviet Union and lessening the repression in Poland.

1. Individual Western governments were obviously unwilling to incur substantial costs - either economic or political - in their half-hearted efforts to promote liberalisation in Poland. The nations of Western Europe had no interest in forgoing Soviet natural gas which was being offered to them at bargain rates and would lessen their reliance on undependable Arab sources of supply. They also were unwilling to embargo their shipments of machinery to the Soviet Union, since industrial equipment makes up approximately 80 per cent of their exports to the Soviet bloc. Similarly, the United States refused to reimpose an embargo on its grain shipments to Moscow which happen to account for some 80 per cent of US exports to the Council of Mutual Economic Assistance (COMECON).[38]

United States policy was especially contradictory. At the very time that Washington was making a major effort to delay the pipeline, the United States agreed to a one-year extension in the Soviet-US grain agreement, and only a week after cancelling Poland's most-favoured-nation status, President Reagan, with his eyes on the forthcoming congressional elections, publicly appealed to the Soviet Union to buy more grain. He even promised that any grain purchased prior to the end of November 1982 would be guaranteed for at least six months against any future embargo![39] A headline in the New York Times effectively captured the President's striking inconsistency: 'Reagan Vows to Bite Warsaw, Feed Moscow'.[40]

Poland was unable to meet her debt payments in 1982. Had Western governments declared Poland in default, this would have done far more to damage her economy than the sanctions that were actually imposed. However, the West feared that such an action would greatly damage its own economic stability, and everything possible was done to avoid taking this step.

2. Conflicting economic interests and divergent perspectives on East-West relations led to disunity within the Western Alliance, and without a united front it was impossible to exert meaningful economic pressure on Moscow or Warsaw. What the Soviet Union could not buy in the United States, it could easily obtain from Japan or Western Europe. United States efforts to delay the pipeline not only failed to impose significant economic costs on the Soviet Union, but actually paid Moscow a handsome political dividend by further weakening the Western Alliance. Far from being willing to pay a political price to see US pipeline sanctions ended, the Soviet leadership probably wished that it could have found some way to induce the US government to continue them.[41]

3. Theoretically, the Polish economy might be considered highly vulnerable to Western economic pressure since it was in such a sharp decline and had made such heavy use in recent years of Western loans and machinery. However, when denied Western assistance, Poland was able to turn to the Soviet Union. Moscow provided billions of dollars to keep Poland afloat and to cushion the impact of Western sanctions.

4. For more than two decades, Western policy toward Eastern Europe has been based on a strategy of 'differentiation' which patiently seeks to encourage - through financial and diplomatic rewards - any evidence of partial autonomy or limited liberalisation (such as that displayed from time to time by Poland, Romania and Hungary). The West's interest in not forcing Poland into total dependence upon the Soviet Union exercises a restraining influence on the choice of sanctions and the degree of pressure that can

be exerted on Warsaw.

5. If Poland can withstand sanctions because it can lean on the Soviet Union, the Soviet economy itself is relatively secure against outside pressure for several reasons. The Soviet Union has long emphasised self-reliance and the avoidance of dependence on foreign sources for critical supplies. The possession of the world's largest land mass, a huge economy (with a Gross National Product exceeding US $1,600 billion) and an abundant supply of energy and raw materials has made such a strategy possible. As Henry Rowen, chairman of the CIA's National Intelligence Council, recently noted, 'the ability of the Soviet economy to remain viable in the absence of imports is much greater than that of most, possibly all, other industrialised economies'.[42] On this basis, he concluded that 'the susceptibility of the Soviet Union to economic leverage tends to be limited'.[43]

6. This relatively high degree of Soviet economic invulnerability is reinforced by the advantages that a highly authoritarian and centralised political system confer upon the Kremlin. Unlike Western leaders, who are forced by slender parliamentary margins and forthcoming elections to pay careful attention to the interests of particular regions or industries that may be harmed by the contraction of East-West trade, the Soviet leadership is much freer to pursue its own conception of the national interest. Workers in the depressed FRG steel industry, US farmers, and US congressmen representing the Midwestern states where International Harvester and Caterpillar Tractor Company are based all speak with a potent voice. Far less audible are the cries of Soviet consumers whose meat supplies have been reduced or the people of Soviet Georgia and Armenia, who in 1978-79 shivered through one of the coldest winters in decades when Iran stopped natural gas exports to the Soviet Union.[44] Thus even if the severing of a particular economic relationship imposes a higher cost on the Soviet Union than the West (which as we have seen is not necessarily the case), the leaders of the Soviet Union may simply be more willing and better able to pay that cost than their Western counterparts.[45]

7. The effectiveness of sanctions depends very much on the perceptions of the leaders in the targeted state. What is important is not just the actual magnitude of the penalties that a country will suffer, but how these are perceived and evaluated by its rulers. It appears that one reason that the Soviet leadership was so eager for detente in the early 1970s and was willing to make a number of conciliatory gestures (such as allowing increased Jewish emigration and ignoring the escalation of US air attacks on North Vietnam in the spring of 1972) was its vast overestimation of the economic benefits to be gained from the importation of advanced US technology. United States

technology was held in high esteem as the most advanced in the world, and it was believed that the introduction of this technology would vastly increase Soviet productivity. It was also expected that a major expansion of Soviet-US trade would strengthen pro-detente forces within the United States and lead to a fundamental improvement in relations between the superpowers. But by the early 1980s, the Soviets had a very different view. They realised that European and Japanese technology was at least as good as that of the United States, and it came with fewer political strings. Even more important, they reluctantly recognised that Western technology would not be the panacea for which they had been searching. It could not easily be adapted to Soviet conditions, and it did not increase productivity to the extent they had expected. Valuing Western technology less than previously, the Soviet leadership clearly had a reduced incentive to make political concessions in Poland or elsewhere simply to prevent a decline in East-West trade.[46]

8. Another factor increasing the Soviet ability to withstand economic sanctions is the Kremlin's knowledge that the capitalist world has little staying power. Even if by some near miracle, Western unity was achieved and damaging sanctions applied, the Soviet leadership knows that the effort is not likely to be of long duration. For impatient Western public opinion, three or four years are an eternity, and Moscow can simply wait things out. Within three years of the bloody Hungarian intervention, Premier Kruschchev received a cordial welcome in the United States, and less than eighteen months after Soviet troops suppressed the Prague Spring, the United States agreed to begin SALT negotiations. By the summer of 1983, the Reagan Administration was so eager for increased trade with the Soviet Union that it happily signed a new long-term grain agreement providing for a 50 per cent increase in minimum Soviet purchase. It also contained a special clause guaranteeing Moscow that during the five-year term of the agreement the United States would not impose any export controls which restricted the Soviet Union's right to purchase up to 12 million metric tons of grain per year.[47] Similarly, as an inducement to Moscow to buy a large number of gas pipe-laying tractors from the Caterpillar Tractor Company, Washington in August 1983 went so far as to accede to Soviet demands that this equipment first be removed from the Commerce Department's list of restricted technology.[48]

9. An often noted drawback of sanctions is that they tend to harden the will of the target state and increase its determination to stand firm.[49] This is especially true in the context of the East-West conflict, where there is a concern on both sides with not appearing weak, irresolute and susceptible to outside pressure. Moscow, no less than Washington, has its nightmares about falling dominoes. A

Soviet leader would have to be very sure of his power within the Politburo before bowing to overt pressure from the West. Thus sanctions directed at the Soviet Union are likely to achieve little and may well be counter-productive in the long run.

10. Lastly, it should be noted that the West's ability to influence the course of events in Poland was seriously constrained by the fact that it was touching upon a fundamental core interest of the Soviet leadership. Clearly, it is easier to find a viable trade-off and to induce change in Soviet behaviour if one is dealing with non-vital or peripheral issues. Various kinds of economic inducements played an important role in the early 1970s in causing the Soviet leadership to permit individual dissidents to leave the Soviet Union, to allow an unprecedented increase in Jewish emigration and to put its signature to the human rights provisions of the Final Act of the Conference on Security and Co-operation in Europe. But when it comes to a vital interest, such as the security of Soviet borders or the maintenance of a protective empire in Eastern Europe, the Soviet commitment is absolute and total, leaving little room for change no matter how great the pressure from the West.

All this points to the rather sobering conclusion that perhaps we should be thankful that the attempt to apply sanctions against Poland and the Soviet Union was so anaemic and half-hearted. Had Western nations moved more forcefully, in all likelihood they would only have done more damage to their own economies and alliance structure, without in any way lessening the cruel repression that has been inflicted upon the Polish people. Punitive economic sanctions can do little to alter Soviet conduct. Perhaps positive inducements for relaxation (such as those employed in the early 1970s) will over the long haul be a more effective means of exercising some influence, however limited, over the future course of events in Eastern Europe.

Notes

The research for this chapter was assisted by the funding provided by the Donner Canadian Foundation through a grant to the Institute of International Relations at the University of British Columbia in support of its research project on 'Canada and International Trade'.

1. New York Times, 13 Dec. 1980, p. 6.
2. Stephen Woolcock, 'East-West Trade: US Policy and European Interests', The World Today, vol. 38, no. 2 (February 1982), pp. 56-7.
3. Hugh MacDonald, 'The Western Alliance and the Polish Crisis', ibid., pp. 42-50.
4. New York Times, 31 Dec. 1981, p. A22.

5. New York Times, 10 Oct. 1982, p. 1.

6. See President Reagan's speech of 13 November 1982, in the New York Times, 14 Nov. 1982, p. 9.

7. New York Times, 19 June 1982, p. 32.

8. Meyer Rashish, 'East-West Economic Relations', The AEI Economist, April 1982, pp. 2-5.

9. New York Times, 25 Dec. 1981, p. 6.

10. New York Times, 15 Nov. 1982, p. A1.

11. New York Times, 12 Jan. 1982, p. A8.

12. Jonathan P. Stern, 'Specters and Pipe Dreams', Foreign Policy, no. 48 (Fall 1982), pp. 31-2.

13. Hans-Dietrich Genscher, 'Toward an Overall Western Strategy for Peace, Freedom and Progress', Foreign Affairs, vol. 61, no. 1 (Fall 1982), pp. 51-7; Ellen L. Frost and Angela E. Stent, 'NATO's Troubles with East-West Trade', International Security, vol. 8, no. 1 (Summer 1983), pp. 179-200.

14. New York Times, 24 Dec. 1981, p. 10.

15. New York Times, 30 Dec. 1981, p. A6. See also Jack Brougher, 'The United States Uses Trade to Penalize Soviet Aggression and Seeks to Reorder Western Policy', in Joint Economic Committee, US Congress, Soviet Economy in the 1980's: Problems and Prospects, Part II, (United States Government Printing Office, Washington, D.C., 1983), pp. 438-41.

16. New York Times, 19 June 1982, p. 1.

17. New York Times, 10 Oct. 1982, p. 1.

18. New York Times, 26 Feb. 1982, p. A3.

19. New York Times, 16 Mar. 1982, p. D4.

20. New York Times, 12 Mar. 1982, p. 6 and 16 Mar. 1982, p. D4.

21. New York Times, 10 Oct. 1982, p. 1.

22. New York Times, 3 Nov. 1982, p. D1.

23. New York Times, 6 Feb. 1982, p. 3.

24. New York Times, 24 Feb. 1982, p. 7.

25. Jan Vanous, 'East European Economic Slowdown', Problems of Communism, vol. 31, no. 4 (July-August 1982), p. 3.

26. Zbigniew M. Fallenbuchl, 'Poland's Economic Crisis', Problems of Communism, vol. 31, no. 2 (March-April 1982), p. 7; Gary R. Teske, 'Poland: Performance and Prospects in Trade with the United States and the West', in Joint Economic Committee, US Congress, East-West Trade: The Prospects to 1985 (United States Government Printing Office, Washington, D.C., 1982), p. 227.

27. New York Times, 24 Dec. 1981, p. 10.

28. New York Times, 14 Dec. 1981, p. A15.

29. New York Times, 15 Dec. 1981, p. A1.

30. Vanous, 'East European Economic Slowdown', p. 4; Fallenbuchl, 'Poland's Economic Crisis,' p. 7.

31. Vanous, 'East European Economic Slowdown', pp.

6-7.

32. Ibid., p. 3.

33. David A. Adelman, 'Economic Crisis and Soviet Trade', The Washington Quarterly, vol. 5, no. 3 (Summer 1982), p. 89.

34. Stern, 'Specters and Pipe Dreams', p. 23.

35. Philip Hanson, 'Economic Constraints on Soviet Policies in the 1980's', International Affairs, vol. 57, no. 1 (Winter 1980-81), p. 36.

36. Stern, 'Specters and Pipe Dreams', p. 31.

37. New York Times, 12 Jan. 1982, p. A8.

38. Woolcock, 'East-West Trade', p. 53.

39. New York Times, 16 Oct. 1982, p. 1.

40. New York Times, 17 Oct. 1982, p. E3.

41. In November 1982 the US government bowed to strenuous allied objections and abandoned its ill-fated attempt to limit European sales of pipeline equipment to the Soviet Union, New York Times, 16 Nov. 1982, p. D6.

42. Henry Rowen, 'Central Intelligence Agency Briefing on the Soviet Economy', Statement Before the Joint Economic Committee, US Congress, 1 December 1982 (mimeo.), p. 17.

43. Ibid., p. 18. Also see Gary Bertsch, 'US-Soviet Trade: The Question of Leverage', Survey, vol. 25, no. 2 (Spring 1980), pp. 66-80.

44. This point is developed in more detail in Jock Finlayson and Paul Marantz, 'Interdependence and East-West Relations', Orbis, vol. 26, no. 1 (Spring 1982), pp. 184-7.

45. For an analysis of the relative economic benefits of East-West trade, see Philip Hanson, Trade and Technology in Soviet-Western Relations (Columbia University Press, New York, 1981), Chs. 12-15; Thomas A. Wolf, 'The Distribution of Economic Costs and Benefits in U.S.-Soviet Trade', Joint Economic Committee, US Congress (United States Government Printing Office, Washington D.C., 1979), pp. 317-41.

46. Finlayson and Marantz, 'Interdependence and East-West Relations', pp. 181-2; M. Elizabeth Denton, 'Soviet Perceptions of Economic Prospects', in Soviet Economy in the 1980's: Problems and Prospects, Part I, pp. 30-45.

47. New York Times, 26 Aug. 1983, pp. A1, D4.

48. New York Times, 21 Aug. 1983, p. 1.

49. James Barber, 'Economic Sanctions as a Policy Instrument', International Affairs, vol. 55, no. 3 (July 1979), pp. 376-7.

PART III

ECONOMIC SANCTIONS IN NON-EAST-WEST CONFLICTS

Chapter Eight

THE ARAB BOYCOTT OF ISRAEL

David B. Dewitt*

Prior to the establishment of the state of Israel in 1948, the countries of the Arab League recognised the vulnerability of the nascent nation to external economic pressure. Already in the 1920s Arab leadership called for a boycott of Jewish businesses in Palestine, and through the 1930s this doctrine spread to include most areas of commerce and trade between Arabs and Palestinian Jews.[1] By December 1945, when the Arab League Council passed its first formal boycott declaration, the distinction between Jew and Zionist had lost significance; the establishment of a Jewish state had become imminent. By 1949, in the wake of Israeli independence, the Arab League Council moved its Central Boycott Office (CBO) from Cairo to Damascus and the rhetoric of previous years was transformed into a formal structure with established procedures and focus. The purpose of the CBO, under the direction of the Commissioner General and with the assistance of Arab governments, was to reverse the decision reached through diplomacy and war. 'The interpretation given by the League is that the boycott will bring about the eventual economic collapse of the state of Israel and will reveal that it is not economically viable in the midst of a hostile world.'[2]

Over the past 35 years the battle between Israel and the Arab world has continued and gradually spread from the borders of the contiguous countries to encompass all regional and many extra-regional state and non-state actors. The Arab economic boycott has been the primary

* In addition to comments received from the participants in 'The Conference on the Utility of Economic Sanctions', I would like to express my thanks to Professor Shmuel Sharir, Department of Economics, University of Alberta, who most graciously conducted a series of interviews for me while he was on sabbatical leave in Israel, and Mr Kassu Gebremarian, who served as a very able graduate student research assistant.

instrument in this broadening of activity, with its potential to encompass the entire world of commerce and trade. While the military option remains open to all sovereign states, its obvious failure in this case has led Arab leaders to observe that '[a] military solution to the problem does not seem easy. But there is a weapon that does not involve steel and fire, a weapon that will help us win - the Arab Boycott of Israel'.[3]

With the October War of 1973, the Arab boycott achieved a new saliency as petrodollar recycling combined with petroleum vulnerability to make the Arab market-place, for the first time, a central factor in the foreign economic policies of most advanced industrialised states, many Third World countries and an increasing number of centrally planned economies. This third phase of the Arab boycott (the first, pre-independence; the second, 1949 to 1973; and the third, since late 1973) resulted in renewed interest and activity, as evidenced by the efforts of a number of key countries in the Organisation for Economic Co-operation and Development (OECD), especially the United States, to enact anti-boycott legislation to counter what was seen as a pervasive threat to the government's decision-making autonomy covering foreign policy and economic affairs. While the Arab world had greater opportunity to employ coercive economic measures in the pursuit of political ends, either because of or in spite of these anti-boycott movements, boycott initiators (mainly Arab League members) became increasingly flexible in interpretation, neither following the CBO directives nor their own publicly stated positions when national self-interest dictated otherwise.

This post-1973 period has exhibited internal contradictions. Increased potential influence and ensuing boycott activity have brought increased compliance, but also responsive government attempts at instituting anti-boycott measures and a resulting flexibility by boycott supporters in order to protect particular economic and political interests. This chapter offers a brief examination of this most recent phase of the Arab boycott of Israel.[4]

Objectives and Sanctions of the Arab Boycott

Until 1945 the objective of economic sanctions against the Jews of Palestine was clear: to inhibit and ultimately prevent the development of a viable economic structure and hence to thwart the emergence of a sovereign political community.[5] The three years between 1945 and 1948 juxtaposed three conflicting national forces - Arab nationalism, Zionism and colonialism - with the emerging US-Soviet rivalry, each having a distinct and exclusive vision of interests and objectives. In this context the Cairo-based Arab boycott was a major expression of Arab nationalism, a unifying force against Western imperialism in the guise of both Zionism and UN mandates, an effort by some anti-secularists to establish the political primacy of Islamic universalism over more radical revolutionary forces, and a statement of self-determination in the face of both Soviet and US penetration. The failure of these efforts, culminating in the establishment of Israel and its expansion and consolidation during the 1948-49 Independence War, undermined much of whatever coherence existed within the Arab world in its pre-1948 anticipation of total Arab victory. With the establishment of the CBO in Damascus, a new structure within the Arab League was empowered to co-ordinate non-military efforts to reassert a cohesive force within the Arab world in its efforts to destroy Israel.

Prior to 1948, the Arab League conducted a primary boycott; with the establishment of the CBO and then the Damascus centre, the more significant secondary and tertiary boycotts became the main instruments of operation.[6] Although the League recognised that to be effective these extensions required centralisation and complementarity in organisation, the political differences between League members resulted in the CBO and its Commissioner General having 'moral' but no legal force within member countries. Hence, while the global Arab objective of undermining Israel's viability was uniformly held, the variation in enforcement severely impeded boycott activities.[7]

During the next 25 years, the Arab boycott was sufficiently important for the Israeli government to establish an anti-boycott office. The office was terminated in 1971 because it was seen to be unnecessary given the obvious failure of the CBO to complete its objective. After the 1973 October War, the Ministry of Finance re-established an anti-boycott bureau - the Authority against Economic Warfare - to co-ordinate the activities of the various Israeli government departments which deal with boycott-related activities. This change in official Israeli perception of the threat posed by the boycott obviously was linked to the emergent petroleum-based Arab wealth. The influence of petrodollar 'diplomacy' can be symbolised by the establishment of an additional type of Arab boycott - the voluntary boycott - in which companies comply implicitly with the threat of being blacklisted by assiduously avoiding conducting business with Israel, Israeli firms, or any company or principal likely to be on the blacklist. By pre-empting the actual boycott instruments and, in turn, anti-boycott legislation, these firms voluntarily act as proxies for the members of the Arab League.[8]

While total numbers of compliant companies are unknown, in the early 1970s there were thought to be at least 6,000 firms on the blacklist which, though substantial in an absolute sense, is relatively few in number when considering the total of all economic actors in the OECD and elsewhere. This reasoning might suggest that the Arab boycott has been successful in its efforts to curtail the diversity of economic partners available to Israel if one were to conclude that non-blacklisted firms were complying with boycott intent. But such an argument seems ill-founded for a number of reasons, especially the fact that among the criteria for blacklisting are the following: (a) the product is not essential to the Arabs; (b) the product strengthens the economy or defence of Israel; and (c) the firm has an important activity in Israel, such as patent rights or manufacturing and distribution headquarters. These criteria have introduced a pragmatic quality to blacklisting procedures which, coupled with the autonomous application by each Arab League member, has undermined the consistency and coherence of Arab boycott efforts. For example, both Saudi Arabia and Israel have purchased Hawk anti-aircraft missiles from Raytheon Corporation, Hilton hotels exist in Israel and throughout the Arab world, Coca-Cola is produced and sold in Israel and in much of North Africa, and the Chase Manhattan Bank participates in financial arrangements with various Organisation of Arab Petroleum Exporting Countries (OAPEC) while remaining the US agent for the sale of Israel bonds. Even items targeted by the primary boycott have found their way between Israel and a number of Arab states.[9]

The objectives and instruments of sanction of the CBO of the Arab League have adjusted both to the reality of Israel and to the changing fortunes of the Arab states. While Israel continues to exist in spite of Arab preference, is there any evidence to suggest that boycott measures have had a significant impact on Israel? Is the boycott slowly eroding the economic viability of the state of Israel? Is it perhaps having its greatest success in the political arena where friends and partners are less easily replaced than markets for products or sources of financial investment?

Israel as a Target

While Israel remains part of the international community of states, its status is continuously being challenged. The Arab boycott is only one of the instruments employed. Both Arab and non-Arab states engage in efforts to isolate Israel from access to the machinery and benefits of multilateral organisations and international regimes. Although Israel is a long-standing member of the United Nations, this institution perhaps more than any other contributes to the world-wide campaign for Israel's delegitimisation, isolation and eventual demise. The extent to which the Arab League boycott has had an independent effect on Israel's plight within the UN forum is difficult to ascertain, although since

1973 the influence of the Arab bloc certainly has spilled over into the foreign policy alignments of member states. The boycott, coupled with the instruments of oil diplomacy and anti-Western rhetoric and behaviour within the United Nations and elsewhere, have placed Israel in an increasingly precarious position.[10]

It is evident that a substantial number of economic actors outside the Arab world do not engage in normal commercial transactions with Israel or those, whether in the private sector or government, who proffer support. Yet it also is evident from the statistical summary provided in Table 8.1 that, even with the difficulties boycott activities may introduce, Israel is a highly productive society maintaining a growing population, an increasingly diversified employment profile, an expanding consumer economy, a sophisticated health and education infrastructure, and a GNP which is growing in both absolute and per capita value. Clearly, in spite of continued runaway inflation, the economic and demographic profiles of Israel reveal a vibrant, albeit severely strained, society. Even the trade component - the primary target of the Arab boycott - has maintained a substantial rate of growth, especially during the 1970s when the increase in Arab oil revenues placed Israel's trading partners in the most vulnerable position. This is not to say that the application of the Arab boycott has not taken a toll, for it is clear that Israel has been prevented from participating in an open market. It is equally evident that markets, products and capital have been found. In addition, although it is difficult to prove, there is some evidence - especially with regard to military materials and strategic resources - that this enforced constraint has provided the incentive for indigenous industrial development and innovative purchasing and credit schemes.[11]

Nevertheless, if the Arab boycott were successful in inhibiting economic interchanges between Israel and others, the starkest evidence would be found in the trade profiles. Tables 8.2 and 8.3 provide such an overview. The data indicate both consistent growth in exports and imports and a reasonable diversification of trading partners. Interestingly, they reveal that Japan and the industrialised countries of Western Europe, so often noted to be the most vulnerable to the Arab boycott, have continued to pursue economic ties with Israel, although it also is well known that major economic actors from these countries - such as the British Norwich Union Insurance and Leyland Motors, and the Japanese firms Mitsubishi, Mitsui, Nissan, Datsun, Toyota and Japan Air Lines - have terminated relations with Israel.[12] However, while macro-trading relations seem healthy, Israel remains vulnerable to strategic resource availability.[13] Table 8.4, which offers an overview of

TABLE 8.1 Statistical Summary

	1950	1960	1970	1980
Population[1]	1,370,100 (4.6)[2]	2,150,400 (3.5)	3,022,100 (2.5)	3,921,700
Polulation Density[3]	67.7	106.2	148.6	191.8
Immigration	170,215 (-17.6)	24,510 (4.1)	36,750 (-5.5)	20,428
Residents leaving	9,987	12,049	7,203	31,856
Tourists	33,100 (13.5)	117,700 (14.1)	441,300 (10.4)	1,175,800
Civilian Labour Force	631,200 (3.1)	735,800 (3.1)	1,001,400 (2.8)	1,318,100
% Unemployed	7.2	4.6	3.8	3.8
% Employed in:				
- Agriculture	17.6	17.3	8.8	6.4
- Industry	21.5	23.2	24.3	23.7
- Commerce	13.5	12.3	13.0	11.7
- Public Service	21.2	22.0	24.0	29.6
Education				
- Teaching Posts	6,500	23,600	41,900	75,700
- Students	138,500	555,300	755,100	1,087,900
Universities				
- Academic Staff	293	293	1,509	9,329[4]
- Students	1,600	11,300	36,200	57,500
National Economy[5]				
- GNP-Total[6]	851.4	2,363.4	5,342.5	8,534.0
- GNP per capita	672 (5.2)	1,116 (4.9)	1,796 (2.1)	2,203
Net Domestic Product[7] (%)				
- Agriculture	11.4	11.6	6.4	5.0
- Industry	21.7	23.9	24.0	23.5
- Finance & Business	2.5	3.8	7.0	8.6
- Public & Community Services	18.2	18.8	19.1	20.8
Foreign Trade[8]				
- Net Imports of goods	300.3	495.7	1,433.5	7,875.1
- Net Exports of goods	35.1	211.3	733.6	5,294.4

(Table 8.1 continued)

	1950	1960	1970	1980
Exports[8]				
- Agricultural Exports	17.0 (19.7)	63.1 (13.2)	129.6 (21.9)	558.1
- Industrial Exports	9.4	92.6	393.1	3,265.3
- Diamonds	8.8	60.9	244.6	1,615.1
- Exports as a per cent of Imports	11.7	42.6	51.2	67.2
Imports[8]				
- Consumer goods	76.7 (5.1)	44.1 (11.2)	142.6 (18.7)	548.6
- Production inputs	169.1	353.5	972.4	6,506.6
- Investment goods	56.2	105.0	347.0	968.9

[1] Includes Jews and Non-Jews and, for 1970 and 1980 figures, Israeli residents living in the Administered Territories.
[2] Average annual per cent change within decades shown in parentheses.
[3] Per km^2.
[4] In 1977.
[5] At 1975 prices.
[6] 10^6 Israeli Shekels.
[7] per cent of current prices.
[8] 10^6 US dollars.

Source: Statistical Abstract of Israel, 1981, No. 32, A. Main Series, Jerusalem: Central Bureau of Statistics.

TABLE 8-2: ISRAEL'S TRADE 1966-1979

($US 10^6 current)

	Exports						Imports					
	1966	1971	1973	1975	1977	1979	1966	1971	1973	1975	1977	1979
Industrial Countries	355.8	675.6	1,096.2	1,351.7	2,052.5	3,181.6	661.5	1,468.6	2,465.8	3,184.1	3,753.6	5,500.3
United States	77.4	185.7	267.0	307.5	569.1	748.7	221.6	429.3	549.5	998.9	981.4	1,511.8
United Kingdom	62.2	97.0	138.8	171.5	226.2	394.5	157.0	273.5	478.8	577.9	463.5	687.7
Industrial Europe[1]	190.8	328.8	559.5	725.0	1,101.2	1,709.3	255.3	687.6	1,608.7	1,746.4	1,970.1	2,707.0
Canada	6.7	15.8	21.2	29.8	40.3	47.5	6.9	20.8	31.7	40.6	55.4	80.6
Japan	18.7	48.2	87.2	99.4	99.5	223.4	20.7	57.4	59.3	88.8	125.4	169.7
Less Developed Countries	74.6	203.9	301.8	526.9	640.6	730.9	120.8	179.3	233.2	285.6	398.1	543.3

1. Industrial Europe

- from 1966 to 1971, includes Austria, Belgium, Denmark, France, Germany, Italy, Netherlands, Norway, Sweden, Switzerland.
- from 1973 to 1979, refers to the members of the European Economic Community.

Sources: International Monetary Fund, Direction of Trade, March 1970, December 1972, and Yearbook, 1980.

TABLE 8-3: ISRAEL'S TRADE 1973-1979

	Exports							Imports						
	1973	1974	.1975	1976	1977	1978	1979	1973	1974	1975	1976	1977	1978	1979
a) Per Cent Distribution														
Industrial Countries	75.1	70.6	69.6	67.7	66.6	65.3	69.9	58.2	59.0	53.1	55.1	69.9	62.9	66.0
Oil Exporting Countries	3.0	4.1	7.5	5.8	4.2	3.3	0.7	0.1	0.1	0.1	0.1	0.1	0.1	--
Non-Oil Developing Countries	17.7	20.7	19.6	17.9	16.6	17.4	15.4	5.4	4.6	4.7	4.5	5.4	5.1	6.5
Eastern Bloc Countries	0.3	0.5	0.7	0.6	0.4	0.3	0.2	0.2	0.2	0.2	0.1	0.2	0.2	0.2
Other Countries	3.9	4.0	2.5	8.1	12.2	13.8	13.8	36.1	36.0	2.0	40.2	29.4	31.7	27.2
b) Annual Per Cent Change														
World	27.0	25.1	6.3	24.4	27.6	26.9	16.4	71.5	28.3	10.3	-5.5	2.1	27.9	12.6
Industrial Countires	28.7	17.7	4.8	20.9	25.6	24.4	24.6	46.3	30.3	-0.9	-1.9	20.1	24.1	18.1
Oil Exporting Countries	-16.1	68.8	95.1	-3.6	-7.6	-0.3	-75.3	89.8	34.3	-26.2	-23.7	67.1	39.5	-69.4
Non-Oil Developing Countries	27.6	46.6	1.0	13.4	18.2	33.0	2.8	58.5	10.5	11.3	-9.0	22.5	19.6	44.4
Eastern Bloc Countries	9.8	106.8	29.5	3.1	-4.3	-18.2	7.5	32.1	-11.1	12.1	-21.1	38.1	27.6	43.7

Source: International Monetary Fund, Direction of Trade Yearbook, 1980, p. 436.

TABLE 8-4: ISRAEL'S TRADE BY SECTOR: 1960-1980
($US 10^6)

	Exports					Imports				
	1960	1965	1970	1975	1980	1960	1965	1970	1975	1980
All Commodities	216.6	429.6	778.7	1,940.7	5,540.0	502.7	835.8	1,462.6	4,172.6	8,024.1
Food & Live Animals	71.1	105.8	160.4	323.9	618.4	70.6	93.0	161.2	499.3	677.6
Crude Materials	7.7	15.1	37.9	95.1	288.1	66.5	104.8	113.2	272.4	419.5
Mineral Fuels & Lubricants	--	--	--	--	1.0	35.0	53.8	70.9	638.5	2,124.1
Chemicals	9.0	37.0	68.2	242.5	774.6	24.3	45.4	99.9	276.9	503.2
Manufactured Goods[1]	91.7	226.5	367.1	874.7	2,495.7	137.0	250.5	479.4	1,298.7	2,293.7
Miscellaneous Manufactured Articles[2]	16.9	25.6	79.8	174.9	540.6	8.8	33.8	69.8	154.9	266.2

[1] Includes mineral manufacturers, precious and semi-precious stones.

[2] Includes high technology products such as professional, scientific, and controlling instruments, photographic and optical goods, and scientific, medical, etc. apparatus.

Sources: Statistical Abstract of Israel, 1981, No. 32, Jerusalem: Central Bureau of Statistics, Table VIII/4.

TABLE 8-5: **PATENT APPLICATIONS IN ISRAEL**

Year	Applications from Abroad	Applications from Israel	Total
1949	428	210	638
1950	378	222	600
1955	448	290	738
1960	1,049	465	1,514
1965	1,785	412	2,197
1970	2,048	247	2,295
1971	2,162	383	2,545
1972	2,331	394	2,725
1973	2,349	374	2,723
1974	2,049	344	2,438
1975	1,915	483	2,398
1976	1,863	561	2,424
1977	2,021	508	2,529
1978	1,989	632	2,621
1979	2,120	595	2,715
1980	2,104	669	2,773

Source: Statistical Abstract of Israel, 1981, No. 32, Jerusalem: Central Bureau of Statistics, Table XXIII/9.

Israel's trade by sector, shows that in foodstuffs, crude materials and, most dramatically, in fuels and lubricants Israel has a negative trade balance. In 1960 the fuels sector accounted for 6.8 per cent of Israel's imports, but by 1980 it had leaped to 26.4 per cent while there were virtually no offsetting exports. This situation is quite different from the manufactured goods sector which currently dominates both imports and exports. Israel's inability to access Middle Eastern oil due to the primary and secondary boycotts results in higher costs (special purchase arrangements plus transport) than might be the case if it could tap directly into proximate sources.[14] Since fuels act as a multiplier factor in the productive cycle, Israeli society has had to adjust its economic structure to absorb simultaneously the additional cost while remaining price competitive in the international market. Yet due to its strategic military placement and its special relationship with a number of OECD states - especially the United States - over the years Israel has been able to purchase sufficient fuel (whether from pre-revolutionary Iran, African oil producing countries, Egypt, Mexico and other Latin American suppliers, or through US conduit arrangements) to maintain its economic position.

Another indication of economic transactions which should be vulnerable to politico-economic coercion, in terms of the criteria set forth by the CBO, is the transfer of patents from the country of origin into Israel. Along with the general trading patterns, this factor is indicative of where foreign actors identify markets of preference for capital investment, manufacturing and sales. Table 8.5 indicates continued growth in patent applications from within Israel while patent applications into Israel from abroad show a slight drop after 1973. Boycott efforts may be responsible for some of the decline, although one cannot make that judgement from these data. A combination of boycott efforts, increased indigenous Israeli competition and the uncertainty of the Israeli economy may have combined to account for this 13 to 15 per cent decline.

In summary, Israel's domestic economic development continues, while economic exchanges expand in both dollar value and diversity of partner. This is not to say that the Arab boycott efforts have not had effect on Israeli development. There is no doubt that they have introduced additional constraints, impeded the free flow of goods and services, and placed in jeopardy Israel's ability to gain secure access to strategic resources, critical advanced high technology and markets. But the record seems to indicate a resilience and adaptability that has undercut the intent of the boycott leaders.

Nevertheless, the Arab boycott has contributed to Israel's relative diplomatic isolation. Voting in the United

Nations General Assembly, the politicisation of functional agencies, the reduction of the status of diplomatic representation and even the complete severing of state-to-state relations have occurred most dramatically since the 1973 October War.[15] The threat to developing countries of lost OAPEC aid and to the OECD of forgone opportunity to penetrate the substantial Arab market-place have been significant factors in the petrodollar experience since 1973.[16] The most dramatic evidence of this, aside from Israel's diplomatic isolation, has been the increased attempts by some to pass anti-boycott legislation to thwart perceived Arab interference and the substantial efforts by others to prevent, hinder, or at least weaken such actions.[17]

Conclusions

In a speech on the Arab boycott to the January 1982 Brussels meeting of the Israel-EEC Co-operation Committee, Mr Ephraim Davrath, Deputy Director General for International Affairs of Israel's Ministry of Finance noted that 'there is no doubt that trade and other fields of economic cooperation would have expanded at a much faster pace, and that Israel's chronic deficit would have been lower, had it not been for the effect of the Arab boycott'.[18] In a word, Israel survives but is hindered by the intrusion of the Arab boycott. There is direct evidence of both Israel's continued presence and the enhanced activities of the Arab boycott, yet there is relatively little direct evidence linking boycott efforts to economic costs, except for the case of oil. While it is likely that production costs, marketing strategies, balance-of-payments ledgers and technological innovation are affected by the presence of the boycott, it is difficult to say more than just that without moving into speculation or rhetoric. On the political side there is little doubt that Israel's position in the strategic calculus of both Middle East and global politics is affected - in some sectors significantly - by constraints imposed on former, current and potential partners through the petrodollar miasma and the boycott instrument.

Yet it is remarkable that, given the concentration of oil wealth, Third World and Eastern bloc support, and strategic location, the Arab League has been unable to implement fully the boycott mechanisms. The primary reason certainly resides in the ideological, structural and strategic differences within the Arab world and the fact that each state ultimately pursues its own interests.[19] While this non-universal character of this boycott effort once again points out the inherent weakness in employing instruments which do not cut off all possibilities at substitution, a contribution to its relative failure must be the inherent qualities of the relationship between the advanced industrialised Western nations and Israel. Whether due to amity or fear of precedent, a successful boycott would not be in the self-interest of any of the OECD members. Finally, one must also acknowledge the ability of the state of Israel to be sufficiently resilient to overcome many of these hindrances, and the critical role of the United States in ensuring substantial credit and technology transfers.[20] With the recent decline in the price of oil, the attendant stresses within OPEC and the Israel-Egypt normalisation process, one might predict the de facto end of the Arab boycott. However, from the Arab perspective the boycott remains a low-cost coercive instrument offering substantial political and diplomatic benefits. For these reasons, in addition to intra-Arab politics, Israel likely will remain the high-profile target of the Arab League boycott.

Notes

1. For an overview of this subject, see Dan S. Chill, The Arab Boycott of Israel: Economic Aggression and World Reaction (Praeger, New York, 1976). In addition, see Donald L. Losman, International Economic Sanctions: The Cases of Cuba, Israel, and Rhodesia (University of New Mexico Press, Albuquerque, 1979), and W. H. Nelson and T. Prittie, The Economic War Against the Jews (Random House, New York, 1977). For examples of some journalists' reports over the years, see 'Arab Boycott Flexible But Determined', The Middle East, 20 June 1976, pp. 31-2; Martin Short, 'Trading with the Enemy' and 'The Arab Boycott in Practice', Middle East International, June 1976, pp. 11-13, and July 1976, pp. 11-13; 'Secret Report Looks at Loopholes in Arab Boycott', The Middle East, April 1978, pp. 108-9; Robert M. Smith, 'The Arab Boycott Is An Elusive But Weighty Ghost', New York Times, 14 Mar. 1976; 'Arabs Step Up Israeli Boycott', Business Week, 23 August 1969, pp. 80-2; and Barry Rubin, 'Challenging the Arab Boycott', Nation 23:7 (1976).

2. B. Y. Boutros-Ghali, 'The Arab League: Ten Years of Struggle', International Conciliation (May 1954) p. 421.

3. Hutik Muhamed Ali Aluba, Palestine and Human Conscience (Dar Elhalal, Cairo, 1964), p. 187 as cited by Chill, The Arab Boycott of Israel, p. 9, fn. 43, who takes it from a Hebrew publication of Yehoshafat Harkabi.

4. The arguments and evidence presented are tentative. While some statistical data, official government pronouncements and secondary literature provide a reasonable basis for initial discussion, the fundamental issue of the real impact of the Arab boycott on Israel is exceptionally difficult to determine. This is due not only to the confidentiality of much data, but also the inherently hypo-

thetical quality of the issue; that is, the cost of lost opportunities to Israel in trade, services and investments. For the general methodological difficulties associated with attempting to assess the effects of boycotts, see Margaret P. Doxey, Economic Sanctions and International Enforcement (Oxford University Press, London, 1971). While there is much published material on responses to the Arab boycott, considering the duration and potential severity of the boycott, relatively little has been written in recent years on the boycott itself or its effectiveness. A number of the more helpful publications in addition to Chill, Losman, and Nelson and Prittie noted above, are Henry J. Steiner, 'International Boycotts and Domestic Order: American Involvement in the Arab-Israeli Conflict', Texas Law Review 54:7 (1976), pp. 1355-1410; Nancy Turck, 'The Arab Boycott of Israel', Foreign Affairs 55:3 (1977), pp. 472-93; Sue Ellen Dodell, 'Comment: United States Banks and the Arab Boycott of Israel', Columbia Journal of Transnational Law 17:7 (1978), pp. 119-43; and Moshe Koby, 'The Arab Boycott', Money, 20 June 1982, pp. 10-12, in Hebrew.

5. Losman, in International Economic Sanctions, Ch. 4, and his earlier 'The Arab Boycott of Israel', International Journal of Middle East Studies 3 (1972), pp. 99-122, argues that in pre-1948 Palestine, the relative separation of Jewish and Arab economic sectors resulting from both specialisation and political considerations imposed very real economic costs, particularly in terms of lost opportunities for intersectional trade and efficiencies of scale. Losman also notes the constraint this imposed on external trade between the Jewish sector and the Arab world, thereby arguing that already in the 1920s and 1930s the boycott exacted a price.

6. Steiner, 'International Boycotts and Domestic Order', pp. 1367-70, separates the boycott into the following categories:

1. Core primary boycott: Arab countries' ban against their trading with Israel; except for oil, affects principally imports from Israel into Arab countries.
2. Extended primary boycott: bars Arab importation of foreign-made products that include Israeli-made components; affects unrelated companies of third countries.
3. Core secondary boycott: the injunction against Arabs trading with third-country firms that maintain proscribed types of commercial relations with Israel.
4. Extended secondary boycott: bans on purchases by Arab nationals of the products or services of a firm otherwise acting consistently with the boycott if those products or services include

components or subcontracted services of a blacklisted foreign firm.

5. Zionist sympathisers and Jews (otherwise known as tertiary boycott): introduces imprecision and exceptional breadth to the ban, since it calls for boycott of all products and services in any way connected with Zionist sympathisers and Jews, although this latter point often is denied or qualified by some Arab states.

7. Ibid., pp. 1362-67; also Losman, International Economic Sanctions, Ch. 4; Chill, The Arab Boycott, Ch. 2.

8. For examples of the impact of voluntary boycotts, see Short, 'The Arab Boycott in Practice', who notes the unwillingness of, for instance, 18 British companies to respond to tender requests from the Israeli Port Authority. The seriousness of this relatively recent (post-1973) aspect of the boycott is evident from the comments made by a number of senior officials in the Israeli Ministry of Finance in confidential interviews, Jerusalem 1982. See also Koby, 'The Arab Boycott', and Howard Stanislawski, Elites, Domestic Interest Groups, and International Interests in the Canadian Foreign Policy Decision-Making Process: The Arab Economic Boycott of Canadians and Canadian Companies Doing Business with Israel, unpublished PhD disseration, Brandeis University, February 1981.

9. In addition to sources already cited, see Jack G. Kaikati, 'How Multinational Corporations Handle the Arab Boycott', Columbia Journal of World Business (Spring 1978), pp. 98-111.

10. For a rather strong introduction to this theme, see, among others, 'The United Nations Campaign Against Israel' (The Heritage Foundation, Washington, D.C.), Backgrounder No. 271 (16 June 1983), pp. 1-22.

11. See Losman, 'The Arab Boycott of Israel'; Nelson and Prittie, The Economic War Against the Jews; Frank Gervasi, The Case for Israel (The Viking Press, New York, 1967); and Ibrahim Shihata, The Case for the Arab Oil Embargo (Institute for Palestine Studies, Beirut, 1975). While Israel's foreign debt of US $24 billion made it the highest per capita debt in the world, the government and private sector still managed to gain credit, grants and technology transfers, primarily from the United States but also from other OECD members and from the International Monetary Fund (IMF). See Thomas Friedman, 'Economic Crisis in Israel May Renew the Country', New York Times, 29 Oct. 1984, p. 1; and Paul Rivlin, 'The Burden of Israel's Defense', Survival 20:4 (July-August 1978).

12. For an insightful commentary on the vitality of Israel's economic exchanges with the OECD, see Fred

Gottheil, 'The Myth of the Pariah Condition: Image and Reality in Israel's External Relations', Middle East Focus 5:5 (January 1983), pp. 4-6.

13. The general concern over the OECD's vulnerability to foreign control of strategic minerals was crystalised by the Arab oil embargo of 1973. For a discussion about one strategic non-fuel mineral, see James T. Bennett and Walter E. Williams, 'Strategic Minerals: The Economic Impact of Supply Disruptions', (The Heritage Foundation, Washington, D.C., 1981).

14. Prior to 1973, approximately 2 per cent of Israel's GNP went for oil imports; by 1984 this figure had reached 12 per cent. Friedman, 'Economic Crisis in Israel'.

15. For example, by the end of 1973 almost all the member-states of the Organisation of African Unity had severed ties with Israel, yet between 1967 and 1971 most of the black African states maintained diplomatic relations with and voted in support of Israel. Ostensibly, the change in position was related to the issue of Israeli occupation of the territories captured in 1967, yet for four years this was not addressed as an issue of concern to black African leaders. The connection seems to be Nigeria's leadership in oil, African concern over foreign aid and the pressure to forge ties with other Third World - especially Muslim - countries. See, for example, Victor T. Le Vine and Timothy W. Luke, The Arab-African Connection: Political and Economic Realities (Westview Press, Boulder, Colorado, 1979). For an important examination of a number of OECD states, see the chapter by Janice G. Stein in Janice G. Stein and David B. Dewitt (eds.), The Middle East at the Crossroads (Mosaic Press, Toronto, 1983).

16. In addition to sources already noted, see Fred Singer, 'Limits to Arab Oil Power', Foreign Policy 30 (Spring 1978); Oded Remba, 'America, Oil Power and Western Response', Middle East Review (1975-76); Robert W. Tucker, 'Appeasement and the AWACs', Commentary 72:6 (1981); and Stephen Emerson, 'The Petrodollar Connection', The New Republic, 17 February 1982.

17. See chapter by Harold Stanislawski in this volume.

18. Press release from the Ministry of Finance, Government of Israel, 11 January 1982.

19. Had the mandate for this chapter been an examination of the strengths and weaknesses, successes and failures of the Arab boycott, then intra-Arab political and socio-economic factors would have been the central focus of the analysis. However, such an interesting and challenging examination is well beyond the scope of a paper which focuses upon the target state, Israel.

20. Although it is difficult to argue a direct cause-and-effect relationship, a reasonable proposition is that the

Arab Boycott of Israel

Arab boycott, while constraining the activities of some private sector actors toward Israel, has contributed to an enhanced commitment of public support toward Israel, most dramatically in United States government assistance to Israel in the form of FMS (Foreign Military Sales), technology transfers, credits and grants. It also has stimulated increased lobbying and public awareness campaigns by pro-Israel organisations, such as Boycott Report published on a regular basis by the American Jewish Congress.

Chapter Nine

THE ARAB OIL WEAPON OF 1973-74

Roy Licklider

The Arab oil weapon of 1973-74 was seen when it occurred as a turning point of some sort in international affairs. It thus inspired a considerable literature, both at the time and since, so much that one may reasonably ask what can be added at this late date. However, most of the writing has concerned the implications of the event for the energy policies of various states of the economic health of the world. Relatively little has been written on the oil weapon as an example of how one group of states attempted to influence another, which is precisely the question we seek to answer in this chapter.

This discussion of the oil weapon is embedded in two separate, although related, theoretical literatures. The literature on economic sanctions can readily be traced back at least 50 years and includes contributions by individuals from different nations with different political ideologies.[1] The more recent literature on coercive diplomacy, the use of force to persuade an opponent to change his behaviour, is also relevant here.[2] These two literatures, based both on theory and historical case studies, agree that it is most unlikely that one country will be able to persuade another to alter its foreign policy significantly by the use of economic sanctions. Indeed, this is one of the few conclusions of applied social science which seems to have become part of the belief systems of Western foreign policy-makers; thus, even when the United States was applying sanctions to the Soviet Union over Afghanistan and Poland, no one in government seemed really to expect Soviet Union policy to change as a result.

Objectives of the Actor Governments

Any discussion of the actor governments should start by identifying them. This in turn requires that we identify the events on which we are focusing, which is a bit more complex than it may at first appear. We can distinguish between at least two kinds of events that took place in 1973-74. The first was a significant increase in the price of oil. This was the result of actions by the Organisation of Petroleum Exporting Countries (OPEC) states for primarily economic goals. The second was the oil embargo and production cutbacks. These actions taken together are often called the 'oil weapon'. They were carried out by most of the Arab oil-producing states (not OPEC as a whole), and they will be the subject of this chapter. Thus the actor governments are the Arab states which participated in the embargoes and export cuts, specifically Abu Dhabi, Algeria, Bahrein, Egypt, Iraq, Kuwait, Libya, Qatar, Saudi Arabia and Syria. Iraq did not reduce production but did participate in the embargo. Iran neither embargoed nor reduced production, although it had been a leader in the price increases.

Why did these governments embargo oil to the United States and the Netherlands and reduce shipments to a number of other countries? What objectives did they hope to attain? We do not know the answers to these questions with any confidence. Indeed, asking the question seriously reveals an interesting bias in the economic sanctions literature: with very few exceptions, it assumes Western governments imposing the sanctions. Thus in this volume the only examples of non-Western governments imposing sanctions are this case and the closely related Arab boycott of Israel.

Moreover, we know remarkably little about the way in which these governments function. We do not have the memoirs of key decision-makers and their aides, which appear in the West almost as they leave office. We do not have a free journalism which works as an effective adversary to government, routinely publishing secret information. There is not even much good writing on the subject by Western academics. Moreover, both the actor and target governments have attempted to conceal crucial aspects of the influence relationship. As a result, we must rely on guessing and inference even more than usual when dealing with motives of governments.

Nonetheless, it is clear that there were in fact several different actor governments and that, while policy was certainly co-ordinated, it was not made and executed from a single command centre. These governments differed among themselves in decision-making structures and policy attitudes; there were also some very strong historical enmities. These divisions often seemed unimportant in declaratory policy; indeed, the competition among the actor governments to support the Arab cause gave each an incentive to match the actions of its rivals, thus quite possibly improving co-ordination. However, this disparity makes it even more difficult to speak with much confidence about the objectives of the actor governments as a group, as most of the literature on the crisis has done.

Given these constraints, we can single out several sets of possible objectives by the actor governments. Later in the chapter we will examine to what extent each predicts the actions of the Organisation of Arab Petroleum Exporting Countries (OAPEC) governments. Such analysis implicitly assumes some version of the 'rational actor' model, an assumption particularly dangerous when analysing individuals from a culture other than our own. Thus it should not be surprising that different observers, looking at the same 'facts', will reach different conclusions about the objectives of the actor governments:

1. Some authors suggest, often only by inference, that the Arab governments intended to use the oil weapon to fundamentally undermine the influence of Western governments in the Middle East and perhaps even to alter the domestic structure of the target states. J. B. Kelly, for example, asserts that:

> Stripped of their specious justifications about past Western exploitation and the intolerable affront to Arab susceptibilities afforded by the existence of Israel, the actions of the Arabs and the Persians before, during and since 1973, if placed in their historical, religious, racial and cultural setting, amount to nothing less than a bold attempt to lay the Christian West under tribute to the Muslim East....The oil weapon, and particularly its financial aspects, has less to do with the Arab-Israeli conflict than with the powerful sentiments of grievance and resentment against the Christian West long cherished by the Arabs, who deem themselves a chosen people, the repository of the true faith, the race of the Prophet, ordained by Providence to receive the submission of others.[3]

Walter Laqueur asserts that Qadaffi suggested 'in passing' that Europe be required to convert to Islam since Europe was after all only the geographical extension of Africa and the Middle East.[4]

2. Another set of objectives involved improving the Arab situation vis-a-vis the Israelis by altering the results of the 1967 war. These were the reasons the OAPEC governments gave when they imposed the oil weapon, so it seems reasonable to give them considerable weight. However, even these 'ostensible' goals of the OAPEC governments are difficult to discern. The key document was presumably the OAPEC resolution of 17 October 1973, which initiated the oil weapon but, as Kelly points out, was a peculiar document.

> Everything about the communique, including the way in which it was issued, was muddled and obscure. Only one copy of it was made available to the newspaper reporters crowding the Kuwait Sheraton Hotel where the meeting was held, and this was handwritten in Arabic, with phrases crossed out and others inserted in pencil - including the reference to the rights of the Palestinians. No translation into any other language was offered; indeed, the OAPEC secretariat refused outright to produce an official English version, either of the communique or of the actual resolution passed by OAPEC ministers.[5]

It is thus not surprising that there are somewhat different versions of the communique in English.[6] Nonetheless, there is agreement that the two key goals were the withdrawal of Israel from all territories captured in the 1967 war and restoration of the 'legitimate rights' of the Palestinians. King Faisal reportedly clarified this to mean self-determination for the Palestinians and added a third goal, 'affirmation of the "Arabism" of Jerusalem'.[7]

Israel was the only country which could in fact give the Arabs these objectives, so if these were the 'real' goals, Israel was the real target. Presumably, the United States was embargoed to induce it to persuade Israel to change its policy. The logic in embargoing the other Western countries is even more complex; since they could not by themselves alter Israel policy, they were apparently supposed to bring pressure on the United States to persuade Israel to alter its policy.

3. A third set of foreign policy goals involves improving the immediate Middle Eastern situation, in particular persuading the United States to pressure Israel not to destroy the encircled Egyptian Third Army in the Sinai and making US policy more 'even-handed'.[8] Presumably, this would leave the Arabs in a better position for negotiations with Israel and other states to try to achieve their goals. Note that this is quite different from the previous set of motives; there is a great deal of difference between negotiating for something and demanding that it be given. One observer asserts that Libya had its own set of conditions for ending the oil weapon, which presumably fall into this category: the supply of modern weapons and technology by Europe to the Arabs and denial of arms and economic assistance to Israel.[9]

4. Another set of goals concerns domestic rather than foreign policy issues. The oil weapon was an important symbolic gesture by the OAPEC governments supporting the Arab cause. Particularly for the conservative governments, the threat of radical revolt or a military coup was a major concern; the oil weapon offered a useful way to defuse some

internal opposition without bringing about major change in their own societies. Thus it may well be that the oil weapon could have been considered a success, at least by some governments, even if it had no impact on the Middle East whatsoever. In fact, there is reason to believe that, despite their verbal support of the Palestinian cause, many conservative Arabs are not happy with the idea of a Palestinian state.

What Particular Sanctions were Adopted?

Two different kinds of sanctions were applied. The first was an embargo, totally cutting off exports of oil to certain countries. In mid-October all ten actor governments embargoed the United States. The Netherlands was embargoed at the end of the month, and Portugal, Rhodesia and South Africa were added to the list as well. There were also some indirect embargoes against countries in which oil was processed or trans-shipped for the Netherlands, the United States or the US Navy. Saudi Arabia listed countries in this category as Trinidad, the Bahamas, the Dutch Antilles, Canada, Puerto Rico, Guam, Singapore and Bahrein (which apparently became both an actor and a target government at the same time). A few European refineries in Italy, France and Greece were embargoed for the same reason.[10] On 18 March 1974 the Arab oil ministers decided, over the protests of Libya and Syria, to lift the embargo on the United States 'provisionally'; on 3 June it was removed altogether. The embargo against the Netherlands ended on 11 July.

The second sanction was a series of oil export reductions. On 17 October the OAPEC oil ministers agreed to cut October exports by a minimum of 5 per cent from the September level with another 5 per cent cut to follow in November. Consumer countries could be exempted entirely or in part from the cutbacks, depending on their positions on the Arab-Israeli conflict. On 4 November it was decided to reduce November exports by 25 per cent of the September level with a further 5 per cent cut scheduled for December. This figure included oil not being sent to embargoed countries, so presumably other countries would be cut less than 25 per cent.

By December Saudi Arabia had developed a very complex classification system of consumer nations, with at least five different categories: (1) Most-favoured countries were to get as much oil as they required; this category included Great Britain, France, Spain, the Arab importing countries, African countries which had broken diplomatic relations with Israel, and Islamic countries. (2) Friendly countries were neutrals which had modified their policies in favour of the Arab positions (Belgium and Japan); they were entitled to their pre-embargo level of imports. (3) The other EEC countries, except for the Netherlands and perhaps Denmark, were subjected to cutbacks but exempted from the December 5 per cent reduction, presumably because of their 6 November declaration which asked Israel to end its 'territorial occupation' from the 1967 war and advocated the 'legitimate rights of the Palestinians'. Denmark and the Netherlands both signed this statement, but it did not save them from embargo. (4) Neutrals were subject to all cutbacks. (5) Embargoed countries (the United States, the Netherlands, South Africa, Rhodesia and Portugal) were to get no Arab oil. Denmark apparently was subjected to a partial embargo. On 25 December OAPEC decided to reduce the December cut to 15 per cent of the September total and not to impose the January 5 per cent cut. All export restrictions were ended 3 June, except for the embargo of the Netherlands.

Economic Impact of the Sanctions on the Targets

The economic impact of the oil weapon can be divided into two parts: the reduction of oil supplies to the industrial countries, and the economic impact of these reductions. Although there is some disagreement on the precise figures, the imports of the industrial countries dropped about 10 to 20 per cent for two or three months. Apparently, there was, for example, at no time any real shortage of oil in Western Europe.[11] Perhaps more importantly, this decline was roughly the same for all industrial countries, regardless of where they stood on the Arabs' preference lists. The major oil companies apparently obeyed orders and denied Arab oil to the appropriate countries but then shifted non-Arab oil toward those countries with shortages. The result was that OAPEC was unable to impose differential penalties on its friends and foes; like a shotgun, the oil weapon was potent but not especially precise.

The direct economic consequences of the oil weapon are more controversial since it is impossible to sort out its particular impact from other factors influencing the world economy. Nonetheless, there seems to be a general agreement that the oil weapon contributed significantly to a world-wide recession and inflation of impressive magnitude. Again, however, the effect seems to have been general; those countries with Arab goodwill did not do significantly better economically than those without it.

However, this focus on direct economic costs misstates the real impact of the oil weapon. Perhaps the most important consequence was the enormous rise in insecurity. Looking back at the oil weapon, we can easily see that the real economic impact, while not trivial, was also not catastrophic. However, it is important to remember that this was by no means clear at the time. Experts seemed divided between those who thought the world was coming to an end and those who thought the price of oil would soon revert to three dollars a barrel. Governments strove desperately to understand what was happening. What did the Arabs really want? What would be the consequences if they didn't get it? How much oil was in reserves? How much on the high seas? How would the major oil companies respond to the crisis? How much advantage would the home countries of such corporations have? What would be the economic impact of higher prices? How would populations and important domestic interest groups react to these changes? No one knew the answers to these questions.

Decision-makers also did not know how long the oil weapon would be maintained. As it happened, it did not last too long; it formally ended in June and July, but in practice the worst effects were over by about January. However, there was no way for the target governments to know this in October and November. The concern was not how to get through the week but whether, in two months or so, there would be sufficient oil to run their societies. Prodi and Clo point out that reserves in Europe never dropped below the 80-day mark,[12] but governments quite understandably were more impressed by the scarcity of reserves before and during the embargo since they didn't know if there would be any more oil after that time.

Perhaps the major effect of the oil weapon was an enormous increase in economic insecurity. The industrial world had grown used to importing large amounts of oil at what now look to have been very low prices; with very little warning governments found they could not count on either the supply or the price of this oil. The result was something very close to panic in high places. Western European governments refused to co-operate to help the Netherlands get oil (at least until the Netherlands in turn threatened an embargo of its gas exports, which constituted 40 per cent of France's gas consumption).[13] Japanese politicians toured the Middle East and made promises of economic assistance, many of which were not honoured by their government later.[14] Even the United States, which was both less dependent on Arab oil and more deeply involved in the Middle East than its partners, apparently did not give the Japanese basic information about oil supplies which could have altered the results of their internal policy debate.[15]

Thus the immediate result of the oil weapon was to increase greatly the sense of vulnerability to supply interruptions, particularly by the Western Europeans and the Japanese, even though the actual economic impact was not too impressive. If a burglar invades a home and leaves without taking anything, the owners may be grateful that it wasn't worse, but the 'lesson' they are likely to learn is that they have a security problem, not that burglary is a benign experience.

Political Impact of the Sanctions on the Targets

Despite the very deep concern among both elites and publics in the Western countries, there was relatively little policy change during the several months when the oil weapon was being used. Concern was higher in Japan and Western Europe than the United States because of different levels of energy imports. The Western European countries decided not to allow the United States to use their ports or air-fields to re-supply Israel; this decision was probably the most substantive, short-term result of the oil weapon.

In addition, there was some change in the rhetoric of these countries toward the Arab-Israeli conflict. The Netherlands, which had pursued a semi-independent Middle Eastern policy that was more pro-Israel than its European Community (EC) partners, signed an EC statement in Brussels on 6 November which asked Israel to return 'territories' (without specifying whether all or some would be included) taken in the 1967 war and acknowledged Palestinian 'rights' (without specifying what they were). The Japanese issued a series of statements, culminating on 22 November when they asked Israel to withdraw from all occupied territories and threatened to 'reconsider' relations with Israel if this were not done. In fact, this threat was never carried out. These statements were seen at the time as acts of appeasement but in retrospect they seem rather innocuous. In addition, several countries (including the United States) attempted to establish new economic relations with the Arabs; interestingly enough, the Japanese apparently did not fulfil a number of their pledges made during this time.

The United States was in a rather special position since, as a superpower and Israel's major ally, it was the only country which might have been able to force Israel to accept the Arab demands. United States policy shifted from supporting the status quo to moving toward disengagement agreements between the Arabs and the Israelis; this process eventually resulted in the Camp David accords and the Egyptian-Israeli peace treaty. However, this shift seems to have been due to the new situation caused by the 1973 war and particularly Henry Kissinger's concern over possible Soviet intervention in the Middle East rather than the oil weapon's impact on the United States.

On the other hand, there has been a significant rhetorical shift of the Western countries in a pro-Arab direction since 1973. This long-term change culminated in the Venice Declaration of 1980 which called for Palestinian self-determination and participation in peace negotiations, although still falling short of recognition of the PLO. Interestingly, there was rather little change in the relative positions of the target countries; before and after the embargo, the United States was the most pro-Israeli, while Japan remained the most pro-Arab country.[16] It is hard to believe that the demonstration of economic vulnerability provided by the oil weapon was irrelevant to this shift. However, my own research suggests strongly that within Europe there is relatively little fear of oil supply cutoffs. The Netherlands, for example, apparently concluded that the oil weapon demonstrated that it could not effectively be embargoed; a more significant factor in its policy shift seems to have been the fact that the Arabs have become major customers, and it is bad business to make unnecessary trouble for customers. Similarly, the United Kingdom, which is now independent of Middle Eastern oil, finds itself dependent on the OAPEC states for trade and finance.

Fulfilment of Actor Goals

This topic again raises the issue of the 'real' Arab goals. We have already noted the problems in answering this question, but it is now appropriate to try to reach some tentative conclusions. How plausible is each set of goals, given Arab behaviour? It may well be that some Arab decision-makers were influenced by a desire to injure or alter the Western countries. However, this does not explain the timing of the oil weapon, the varying degrees of co-operation, or its conclusion. Therefore, it is unsatisfactory as the central goal of the Arab governments. Desires to alter fundamentally the Arab situation in the Middle East, to improve the Arab negotiating position, and to appeal to Arab domestic opinion, on the other hand, all seem more useful in predicting policy acts such as the oil weapon.

However, these three goals were not equally satisfied. No fundamental change in the Arab-Israeli dispute occurred because of the oil weapon. None of the three goals laid out by OAPEC (Israeli withdrawal from all the 1967 territories, self-determination for the Palestinians and alteration of the status of Jerusalem) was achieved. The closest approximation was the withdrawal of Israel from the Sinai in the Camp David accords, but the immediate consequence of this was the virtual secession of Egypt from the Arab world, making it an unlikely Arab victory. Indeed, some commentators contend that by freeing the Israelis from an Egyptian threat, the return of the Sinai allowed the Begin government to invade Lebanon to attack the PLO.

On the other hand, there is no doubt that the oil weapon did strengthen the bargaining position of the Arabs with the West, if not necessarily with the Israelis. The

European rhetorical shift on the Middle East toward the Arab position is not solely the result of the oil weapon. It seems to start after the 1967 war, when Israel emerged as the dominant regional power rather than an underdog and when the Palestinian issue became more prominent, and it can be fairly dated from 1971.[17] Moreover, the Western states did not simply cave in to Arab pressure during the time of the oil weapon. Nonetheless, the perceived vulnerability to oil cut-offs certainly made such positions easier to support domestically. Moreover, the Third World countries have generally supported the Arab position, as shown in UN resolutions for the past several years, probably largely because of the oil weapon. As suggested above, however, the substantive consequences of all this rhetoric have so far been rather minimal.

It is more difficult to judge the utility of the oil weapon in curbing potential domestic disorders. In the short run it was probably successful. The international publicity, the willingness of Western leaders to come to the Middle East, in many cases almost as supplicants, and the immense increases in oil revenues may have strengthened the OAPEC governments at home. However, in the long run this may be counter-productive by raising expectations for actually having an impact on the Arab-Israeli conflict which may be impossible to meet. We will note later the unpredictable consequences for long-term stability in the Arab countries of the increased oil revenues.

Why Were Some Objectives not Attained?

Why were the OAPEC governments unable to change fundamentally the Middle Eastern situation? They mustered a very impressive threat (to undermine the basis of Western economies), had sufficient reserves to do so without too much risk to themselves, and asked for changes in an area which was not of critical importance to most of their targets. If any economic sanction could have produced real political changes, surely this was the one.

But this ignores a series of important problems. The central difficulty was that only Israel could bring about real change in the Middle East, and the oil weapon had no impact on Israel. Thus the Arabs were attempting indirect influence. Embargoing the United States was presumably supposed to persuade the United States to persuade the Israel to change its position. Injuring the Europeans was supposed to persuade them to persuade the United States to persuade Israel, a somewhat unlikely exercise on its face.

Second, the Arabs were unable to manipulate the international flow of oil to reward their friends and punish their enemies. This occurred because the non-Arab OPEC governments never joined the embargo or production cutbacks, allowing the major oil companies to spread the cost of the oil weapon roughly equally among all importing countries. The Arabs also did not control the world supply of tankers or refineries.[18]

Third, the Arabs apparently had other foreign policy goals. Thus they do not seem to have pressured the major oil companies much, even when it must have become clear that the corporations were fundamentally undercutting the oil weapon. How, for example, would the majors have reacted to an ultimatum that any oil company which supplied an embargoed country with oil from any source would be denied any oil by all the OAPEC countries? Moreover, the Arabs did in fact lift the oil weapon before too much economic damage was done but before any substantive changes had occurred or even been promised.

What were these other goals? The conservative Arab governments may have been concerned not to alienate the United States by applying too much pressure. The unpredictable effects of a financial collapse originating in Western Europe may have been a factor. It was always possible that the United States might react to extreme economic pressure by taking military action against the Arab states. Peace negotiations were beginning, and some disengagement agreements were reached. Egypt seems to have encouraged OAPEC to end the oil weapon. Lastly, the Arab governments may have decided that it simply was not working very well, either because they could not damage their enemies and help their friends or because it was not getting the desired political results. The effective motives were apparently felt more strongly by the conservative Arab governments since Algeria, Syria and Libya, to varying degrees, opposed ending the oil weapon.[19]

Unintended Consequences of the Oil Weapon

The word 'unintended' implies that we know the intentions of the OAPEC governments. As explained throughout this chapter, we do not. My use of the term depends on two personal assumptions which may not be widely shared and therefore should be spelled out: (1) OAPEC leaders did not anticipate correctly and with confidence any of the real consequences of the oil weapon. This is not a slur on the analytic competence of OAPEC personnel. Rather, it reflects a general belief that people cannot anticipate the consequences of major social changes, of which the oil weapon is admittedly a rather small example. It seems more likely that the OAPEC leaders hoped for certain consequences (as shown by their willingness to alter and eventually terminate the oil weapon). (2) These hopes centred on the political goals which were set forth, although they undoubtedly knew that the oil weapon would assist the price-raising process of OPEC, which had started earlier and was simultaneously proceeding on a parallel track. However, I do not believe that the OAPEC leaders knew how high oil prices would go; indeed, the Saudi government seems to have preferred a somewhat lower price than eventually resulted.

The first important unintended consequence, then, was the fourfold increase in oil prices. This placed severe strains on the international financial structure, weakened the economic position of some important Third World countries, increased world-wide inflation, helped extend a world-wide recession, and forced the world to alter its energy consumption patterns. In addition, it resulted in enormous increases of funds for the Arab governments with domestic consequences that, ten years later, remain difficult to ascertain clearly. It is probably not reasonable to blame the current Iranian government for the oil weapon, but the enormous amount of money which it produced clearly contributed to the Iranian revolution. In foreign policy terms, the new oil money clearly increased Arab prestige immensely; indeed, the European shift on the Middle East may well stem more from the increased markets provided by the new wealth of the Arabs than from a direct calculus of vulnerability caused by the oil weapon. This is an important point since economic sanctions do not normally produce great wealth for the actor governments; if the oil weapon's limited success as an instrument of coercion was due to Arab wealth, other embargoes are unlikely to work as well.

A second consequence was increased strain within the Western alliance. Since 1973 the Middle Eastern policies of these countries have polarised into two groups: the United States and everyone else. This difference did not matter much until the oil weapon suddenly made the Middle East into a high priority issue for practically everyone, at least rhetorically. The Europeans became increasingly unhappy because they felt the United States was risking their economic security for either ideological or domestic political considerations, while the United States tended to see the Europeans as actively undercutting its efforts to get a lasting solution to the problem.[20] By itself, this difference is unlikely to wreck the alliance, but it has become a factor in what is broadly perceived as a fundamental crisis in the relationship.

Conclusion

In sum, the Arab oil weapon appears to fit rather well within the general theoretical and historical literature on economic sanctions and coercive diplomacy cited earlier. These literatures argue strongly that it is very difficult for one state to influence an important policy of another state by economic sanctions alone.[21] It is difficult to imagine a real-world case where the actor governments had more advantages than this one; if sanctions cannot influence other governments here, they are unlikely to do so elsewhere. Moreover, to the extent that the embargo did at least alter rhetoric about the Middle East among the industrial target states over time, it seems to have been successful only because it helped make the Arabs rich, which in turn means that its success is unlikely to be repeated.

However, the fact that the oil weapon did not achieve its stated goals need not mean it was a total failure. In fact, it was probably useful in improving the Arabs' negotiating position and, at least in the short run, may have strengthened the domestic position of the actor governments; either or both of these may have been the 'real' goal all along. Perhaps everyone benefits: the targets because they were not really coerced, and the actors because they seem to have been successful.

Unfortunately, there remains at least one problem with this optimistic analysis - the apparent success of the actor governments may increase the probability that the sanctions will be reimposed in the future. Some people, including myself, have justified analysis of such situations as providing information necessary to prevent future imposition of economic sanctions. However, if the domestic consequences of sanctions are crucial for the actor governments, they may have a vested interest in pretending that the sanctions worked, even if they know they did not. It is not impossible that they may thus talk themselves into having to repeat the experience.

Notes

1. See the many works footnoted elsewhere in this volume.

2. Thomas C. Schelling, Arms and Influence (Yale University Press, New Haven, 1966); Alexander L. George, David K. Hall and William Simons, The Limits of Coercive Diplomacy: Laos, Cuba, Vietnam (Little, Brown & Co., Boston, 1971); Oran Young, The Politics of Force (Princeton University Press, Princeton N.J., 1968); Edward N. Luttwak, The Political Uses of Sea Power (Johns Hopkins University Press, Baltimore, 1974); Edward N. Luttwak, The Grand Strategy of the Roman Empire (Johns Hopkins University Press, Baltimore, 1976); Wallace C. Thies, When Governments Collide: Coercion and Diplomacy in the Vietnam Conflict 1964-1968 (University of California Press, Berkeley, 1980); Barry M. Blechman and Stephen S. Kaplan, Force Without War: U.S. Armed Forces as a Political Instrument (The Brookings Institution, Washigton,

D.C., 1978); Gordon A. Craig and Alexander L. George, Force and Statecraft: Diplomatic Problems of Our Time (Oxford University Press, New York, 1983).

3. J. B. Kelley, Arabia, the Gulf and the West (Basic Books Inc., New York, 1980).

4. Walter Laqueur, Confrontation: The Middle East and World Politics (Quadrange/The New York Times Book Co., New York, 1974).

5. Kelley, Arabia, the Gulf and the West.

6. Sygliowicz in Joseph A. Sygliowicz and Bard E. O'Neill, The Energy Crisis and U.S. Foreign Policy (Praeger Publishers, New York, 1975), p. 185; and Stockholm International Peace Research Institute, 'Oil and Security: A SIPRI Monograph' (Humanities Press, New York, 1974), p. 118.

7. Sygliowicz in Sygliowicz and O'Neill, The Energy Crisis and U.S. Foreign Policy, p. 204.

8. Dankwart A. Rustow, 'U.S.-Saudi Relations and the Oil Crisis of the 1980s', Foreign Affairs 55 (April 1977), p. 507.

9. George Lenczowski in Raymond A. Vernon (ed.), The Oil Crisis (W. W. Norton & Co., New York, 1976), p. 64.

10. Ibid., p. 65.

11. Hanus Maull, 'Oil and Influence: The Oil Weapon Examined', Adelphi Papers no. 117 (International Institute for Strategic Studies, London, 1975), pp. 6-7; R. Stobaugh in Vernon, The Oil Crisis; Prodi and Clo in Vernon, The Oil Crisis, p. 101.

12. Prodi and Clo in Vernon, The Oil Crisis, p. 101.

13. Robert J. Lieber, 'Oil and the Middle East War: Europe in the Energy Crisis', Harvard Studies in International Affairs no. 35 (Harvard University Center for International Affairs, Cambridge, Mass., 1976).

14. Kenneth L. Juster, 'Foreign Policy-making During the Oil Crisis', Japan Interpreter 11 (Winter 1977), p. 308.

15. Lieber, 'Oil and the Middle East War', pp. 299-301.

16. Stein in Steven L. Spiegel (ed.), The Middle East and the Western Alliance (George Allen & Unwin, Boston, 1982), pp. 59-60.

17. Maull in J. C. Hurewitz (ed.), Oil, the Arab-Israeli Dispute, and the Industrial World (Westview Press, Boulder, Colorado, 1976), p. 118.

18. Maull, 'Oil and Influence', p. 12.

19. For an elaboration of these arguments, see Roy Licklider, 'The Failure of the Arab Oil Weapon of 1973-74', Comparative Strategy 3 (1982), pp. 370-5; the section as a whole draws heavily on Roy Licklider, 'Targets of the Oil Weapon', manuscript, Political Science Department, Rutgers University, New Brunswick, N.J., 1984.

20. David Allen and Michael Smith, 'The Ten, The U.S. and the Camp David Process', paper prepared for the Colloquium on European Policy Making and the Arab-Israeli Conflict, Europa Institut, University of Amsterdam, February 1983.

21. For an attempt to exlain why this is true and why governments continue nonetheless to use such sanctions, see H. Peter Gray and Roy Licklider, 'Economic Warfare', mimeo. Rutgers University, New Brunswick, N.J., 1983.

PART IV

IMPACT OF ECONOMIC SANCTIONS ON THE INITIATOR

Chapter Ten

THE 1980-81 US GRAIN EMBARGO: CONSEQUENCES FOR THE PARTICIPANTS

Robert L. Paarlberg

When US President Jimmy Carter decided to place a partial embargo on grain sales to the Soviet Union in January 1980 to punish the Soviets for their military invasion of Afghanistan, the potential impact of the embargo seemed large. Soviet grain production in 1979 had fallen to 179 million tons, 58 million tons below the harvest of the previous year. To compensate for this harvest shortfall, Soviet planners were hoping to import a record volume of more than 30 million tons of grain, roughly twice the import volume of the previous year. As in years past, nearly three-quarters of these imports was expected to come from the United States. Without such large grain imports, the Soviet Union would be obliged to reduce sharply the feeding of grain to livestock, a step which would in turn reduce domestic meat production at a time when the leadership was pledged to rapid dietary improvements. If the Soviet Union would ever be vulnerable to US economic sanctions, to the threat of US 'food power', this seemed the time.

The eventual failure of the 1980-81 grain embargo to reduce Soviet grain imports enough to trigger a 'distress slaughter' of livestock herds is therefore an instructive development. Since the embargo failed under circumstances which were uniquely favourable to its success, we may tentatively conclude that an embargo policy adopted under any less favourable circumstances will fail as well.

But the manner in which the 1980-81 grain embargo failed - through substitute sales of grain to the Soviet Union from non-US exporters - is also an instructive point of observation. It was through these substitute sales, which were accompanied by a more general redirection of trade, that the international market-place absorbed and nullified the intended effects of the embargo world-wide. A number of grain importers and exporters 'switched partners' during the embargo, but at no point were Soviet grain imports or, for that matter, US grain exports seriously impaired. For those exporting nations that participated in the embargo, as well as those who declined to participate, not to mention the United States itself, which led the embargo, the trading consequences were surprisingly uniform. With only marginal exceptions (and despite intense political controversy over who was selling what to whom), during the embargo the grain exports of all nations continued apace. In a strictly commercial sense, the short-run consequences of the embargo, for participants and non-participants alike, were remarkably modest and benign.

In the process of making their original embargo decision, US officials spent little time considering the possibility that other suppliers would nullify its effects by stepping in to meet Soviet grain import needs. Statements made at the time the decision was announced reveal mostly official confusion on this matter. While briefing the press just prior to the President's 4 January embargo speech, White House Press Secretary Jody Powell was asked whether the US embargo would be supported by other exporters. 'Yes for the EC, Canada and Australia,' Powell replied. When asked directly if Argentina would co-operate, Mr Powell stated erroneously: 'They don't count for these products'.[1] The President's announcement speech was likewise confused and misleading in its references to other grain exporters. The President offered a brief but hopeful statement on allied co-operation: 'After consultation with other principal grain exporting nations, I am confident that they will not replace these quantities of grain by additional shipments on their own part to the Soviet Union'.[2]

In fact, the President was in no position to offer such reassurances, since high level consultations had not yet been undertaken.[3] About a week before the President's speech the State Department did instruct US embassies abroad to inform foreign ministries of the economic sanctions - including a grain embargo - which were then under consideration in Washington and to ascertain the likelihood of international support. But such low-level inquiries produced little response. Not until the evening of 4 January, just prior to the President's speech, were direct contacts initiated on the specific question of a grain embargo. These contacts, however, were also undertaken at a low level - by the Associate Administrator of the United States Department of Agriculture's (USDA) Foreign Agriculture Service. The Secretary of Agriculture and his principal deputies were too busy notifying <u>domestic</u> farm leaders and grain traders, another indication of the inward-looking preoccupation of most participants in the embargo process.

Undertaken at the last minute by low-level officials, the consultation process with other exporters probably did more harm than good. Among those officials who could be contacted on short notice in the European Community (EC), Canada and Australia, none responded with an immediate commitment to co-operate. Efforts to reach ranking officials in Argentina failed entirely; the leaders of the junta in Buenos Aires learned about the grain embargo in the newspaper the next morning.

There was a practical limit, of course, to the range of consultations that could have preceded the embargo announcement. An element of surprise was necessary to ensure a maximum advantage over the target country, as well as to pre-empt political opposition to avoid a premature disruption of commercial markets at home. Even so, the consultations undertaken with other grain-exporting countries were, in this case, too little as well as too late. Prior notification at the head-of-state level might not have been enough to ensure the full co-operation of other exporters, but lacking this diplomatic courtesy, the likelihood of full co-operation was probably nil from the start.

Belatedly, after the embargo decision had been publicly announced, a more energetic effort to secure the co-operation of other Western grain exporting nations was initiated. On 6 January Secretary of Agriculture Bergland called for a 12 January meeting in Washington of sub-cabinet level officials from the European Community, Canada, Australia and Argentina. On the eve of this meeting officials from Canada, Australia and the European Community came forward with a series of public statements interpreted by the United States as promises of support. Canadian Prime Minister Joe Clark was particularly forthright, stating on 11 January that the Canadian Cabinet had decided that 'It will not be business as usual [with the Soviet Union]....No quantity [of Canadian grain] above the normal and traditional amounts will be sent'.[4]

The EC Commission in Brussels also offered formal support, agreeing not to undertake larger than normal sales of cereals from Europe. The United Kingdom wanted the EC to go further by restricting sales of butter, meat and sugar as well as grain; but France, the major EC food exporter, argued that EC food trade sanctions should not go beyond those of the United States.[5] Still, the French gave an early impression of supporting the embargo on grain. President Giscard d'Estaing himself explained that 'The Soviets have broken the principles of detente. The actions of the United States as a superpower are justified. France will not substitute embargoed items, and will make no grain sales'.[6] When similar public assurances were then received from Australia, prior to the 12 January meeting in Washington, only Argentina loomed as a likely holdout to allied co-operation. On 10 January in Buenos Aires the military government of Jorge Rafael Videla had issued an eleven-paragraph communique which announced its plans to send a representative to the meeting, but at the same time not to participate 'in decisions or punitive actions that have been adopted without our prior intervention or that come from decision-making centers not of our country'.[7]

With this foreboding Argentine statement as its prelude, the 12 January meeting in Washington produced an ambiguous result. United States Under-Secretary of Agriculture Dale Hathaway, after chairing the meeting, announced that 'there was general agreement these governments would not directly or indirectly replace the grain the United States would have shipped to the Soviet Union'. Mr Hathaway even quoted a statement written by the Argentine representative subscribing to this viewpoint. Upon its being monitored in Buenos Aires, however, this statement was promptly denied, and four days later, on 16 January, the Argentine Minister of Agriculture stated outright that his country would not participate in the US embargo.[8]

Argentina's early decision not to support the embargo was based on much more than its displeasure over not having been consulted prior to the embargo announcement. First, Argentina was understandably reluctant to follow the US lead because of its much larger relative dependence on grain exports. Argentina could less well afford to play 'stop and go' with its commercial grain exports, since they accounted for about 30 per cent of total export earnings, compared to only 8 per cent of total export earnings for the United States. Even before the embargo, roughly 15 per cent of Argentina's grain exports had been going to the Soviet Union. Argentine trade with the Soviet Union in 1979 had reached US $470 million, and from the perspective of the Argentine government, this was not a market to be lightly sacrificed.[9]

Argentina had diplomatic as well as commercial interests in a continued expansion of its trade ties with the Soviet Union in 1980. Despite conspicuous ideological differences, these two regimes had found a common cause in resisting US human rights policies. Since President Carter had repeatedly annoyed the Argentine leadership with disparaging references to its human rights record (which he had judged 'abominable'), the junta felt little inclination to respond to diplomatic pleas for co-operation from Washington.

But the greatest enticement facing the Argentine government immediately following the US embargo announcement was simply the high price for grain that Soviet purchasing agents were suddenly willing to pay. Argentina was not in a position in the short run to expand the <u>total volume</u> of its grain exports, since its maturing crop was just then suffering from a significant drought (one which would eventually reduce total production from the previous year's level by more than 40 per cent). Total Argentine grain exports in 1980 actually <u>fell by nearly 50 per cent.</u>[10] But with adequate price incentives, Argentina could be persuaded to redirect a substantial portion of these reduced grain exports away from traditional customers and toward the Soviet Union. The Soviet Union wasted no time in providing those incentives. A high-level Soviet trade mission - led by Viktor Pershin, the Director of Exportkhleb - visited Buenos Aires at the end of January and contracted for grain deliveries directly with Argentine grain co-operatives, at prices well above those offered by Argentina's traditional foreign customers. At a time when Argentine wheat normally would have been priced four to ten dollars per ton below US wheat, the f.o.b. price in Buenos Aires suddenly moved up to more than US $23 per ton above the US export price. By late April, due to Soviet price premiums, f.o.b. corn prices in Buenos Aires had risen to about US $150 per ton (compared with US corn at US $112 per ton), and Argentine grain sorghum was selling for export at US $145 per ton (compared with the US export price of US $117 per ton).[11]

The Argentine government tried to argue that its high priced sales to the Soviet Union were simply the result of 'free market competition'. It was true that the junta had lifted Peronist controls on grain prices some years before and was no longer playing such a dominant role in the management of grain exports, but Argentina's commercial response to the high prices being offered by Exportkhleb nonetheless had plenty of official support. At the time of Director Pershin's visit to Buenos Aires, the Argentine government had in fact negotiated a formal agreement with the Soviets to ensure sales of at least 4.5 million tons of corn, sorghum and soybeans in 1980, in addition to the 1.6 million tons of wheat that had already been sold. These officially guaranteed sales would cover the equivalent of roughly 75 per cent of all Argentine corn then available for export.

By June 1980 the premiums being offered by the Soviet Union for Argentine corn reached their peak level of 83 cents per bushel, pushing prices to 29 per cent above the US Gulf price of US $2.90. Thereafter, with the Russians own summer harvest soon to begin and with an additional 8 million tons of US grain scheduled to be available after 1 October, Soviet purchasing agents felt less need to pay such exorbitant prices.[12] An enduring re-direction of Argentine trade had nonetheless been accomplished. Argentina wanted its larger sales to the Soviet Union to continue even at a lower price, since its traditional export customers had begun to fill their grain needs elsewhere - primarily from the United States. So long as the embargo continued, this also suited the Soviet Union. Following a full recovery of Argentine grain production in 1981, total exports to the Soviet Union thus continued to increase, to more than 40 per cent above the 1980 level.

In fact, both Argentina and the Soviet Union were eager that this expanded volume of trade be continued into the future, with or without a termination of the US embargo. During a visit to Argentina by Soviet Vice-Minister of Foreign Trade Alexei Manzhula in April 1980, the two governments concluded a long-term bilateral grain trade agreement (signed in July) ensuring for the next five years annual exports to the Soviet Union of at least 4 million tons of feedgrains and one-half million tons of soybeans.[13] For a nation such as Argentina, as yet lacking the means to store large quantities of grain between harvests, a five-year guarantee of annual exports at this level became just the incentive needed by producers to go full-speed ahead with expanded production.

It was precisely this further expansion of Argentine grain production and sales to the Soviet Union early in 1981 that blunted the US embargo during its second winter season, following the Soviet Union's second poor harvest at home. While harvesting its new bumper crop, between January and June 1981, Argentina shipped a hefty 8.5 million tons of this grain directly to the Soviet Union. This was more than twice the export level of the January-June 1980 period and nearly ten times the pre-embargo shipment rate.[14] Knowledge that these vastly expanded Argentine grain shipments would be available during the first six months of 1981 was no doubt comforting to Soviet planners, who were just then exhausting their latest 8 million ton allotment from the United States and might have otherwise been forced into deeper livestock feed cutbacks. Indeed, the Soviet Union enjoyed access to so much Argentine grain during the early months of 1981, that it felt no need to make any additional purchases from the United States when the embargo was finally lifted in April. Significant Soviet purchases of US grain were not resumed until late summer 1981, when these large shipments from Argentina had been completed and it had become clear to the Soviets that their third successive bad harvest was in prospect.

During the total 16-month period of the embargo between January 1980 and April 1981, Argentina exported 11.1 million tons of grain to the Soviet Union. These exports were more than an isolated blow to the embargo. Argentina's success in taking commercial advantage from the embargo inspired others to reconsider their earlier pledges of restraint and eventually to follow suit. The grain export policies of Australia, Canada and the EC never became so damaging to the embargo as those of Argentina. But each was inspired by Argentina to limit its support for the embargo in due course.

Among this group of allied grain exporters, Australia showed the least restraint. Australia was not so heavily dependent upon its foreign grain sales as was Argentina, since grains made up only about 13 per cent of its total export earnings. Nor had Australia ever been a heavy supplier of grain exports to the Soviet Union. During the last two complete marketing years prior to the embargo, Australian grain exports to the Soviet Union had averaged annually only 0.2 million tons (less than 3 per cent of total grain exports).[15] When Australia proceeded to increase these exports several-fold in 1980 and 1981 while the US grain embargo was in place, it was clearly violating its official promise to hold sales within 'normal and traditional' bounds.

During the first calendar year that the embargo was in place, grain shipments from Australia to the Soviet Union increased from the 1979 level of 1.2 million tons to an unprecedented level of 4.3 million tons. Australian officials tried to point out that most of these expanded grain shipments had actually been contracted prior to President Carter's surprise embargo announcement. In fact, Australia used its innocence on this score to maximum advantage. During the first months of 1980, simply by refusing to cancel any of these pre-embargo contracts, the Australian government could claim to be supporting the US embargo (by making no new sales) while all the time exporting larger volumes of grain than ever before to the Soviet Union.[16]

Prime Minister Malcolm Fraser did not wish to antagonise the United States. Nevertheless, he was under intense pressure from the Australian Wheat Board (AWB) not only to deliver on all pre-embargo contracts, but also further to expand sales to the Soviets. In May, therefore, the Australian government announced that it would authorise a limited number of forward export contracts for sales to the Soviet Union of feedgrains - barley, oats and grain sorghum. These sales, in combination with 2.3 million tons of wheat sales to the Soviet Union already under contract for delivery through July, would bring Australia's total July 1979-June 1980 grain shipments to the Soviet Union to an unprecedented level of roughly 4 million tons.

Prime Minister Fraser delayed for as long as he could any public decision on expanded sales for the 1980-81 year, and so into the summer of 1980 some US officials continued to express hope that Australia would show restraint: 'I've talked with the Australians and they're going to hold the Russians' feet to the fire', said Secretary Bergland in late June.[17] Despite its record exports already completed, however, the AWB was still expecting to carry relatively large quantities of unsold grain into the new season, and therefore it argued that its unusually large 1979-80 sales to the Soviets ought to be established as the new 'normal and traditional' level and hence permitted to continue in the coming year. In July 1980 the Australian government finally accepted this argument, and the AWB went ahead immediately to arrange new sales of an additional 2 million tons of wheat to the Soviet Union for delivery between August 1980 and May 1981. As a public justification for this new sale, AWB Chairman Leslie Price explained that Australia was forced into expanded sales to the Soviets because of certain 'aberrations' in world grain trade patterns that had been caused by the embargo - most notably a large increase in US wheat sales to China, a growing market which Australia coveted as its own. In private, however, AWB officials had come to view the embargo as a rare opportunity to gain access to the Soviet market on a long-term basis. In negotiations with Soviet officials prior to concluding the new 2 million ton wheat sale, the AWB sought informal assurances that the Soviet Union would also be a more regular customer in the future.[18]

United States officials accepted these new Soviet-Australian wheat contracts with a certain resignation. Although Australian grain shipments to the Soviet Union in the July 1980-June 1981 year would total 2.9 million tons, once again well above the pre-embargo level, the United States chose not to challenge the dubious assertion that these sales were still within the 'normal and traditional' range.[19]

But as Argentina and Australia went ahead with larger than normal post-embargo grain sales to the Soviet Union, the pressure on Canada to do likewise would eventually become irresistible. Canada, though resentful at not having been consulted prior to the embargo decision, showed exceptional restraint during the early months of 1980. Unlike Australia, Canada was caught not having signed a new round of export contracts with the Soviets at the time the embargo was announced. It had been waiting for an expected rise in export prices in the new year. Simply to maintain a normal pace of grain sales to the Soviet Union, therefore, Canada was obliged to enter into an awkward agreement on new sales within a month after having pledged not to take advantage of the embargo. In February 1980 the Canadian Wheat Board (CWB) announced plans to sell an additional 2 million tons of grain to the Soviet Union during the balance of the marketing year that would end in June.[20] While denounced by some in the United States as early evidence of a Canadian betrayal, these sales would bring total Canadian grain exports to the Soviet Union during the July 1979-June 1980 year to only 3.5 million tons. This was a sales volume somewhat above the average of the three previous years, but actually below the volume recorded following earlier harvest failures in the Soviet Union in both 1975-76 and 1972-73. In fact, the ratio of Canada's total wheat exports going to the Soviet Union actually fell in 1979-80, during the first year of the US embargo, from 14 per cent down to 12 per cent.[21]

This early Canadian resolve not to take commercial advantage of the US embargo began to weaken following the defeat of Prime Minister Joe Clark's Progressive Conservative government and its replacement by the Liberal government of Prime Minister Pierre Trudeau, which felt less personally committed to the embargo.[22] By early summer Canadian grain producers were also becoming more vocal in their resentment, noting estimates that unrestrained sales to the Soviet Union could have boosted the prices they were getting by as much as 75 cents a bushel.[23] In early June the Saskatchewan Wheat Pool announced that it would independently withdraw its support for the embargo on 31 July, when the current crop-year came to an end. The President of the Pool, Ted Turner, had argued that Canadian restraint was no longer called for, since the United States was selling so much grain to Eastern Europe, a region which he characterised as a likely trans-shipment point to the Soviet Union. A sure sign that support for the embargo was also eroding in Ottawa came in early July, when Senator Hazen Argue, the Minister in the Trudeau Cabinet responsible for the CWB, announced that Canada had definitely suffered as a result of limiting its grain shipments to the Soviet Union. As a consequence, Canada would have to seek a 'change in the rules' governing its grain exports during the new crop-year to begin on 1 August. Canada, said Argue, should be credited with 'normally and traditionally' supplying the Soviets with 'up to 5 million tons or more' of grain. In 1972-73, to be sure, Canada had supplied the Soviets with 5.1 million tons of grain. But US officials felt it was hardly accurate to characterise this one-time-only record volume as 'normal and traditional'.[24]

Early in August, despite US misgivings, Canada went forward with an authorisation of new grain sales to the Soviet Union at an annual level of about 5 million tons. New Canadian sales to the Soviets from that point onward would be limited mostly by Canada's own constrained handling capacity and by the final size of the summer crop. The government still claimed that it was standing by the earlier pledge to hold sales to normal and traditional levels, but for all practical purposes it had abandoned its original position of support for the embargo.[25]

Canada did not formally announce its withdrawal from the embargo until late November, by which time President Carter's election defeat at last seemed to render any future Canadian support for the embargo meaningless. Upon withdrawal, it simultaneously announced that a new sale of 2.1 million tons of wheat and barley had just been arranged by a CWB delegation in Moscow. This sale actually pushed Canada's 1980-81 grain exports to the Soviet Union above the 5 million ton level, which Senator Argue had just recently described as 'normal'.[26] The public justification offered for abandoning the embargo in this fashion was a US decision, made public the month before, to sign a long-term bilateral grain trade agreement with the People's Republic of China. Canada (much like Australia) had long coveted for itself the Chinese grain market and resented the rapid growth in US wheat sales to that market seemingly occasioned by the embargo. With the United States unloading its embargoed grain in Canada's export market, why should Canada show restraint? Equally upsetting to Canadian grain producers had been the October resumption of US sales to the Soviets - the annual allowance of 8 million tons of US grain that President Carter had exempted from the embargo. If US producers could continue to sell 8 million tons of grain to the Soviet Union every year, why should Canadian producers agree to retrict themselves to less?

Over the course of the entire July 1980-June 1981 year, Canadian grain exports to the Soviet Union would actually reach a record-breaking level of 6.8 million tons. Considering specifically the 16-month period of the embargo, Canadian grain exports to the Soviet Union totalled 6.5 million tons. Two-thirds of these exports were recorded during the second half of the 1980 calendar year, helping to sustain the Soviets in the aftermath of their second bad summer grain harvest.[27] The early restraint shown by the Canadian government was therefore not maintained. By 1981 Canada had emerged second only to Argentina as a supplier of larger than usual quantities of grain to the Soviet Union, spelling further problems for the embargo.

Argentina, Australia and Canada were by far the largest suppliers of non-US grain to the Soviet Union during the period of the embargo, but other traders got into the act as well. The response of the European Community to the US grain embargo was of particular interest in this regard. To a surprising degree, the European Community lived to at least the letter of its original pledge not to take commercial advantage of the embargo. Grain exports from the European Community to the Soviet Union did increase during the July 1979-June 1980 year, up from the previous year's level of 200,000 tons to about 800,000 tons. But most of these larger 1979-80 shipments were delivered under licences issued before the US embargo announcement and so did not represent any wilful European effort to undercut the embargo.[28] In the 1980-81 year, even though most others had abandoned all restraint, EC grain sales to the Soviet Union expanded only modestly to a total of just 1.1 million tons. This, despite the fact that the European Community had plenty of grain to sell. Total exportable supplies of EC wheat were actually increasing during the embargo period from 10 million tons in 1979-80, up to 11.5

million tons in 1980-81.[29] Pressure from grain producers within the European Community to boost exports was also on the rise during the embargo period. Early in 1980 French representatives within the European Community had specifically urged additional authorisations for subsidised wheat exports to further strengthen internal prices and hold down surplus stocks, which then stood at about 6 million tons.[30]

This restraint of EC grain sales to the Soviet Union during the 16-month period of the grain embargo did not, however, reflect any exceptional European deference to the US sanctions policy. It must be remembered that the European Community only recently had become a wheat surplus region and had no history of providing significant quantities of grain to the Soviet Union. Over the six-year period prior to the embargo, the European Community had sold to the Soviet Union no wheat at all and only modest quantities of barley. Just as important, the budgetary cost to the European Community of a dramatic increase in its subsidised grain sales to the Soviet Union might have been prohibitive. European Community grains, grown behind a protective barrier of variable import levies, are priced so high that they cannot be sold abroad without the application of expensive 'restitution payments'. It has been the budgetary cost of these export subsidies, rather than physical availability of surplus grain, that has most often constrained the recent growth of EC grain exports. When EC officials discontinued offering grain export subsidies to the Soviet Union in January 1980 as their way of supporting the US grain embargo, they were actually saving money. It was a reluctance to increase EC spending on export subsidies more than any reluctance to defy the United States, that held down EC grain exports to the Soviet Union during the period of the embargo.[31] As one indication of this, just before the embargo was lifted, the EC Commission actually refused to authorise an additional 600,000 tons of EC wheat sales to the Soviet Union despite the fact that the French Ambassador in Washington had already solicited and received approval for the sale from the US Secretary of State.[32]

Because of its unique budgetary exposure, the European Community was actually obliged at times during the embargo to place extra restraints on EC food sales to the Soviet Union. Soviet purchasing agents, eager during the embargo to find affordable supplies of animal feed, had discovered in 1980 that the EC export subsidies no longer available for most grain products were still available for some kinds of EC grain 'mixtures'. European Community officials were upset to discover in late October that the Soviet Union had used this loophole to purchase an unprecedented 500,000 tons of mixed animal feed from two West German firms at a cost to the EC budget of US $23 million in export subsidies. Export subsidies on mixed grains were thereafter suspended and overseas grain sales were more tightly monitored.[33]

Whenever the European Community found itself in a position to sell food products that did not require costly subsidies, it showed much less restraint. Soybeans, for example, which could be purchased duty free from abroad by EC processors, could then be re-exported to the Soviets without subsidy at competitive prices. Taking every advantage of this option, European companies imported and processed as much as 1 million tons of US soybeans during the period of the embargo for resale to the Soviet Union as soybean meal (a high-protein animal feed).[34] European millers meanwhile used a parallel scheme to expand wheat flour exports to the Soviet Union. The rules of the European Community permitted European companies to import inexpensive foreign wheat, levy-free, so long as they re-exported that wheat in the form of milled flour. Taking maximum advantage of this loophole, North German millers were able to sell a record volume of wheat flour to the Soviet Union (as much as 250,000 tons by mid-summer 1980), much of it processed from US wheat.[35] Prior to the embargo, the Soviet Union had been only a minimal buyer of foreign wheat flour, but by February 1981 Soviet purchases from European mills had reached 700,000 tons, or roughly 15 per cent of the world trade total.[36]

The US grain embargo was not, therefore, supported in every respect by the European Community. For reasons of financial convenience to the European Community, direct sales of European grains were not conspicuously expanded. The expansion of food sales that occurred took a less conspicuous but more profitable form: re-sales to the Soviet Union, after processing, of various US food products, including wheat and soybeans, which captured value-added tax along the way.

Additional embargo slippage was encountered at a variety of less prominent points within the world's food trading system. Having noticed the price incentives being offered, a number of much smaller exporters joined the major suppliers in providing grain to the Soviet Union during the 16-month period of the embargo. These smaller exporters - including Hungary, Thailand, Spain, Sweden and India - combined during the embargo to provide the Soviet Union with roughly 4.7 million tons of much needed non-US grain.[37] United States efforts to discourage these sales were fitful and unavailing. Thailand, for example, remained defiant in the face of early US diplomatic pressures to restrain its exports to the Soviet Union of rice, corn and tapioca. 'We are not a satellite of the US,' announced the Thai Deputy Minister of Commerce in March 1980; in December his government entered into a ten-year bilateral trade agreement with the Soviet Union to cover annual Soviet purchases of roughly 500,000 tons of tapioca (a high-value animal feed), plus 450,000 tons of corn and 230,000 tons of rice.[38] One month earlier, in November 1980, Spain had seized upon the occasion of an unusually large wheat harvest at home (up 33 per cent from the level of the previous year) to announce that it would begin direct wheat sales to the Soviet Union. Spain, which until then had been consistently a net importer of wheat, supplied the Soviets with 700,000 tons of wheat and barley in the new year beginning January 1981.[39] India's rice exports to the Soviet Union were expanded, and the repayment of a 2 million ton wheat loan was also accelerated during the period of the embargo.

The cumulative effect, during the 16-month period of the embargo, was the continued expansion of total Soviet grain imports despite a significant reduction in grain imports taken directly from the United States (see Table 10.1).

Amid so much shifting in global trade patterns, it is noteworthy that several events which some feared might weaken the embargo did not occur. First, large quantities of US grain were not trans-shipped to the Soviet Union through satellite states in Eastern Europe. About 1.4 million tons of grain was shipped to the Soviet Union from Hungary, Bulgaria and Romania in 1979-80, but US analysts concluded that this was only slightly more than the quantity of grains normally traded between these countries.[40] Hungary's wheat exports during the first calendar year of the embargo increased to a significant 1.1 million tons (or more than twice the average level of the three previous years), but these larger exports were facilitated, at least in part, by a record domestic harvest. Hungary was a regular exporter of its own agricultural products in Eastern Europe, and not a trans-shipment point for Western origin grains. Romania, which did increase both its imports and exports of grain in 1979-80 to levels approaching 2 million tons, was the more likely focal point for those few trans-shipments through Eastern Europe that did occur.[41]

Suspicion that grain was being heavily trans-shipped was understandably aroused when US grain sales to Eastern Europe suddenly increased during 1979-80, up to 11.6 million tons, in contrast with only 5.6 million tons the previous year. But USDA later stated that it had found no evidence that this grain, most of which had been sold to Poland, was moving on to the Soviet Union. Grain shipments from the Soviet Union to Poland were in fact on the rise while the embargo was in place.[42] Poland's larger grain imports in 1980 were an independent response to its own much larger internal needs, due to a very poor harvest of its own in 1979 and then following the labour unrest which subsequently broke out as one result of domestic food price increases.

A second kind of anticipated slippage which did not occur was the wide-spread sale of US grain to the Soviet Union through the foreign subsidiaries of US-based multinational grain trading companies. Such firms, which handle the vast majority of US grain exports, enjoy a well-deserved reputation for both ingenuity and discretion when servicing the import needs of a large and steady cash-paying customer such as the Soviet Union. The US government could scarcely hope to monitor, let alone control, all of the highly secretive sale and re-sale operations that these firms conducted overseas. During the period of the embargo, however, most fears of corporate duplicity were quickly laid to rest. The private companies had apparently been mollified by the marketing opportunities that had become available elsewhere and by the extraordinary protection and compensation provided to them under the terms of an 'exporter's agreement' patched together in Washington immediately following the embargo announcement. To protect themselves from too much unwelcome federal investigation, they went out of their way to demonstrate good faith, even to the extent of honouring an informal request from the administration, made on 12 January 1980, that they refrain from using their foreign subsidiaries to sell non-US grain to the Soviet Union. This so-called 'gentlemen's agreement', which went well beyond the official scope of the embargo, was terminated at the end of the crop-year in June, by which time official suspicions of company behaviour had been eased.[43] Investigations of 'alleged' instances of diversion of trans-shipment of US grain to the Soviet Union continued under the direction of the US Department of Commerce, but in mid-summer 1980 it was announced by the USDA that no violation of the terms of the embargo by any private trading firm had yet been demonstrated.[44]

Food power advocates should not conclude too much, however, from the 'leak-proof' appearance of the embargo. United States grain did not 'leak' through the 1980-81 embargo because it did not have to. Recall that the Soviet Union had found ways to meet almost all of its import needs through the purchase of non-US grain. United States exporters were likewise finding ways to keep their sales volume up without resorting to duplicity. As larger quantities of non-US grain began to move toward the Soviet Union, embargoed US grain had found compensating opportunities to move elsewhere. International grain shipments were substantially re-routed following the embargo announcement, but neither the Soviet Union nor the United States had been forced by the embargo into a dramatic downward adjustment in the total volume of its trade. On the contrary, both Soviet grain imports and US grain exports continued to grow during the embargo (see Table 10.2). These compensating shifts in trade patterns were enough to permit both importers and exporters, including both the United States and the Soviet Union, to continue to meet their customary needs without the deceptions, diversions or trans-shipments of grain that might well have occurred otherwise.

Here, once again, is the key to understanding the 16-month duration of the embargo. Within the international grain trading system, that embargo not only failed to deny short-run import opportunities to the Soviet Union, it also failed to deny short-run export opportunities to the United States. Soon after the embargo was declared, the United States and its export competitors in effect merely 'traded customers'. The United States gave up in the process a large share of its annual sales to the Soviet Union, but gained a compensating share of annual sales to numerous non-Soviet customers, such as Mexico and China, who didn't wish to compete with the Soviets for the purchase of Argentine, Australian or Canadian grain. The fact is that total US grain exports never did decline during the period of the embargo. The volume of those sales <u>increased</u> (as the USDA had earlier forecast) by no less than 22 per cent during the first marketing year affected by the embargo, from 89.2 million tons in 1978-79 to 108.8 million tons in 1979-80. Total US grain exports were then forecast to continue to increase by another 5 per cent, even on the assumption that the embargo would not be lifted, to reach 114.5 million tons in 1980-81.[45] Even the United States' share of world grain exports managed to increase during the period of the embargo, being greater when the embargo finally ended than it had been in 1978-79, the last complete marketing year prior to the embargo. Since US grain export prices were also on the rise from the middle of 1980 into 1981, this unbroken expansion of US grain exports during the embargo period also produced record export earnings for US grain traders and producers (see Table 10.3). The fact that the embargo did such little short-run damage to US grain exports helps to explain how it survived for as long as it did. If the embargo had at any time placed a tighter lid on commercial export opportunities for US producers and traders, domestic pressures to end the embargo would have been much stronger and had an effect much sooner. No doubt aware of this danger, the Carter Administration had done its best, from the start, to encourage a prompt shift in US export patterns so as to take full advantage of new openings in non-Soviet markets. As early as 16 January 1980, following two days of hasty negotiations, the United States had announced an agreement whereby Mexico would purchase larger than expected quantities of US agricultural commodities in 1980 (4.76 million tons in all), a portion of which (about 1 million tons of corn) would come directly from embargoed grain supplies previously destined for the Soviet Union. In September the total quantity of Mexican agricultural purchases covered by this agreement was then increased to 7.2 million tons, roughly twice the level of Mexico's annual imports from the United States over the three previous years.[46] In October 1980 the United States then signed an equally significant four-year grain supply agreement with the People's Republic of China.[47] As President Carter would later write:'Secretary Bob Bergland and other administration officials marshaled a world-wide effort to sell American corn and wheat, concentrating on such countries as Mexico and China....We were to be very successful, breaking all-time world records in grain sales during 1980, in spite of the restraints on Soviet trade'.[48] By working so hard to push its grain into these non-Soviet markets, of course, the United States gave its export competitors further cause to ignore the embargo and to redirect their own sales to the Soviet Union.

In the last analysis, therefore, perhaps the 1980-81 grain embargo was not such a clear test of the ability of the United States to deny grain sales to the Soviet Union. Such a test would have required that steps be taken which were politically unacceptable at home. First, it would have required that the United States first discontinue all sales to the Soviet Union - including the 8 million tons guaranteed under the Long Term Agreement. And, if seriously seeking multilateral co-operation for the embargo, the United States should also have restrained the impulse to dump its own embargoed grain into non-Soviet markets. By behaving otherwise, so as to protect its share of the world market and to relieve some short-run domestic political and economic pressures to terminate the embargo, the United States only aggravated the problems of non-co-operation already being encountered within the international grain trading system.

Notes

1. John C. Roney, 'Grain Embargo as Diplomatic Lever: Fulcrum or Folly?', SAIS Review, no. 4 (Summer 1982), p. 197.
2. Ibid., p. 195.
3. Ibid.
4. New York Times, 12 Jan. 1980, p. D1.
5. New York Times, 11 Jan. 1980, p. D1; The Economist, 19 January 1980, p. 44.
6. Jimmy Carter, Keeping Faith (Bantam, New York, 1982), p. 477.

7. New York Times, 11 Jan. 1980, p. D13.
8. Roney, 'Grain Embargo', p. 198.
9. United States Department of Agriculture, Foreign Agricultural Circular, FG-4-81, 28 January 1981; U.S. Wheat Associates Newsletter, Washington, D.C., 11 April 1980 p. 2.
10. United States Department of Agriculture, Foreign Agriculture Circular, FG-4-81, 28 January 1981.
11. U.S. Wheat Associates Newsletter, Washington, D.C., 8 February 1980, p. 2; United States Department of Agriculture, Foreign Agriculture Circular, FG-15-80, 9 May 1980, p. 3.
12. National Farmer's Union Washington Newsletter, 20 June 1980, p. 3; United States Department of Agriculture, Foreign Agriculture Circular, FG-23-82, 15 July 1982, p. 28.
13. U.S. Wheat Associates Newsletter, Washington, D.C., 11 July 1980, p. 3.
14. United States Department of Agriculture, Foreign Agriculture Circular, FG-25-82, 12 August 1982, p. 5.
15. Roney, 'Grain Embargo', p. 198; United States Department of Agriculture, Foreign Agriculture Circular, FG-34-80, 11 December 1980, p. 6.
16. United States Library of Congress, Congressional Research Service, 'Agriculture: U.S. Embargo of Agricultural Exports to U.S.S.R.', Issue Brief IB 80025, August 1981, p. 13.
17. Lafayette Journal Courier, 24 June 1980, p. 1.
18. U.S. Wheat Associates Newsletter, Washington, D.C., 11 July 1980, p. 1; see also Department of State Telegram, UNCLAS STATE 2306 19, FM SECSTATE Wash DC to AMEMBASSY Moscow, R291727Z, AUG 80.
19. Milling and Baking News, 8 July 1980, p. 14.
20. New York Times, 3 Mar. 1980, p. D5.
21. Allan P. Mustard, 'Impact of the U.S. Grain Embargo on World Grain Trading Patterns and Soviet Livestock Output', unpublished Thesis, Master of Science in Agricultural Economics, Graduate College of the University of Illinois at Urbana-Champaign, 1982, p. 41.
22. Dale Hathaway, 'Foreign Policy and Agricultural Trade', speech presented at Seminar on Agriculture and Foreign Policy, University of Minnesota, 29 April 1982.
23. Milling and Baking News, 8 July 1980, p. 14.
24. National Farmer's Union Washington Newsletter, Washington, D.C., 13 June 1980, p. 3; Milling and Baking News, 8 July 1980, p. 14.
25. Milling and Baking News, 5 Aug. 1980, p. 12.
26. New York Times, 29 Nov. 1980, p. D1.
27. United States Department of Agriculture, Foreign Agriculture Circular, FG-25-82, 12 August 1982; FG-19-81, 12 May 1981.

28. Wall Street Journal, 27 Oct. 1980, p. 32.

29. United States Department of Agriculture, Foreign Agriculture Circular, FG-25-82, 12 August 1982, p. 5; Milling and Baking News, 11 November 1980, p. 12.

30. U.S. Wheat Associates Newsletter, Washington, D.C., 18 April 1980, p. 2.

31. Le Monde, 8 Jan. 1980, p. 5. This was the explanation offered in public by French Foreign Minister M. Francois-Poncet in Paris, two days after the embargo announcement:

'La France ne dispose pas de cereales exportables vers Union Sovietique pour une raison extremement simple: les courants commerciaux francais en matiere de cereales sont exclusivement, ou a peu pres, orientes vers la Communaute economique europeenne et les prix que nous obtenons dans cette Communaute n'ont rien a voir avec les prix du marche mondial. Par consequent, il n'y a pas de cereales disponibles pour l'ajaire que vous dites...'

32. U.S. Wheat Associates Newsletter, Washington, D.C., 10 April 1981, p. 1.

33. New York Times, 30 Oct. 1980, p. D1; U.S. Wheat Associates Newsletter, Washington, D.C., 30 October 1980, p. 1.

34. US Library of Congress, CRS, 'Agriculture: U.S. Embargo', p. 15.

35. Department of State Telegram, UNCLAS PARIS 27224, TOFAS 433, R281731Z AUG 80, FROM AMEMBASSY PARIS TO USDA WASHDC, 'EC Flour Sales to USSR'.

36. Milling and Baking News, 3 February 1981, p. 1.

37. United States Department of Agriculture, Foreign Agriculture Circular, FG-25-82, 12 August 1982, p. 5; FG-19-81, 12 May 1981, p. 5.

38. The Economist, 15 March 1980, p. 36; United States Department of Agriculture, Foreign Agriculture, April 1982, p. 21.

39. United States Department of Agriculture, Foreign Agriculture Circular, FG-2-81, 15 January 1981; New York Times, 29 Nov. 1980, p. D30.

40. United States Library of Congress, 'Agriculture: US Embargo', p. 15.

41. United States Department of Agriculture, Foreign Agriculture Circular, FG-4-81, 28 January 1981.

42. US Library of Congress, 'Agriculture: U.S. Embargo', p. 15.

43. Milling and Baking News, 24 June 1980, p. 9.

44. United States Department of Agriculture, 'Update: Impact of Agricultural Trade Restrictions on the Soviet Union', Foreign Agricultural Economic Report, No. 160, July 1980, p. 2.

45. United States Department of Agriculture, Foreign Agriculture Circular, FG-15-81, 13 April 1981, p. 2.

46. United States Library of Congress, 'Agriculture: U.S. Embargo', p. 28; Boston Globe, 17 Jan. 1980, p. 9.

47. United States Library of Congress, 'Agriculture: U.S. Embargo', p. 25.

48. Carter, Keeping Faith, p. 478.

TABLE 10.1

Total USSR Grain Imports by Country of Origin
(Million Metric Tons)

Country of Origin	Calendar Year 1979 Volume	% of Total	Jan. 1980-Apr. 1981 Volume	% of Total
United States:	19.4	77.6%	10.96	27.1%
Non-U.S. Total:	5.6	22.4	29.51	72.9
Argentina	1.9	7.4	11.13	27.5
Australia	1.2	5.0	5.34	13.2
Canada	2.1	8.3	6.48	16.0
EC	.2	.8	1.38	4.6
Other	.2	.9	4.68	11.6
All-Origin Total:	25.0	100.0%	40.47	100.0%

Sources: USDA, FG-25-82 Aug. 12, 1982, p. 5. FG-19-81, May 12, 1981, p. 5. January-June and CY 79 figures from private communication with USDA.

TABLE 10.2

U.S. Grain Exports & Soviet Grain Imports,
Calendar Years 1979-1980

	1979 (Pre-Embargo)	1980 (Embargo)	ROG
U.S. Grain Exports			
Total Volume:	100.8 MMT	109.8 MMT	8.9%
% to USSR:	21.3%	6.2%	
% to Other:	78.7%	93.8%	
Soviet Grain Imports	25.0 MMT	28.7 MMT	4.8%
% From U.S.:	77.6%	24.0%	
% From Other:	22.4%	76.0%	

Sources: U.S. Department of Agriculture, FG-19-81, May 12, 1981, p. 5. Calendar Year trade figures provided by Trade and Economic Information Division, International Agricultural Statistics, Foreign Agricultural Service, USDA.

TABLE 10.3

U.S. Share of World Exports (July-June Year)

	1978-79	1979-80	1980-81
Wheat & Wheat Flour:	44.9%	43.3%	44.8%
Course Grains:	63.1%	71.0%	69.0%
Total Grains:	55.0%	58.2%	57.5%

Source: FG-26-82, August 16, 1982.

TABLE 10.4

USSR Total Grain Imports Quarterly
(Million Metric Tons)

Quarter	1979	1980	1981
I	2.3	7.0	9.1
II	6.2	6.9	10.2
III	9.0	5.9	10.8
IV	7.5	8.9	10.0
Total:	25.0	28.7	40.1

Source: FG-19-81 May 12, 1981; FG-25-82, August 12, 1982; 1979 quarters I and II supplied by USDA, ERS.

TABLE 10.5

Soviet Grain Imports and Feed Use, 1979-80 (July-June Year)
(Million Metric Tons)

	Imports	Feed Use
Pre-Embargo Projection:	37.5	128
Actual:	31.0	123
Estimated Reductions Attributable to Embargo:	6.5	5

Source: USDA, FG-23-79, Dec. 11, 1979; FG-35-82, Nov. 12, 1982; FG-12-80, Apr. 10, 1980.

TABLE 10.6

USSR Cattle, Hog, and Poultry Inventories on State & Collective Farms as of November 1 (Millions Head)

Year	Cattle	Hogs	Poultry
1978	88.6	57.7	573.1
1979	89.3	57.5	616.1
1980	90.0	57.7	655.5
1981	90.3	57.6	674.2

Source: USDA FG-45-81, Dec. 11, 1981, p. 3.

TABLE 10.7

January-October Average Liveweights at Slaughter for Cattle and Hogs (Kilograms)

Year	Cattle	Hogs
1978	366	105
1979	363	104
1980	355	101
1981	350	101

Source: FG-45-81, December 11, 1981, p. 3.

TABLE 10.8

Soviet Production of Meat and Milk (Million Metric Tons)

Year	Total Meat	Milk
1978	15.5	94.7
1979	15.3	93.3
1980	15.0	90.6

Source: Cole, Table 4, p. 24.

Chapter Eleven

ECONOMIC IMPACT ON THE UNITED STATES OF THE PIPELINE SANCTIONS

Bernard M. Wolf

This chapter deals with the economic impact on the United States of imposing an embargo on US exports and on goods made elsewhere employing US technology, both of which were destined for use in the Soviet Union's project to build additional pipelines to transport natural gas from Siberia to Western Europe. The embargo on the re-export of US-origin goods was applied unilaterally in December 1981, ostensibly in reaction to the events in Poland. In June 1982 the embargo was tightened by extending it to goods produced outside of the United States, both by foreign subsidiaries of US firms and by other firms operating under US licences. After vigorous protests from Western European governments and orders by these governments for firms to proceed with the production and shipping of goods for the project, the United States lifted the embargo in November 1982.

Background

The Soviet Union in the late 1960s began concluding agreements with Western European countries and firms to supply natural gas from the Siberian fields, discovered in the mid-1960s. The agreements were essentially 'gas for pipes' deals which utilised Western capital to develop the export capacity. By 1980-81 the Soviet Union was eager to increase its supplies to Western Europe and began discussing the possibility of agreements involving $10-$15 billion of European capital.[1] For the Soviet Union the increased pipeline capacity would provide badly needed foreign exchange and would be a relatively inexpensive way of developing the gas fields, both for export and domestic use. This was of high priority in view of the Soviet Union's dwindling oil supplies. On the other side, the Western Europeans found the prospects attractive since it would provide a relatively inexpensive supply of energy, the means to diversify their energy sources (away from the Middle East), and the ability to conserve European energy supplies. It would also result in potentially large contracts for equipment. The latter is particularly welcome in times of recession since the equipment purchases would be largely from depressed industries such as steel. Moreover, some governments suggested that these dealings with the Soviet Union might contribute to improved political relations between them and the Soviet Union.[2]

The United States was extremely hostile to the proposals, citing: (1) that increased dependence by Western Europe on Soviet gas might make the region more receptive to the Soviet view of the world; and (2) that the increased foreign exchange would be used by the Soviet Union to bolster its sagging economy. In response to US criticism, the Europeans argued that only about 4 per cent of their energy supplies would be Soviet-sourced, which would not give the Soviet Union a great deal of leverage over their economies. In addition, if the pipeline were indeed a good source of foreign exchange for the Soviet Union, it was not too likely to jeopardise this by threatening to cut off gas supplies.

As talks between Western European governments and the Soviet Union moved to 'a more concrete stage' in 1981, the project was reduced in scale.[3] Only US $5 billion in official and private credit lines were required. These would be used chiefly for turbines, compressors, pipes and auxiliary equipment for the line which was scheduled to open in 1984 and be in full operation by 1987 or 1988. The project shrank in size, perhaps in part due to the US government's efforts to squash the agreement. However, Hewett cites as a more important reason the downward revision by Europeans of 'their likely future energy needs (reflecting both energy conservation achievements and falling GNP growth rates)'.[4] In addition to the equipment requirements for the pipeline to the West, Europeans might receive further contracts for an additional US $10 to $15 billion for the construction of domestic gas lines.[5]

The US Embargo

Unable to persuade the Europeans not to go ahead with the scaled-down pipeline project, the Reagan Administration, citing its authority under the Export Administration Act of 1979, in December 1981 declared that US-made goods could not be exported for use in the pipeline. Previously-approved export licences were cancelled. The embargo was part of a package of measures announced as a response to the imposition of martial law in Poland.

Given that the equipment supplied by the United States for the pipeline was not that close to the frontiers of knowledge, it could readily be duplicated in Europe or Japan, albeit with some delays. Realising that the export embargo was having little effect, the United States on 18 June 1982 extended the embargo, apparently without consulting its allies in Europe, to include goods manufactured outside of the United States by either foreign subsidiaries of US firms or other firms operating under US licences. Thus, goods produced in the United States or by US-controlled corporations abroad or those embodying US technology would not be permitted to be shipped to the Soviet Union for use in the pipeline project. Contracts already signed, which came under the ruling, could not be fulfilled so that the regulations included retroactive application. Sanctions would be imposed on those firms violating the regulations. No compensation was offered to those firms suffering losses as a result of the embargo. The action was taken just after the Versailles Summit, in which the allies had agreed on their economic approach to the Soviet Union (see Versailles Communique), although the United States clearly felt that the accord had not gone far enough. The United States was asserting a right to control

> the re-exports of US origin goods and technology, no matter how many hands the goods pass through, entailing the imposition of penalties on any person of whatever nationality or residence, however remote from the original export transaction, who fails to observe the control. The penalties include 'denial of export privilege's (blacklisting of companies against receiving further export or re-export licences) and fines, and, for individuals, imprisonment.[6]

The United States was applying its economic regulations extraterritorially in order to pursue foreign policy objectives.

European reaction to the Reagan Administration's embargo was swift. The British, French, Germans and Italians (and the European Community as a whole) protested loudly. In one way or another, companies incorporated in these countries, were told by their respective governments to ignore the embargo. In July the FRG government permitted a consortium of banks to provide up to US $1.6 billion in credits for the pipeline.[7] The United Kingdom, France and Italy, with much publicity, allowed goods to be shipped to the Soviet Union in defiance of the ban. With respect to the latter, in August and September 1982 the United States Department of Commerce felt forced to issue regulations that penalised companies which were violating the embargo. It was clear that the Europeans were able to circumvent the US regulations even in the short run. In the longer run, European production could replace US exports since the US firms had already supplied the technology. As Hewett points out, 'the most critical and technically sophisticated parts - the turbine rotors and blades' were, in part, to be produced by the French firm Alsthom Atlantique under a licence from General Electric (U.S.). The French firm could expand its capacity to replace those rotors and blades which were to be exported by General Electric. This would take additional time and expense, but it could be done.[8]

Finally, realising that the ban was a bit like closing the barn door when the horse was already out (and perhaps recognising the other costs, which will be enumerated below), President Reagan on 13 November, 1982 lifted the ban. He did so under a face-saving gesture by announcing that the United States had reached an agreement on East-West trade with some of its Western European allies. It would seem that the United States achieved very little in terms of utility from the sanctions. The Europeans contend that the agreement involves no major concessions on their part. With one apparent exception, the agreement does not go beyond the Versailles Communique.[9] The one exception is an undertaking not to sign or approve new contracts for the purchase of natural gas while a series of studies is carried out. However, this concession seems to mean little since it is unlikely that any new agreements would have been signed during the current oil glut and the studies should take only a matter of months to complete.[10] It is interesting that France refused to be a party to the agreement. The French maintained adamantly that the June regulations were 'unilateral and unjustified'; they had to be removed without any element of *quid pro quo*.[11]

Martin Feldstein, the Chairman of the US President's Council of Economic Advisors, indicated, according to the *New York Times*, that the sanctions had 'worked temporarily'. 'I think we have inflicted some pain,' he said, 'but we were also creating some side effects for our allies and ourselves so it was an inefficient way to penalize the Russians. We were hurting the allies and ourselves.'[12] In the next section, the costs of the pipeline sanctions are analysed.

Costs of the Embargo to the United States: Immediate Effects

In discussing the costs of the embargo to the United States, initial consideration will be given to the immediate effects. These include the impact on exports and the impact on revenue received from licensing the technology both to subsidiaries of US firms and to foreign-controlled firms, as well as the impact on profits earned by the foreign subsidiaries.

The only estimates which are available are those provided by the Under-Secretary of the Department of Commerce, Lionel Olmer, while the sanctions were still in effect:

> Over the next 3 years, the United States will probably lose $300-600 million in exports, direct and through third countries, to the U.S.S.R. as a result of the December 29, 1981 controls relating to oil and gas equipment and technology.
> Over the next 3 years, foreign subsidiaries as well as technology licensees of U.S. firms could lose as much as $1.6 billion in business with the Soviet Union as a result of the June 18 amendment and expansion of the controls.[13]

Even when these estimates are adjusted to take into account the multiplier effect on income associated with those costs, the per annum overall fall in gross national product for an economy operating at a rate of three trillion dollars would not be significant.

However, the loss would not be distributed evenly within the United States. For example, with respect to exports, the most heavily involved firms, General Electric and Caterpillar, already suffering from the recession, would be the big losers.[14] Their employees and suppliers would also be directly affected as would the communities in which General Electric, Caterpillar and their suppliers would have manufactured the lost exports.

Thus, the immediate losses from exports (as well as from subsidiary dividends and licensing revenue) would have been consequential for individual firms or regions of the United States. In fact, their losses were large in spite of the fact that the sanctions were lifted in November 1982.[15] However, the overall US economy was hardly affected over the period. The large losses to the US economy do not lie in the immediate effects stemming from totalling the dollars associated with the cancellation of existing contracts but in the longer-term consequences.

Longer-Term Effects on US Firms

United States firms can service an international market through exporting, licensing or foreign direct investment. Any of these forms allows the firm to utilise its specific know-how in additional markets and thereby collect quasi-rents on the knowhow.[16] For example, the know-how may be based on research and development done by the firm leading to a product or group of products that is technologically advanced, or the know-how may be in the form of adept product differentiation. Either way, additional sales to the firm from servicing an international market help reduce the average cost of developing the firm's specific advantage. Moreover, with some types of technology, an industry standard becomes established. Firms whose products serve as the standard often accrue advantages of being first in the market. Moreover, with large volumes, they can advance along the 'learning' or 'experience' curve more quickly and hence reduce their costs.[17] Interference with the ability of US firms to service foreign markets reduces their international competitiveness and strengthens foreign competitors. Hence, the pipeline sanctions represent a long-term cost to the United States.

The pipeline sanctions have made it more difficult for US firms to be seen as reliable exporters not only to the Soviet Union, but also to areas where an embargo is a possibility, albeit remote, or on products in which such an embargo could occur. Thus trade may be diverted from US suppliers. The Economist reported that 'since business hates uncertainty, American multinationals are beginning to complain that they are being excluded from consortia formed to win contracts in sanction prone Middle Eastern, third world and communist countries'.[18] United States competitors do not hesitate to mention the possibility of an embargo in their sales promotions. With respect to military goods, The Economist quoted a vice-president of the French aircraft manufacturer, Dassault, as saying that 'Greece needs a plane that is not subject to embargoes on its missiles, spaces or ammunition'. Hence, the Greek government should buy a French plane rather than a US one.[19] In the area of agricultural products there is evidence of this difficulty from an earlier export ban. According to Rosenthal and Knighton, as a result of the United States' decision to embargo soya beans in 1973 in order to reduce pressure on domestic prices, Japanese trading companies found new sources of supply in Brazil, and that country continued to supply substantial exports of soya beans to Japan after the United States resumed exporting.[20]

Not only with respect to exporting may the United States be shunned; it may also find greater difficulty in licensing technology to foreign firms if there are strings attached to the use of the technology. The limitations may be enough for firms to choose other rival technologies or to attempt developing the know-how themselves, thereby reducing US royalties from the licensing of technology.[21] They may in fact be encouraged to create their own high technology through a variety of incentives provided by their home governments so as to establish their 'independence' from the United States.[22]

US multinational enterprises (MNEs) operating abroad may also find themselves discriminated against by foreign governments. The OECD Declaration of National Treatment on Investment stipulates 'that host countries should not, except in exceptional circumstances, discriminate between domestic enterprises and those with foreign shareholdings'.[23] However, the case for such non-discrimination or 'national treatment' clearly is weakened if the subsidiary is subject to directives from the source country. One cannot expect equal treatment when a subsidiary is subject to potentially conflicting laws.

As a consequence of the pipeline sanctions, foreign direct investment through takeovers may become more difficult for US multinationals. When the British Monopolies Commission in 1981 'came out against a bid by Enserch Corporation of America for Davy Corporation, The United Kingdom's largest international contracting firm, it cited the threat of extraterritorial application of US export controls'. The Economist indicated that the Commission was criticised for using such an alarmist argument, but it concluded 'Today it cannot be'.

> The Reagan administration's attempt to compel American subsidiaries incorporated in foreign countries to disobey the laws of their host governments, and compel foreign companies of all sorts to break contracts to supply equipment for a pipeline bringing gas from Siberia to Western Europe, is exactly the sort of outreach Britain's monopolies commission had in mind.[24]

The possibility that the earlier application of extraterritoriality by the United States has led to restrictions on foreign direct investment is cited by Rosenthal and Knighton.[25] They suggest that it may have been one of the considerations for the setting up of the Canadian Foreign Investment Review Agency. Both the inability to rationalise manufacturing in Canada because of the applicability of US anti-trust laws,[26] and the US attempt to block the Canadian subsidiary of a US MNE from shipping locomotives to Cuba tended to make the Canadian public more receptive to the idea of screening incoming foreign direct investment.

Another fallout from the pipeline sanctions is that the United States will find it more difficult to resist retroactive legislation by other countries detrimental to US MNEs when the United States itself imposes such measures. Disallowing exports already under contract was certaintly retroactive. In the case of Canada, the National Energy Programme contained some retroactivity by giving the Canadian government claim on part of the oil discoveries made on off-shore tracts. The United States was vigorous in its criticism, but in future that may be looked upon as engulfing the same kind of hypocrisy as that of the United States instituting the pipeline sanctions almost simultaneously with extending grain sales to the Soviet Union.

At the same time that US foreign direct investment may

be less welcome in some host countries because of extraterritoriality, US MNEs may in some limited circumstances seek out additional foreign direct investment to circumvent US export laws. Such a case occurs when it is widely held that the United States can forbid exports from domestic firms but is powerless because of the actions of host governments to stop exports form overseas subsidiaries. This, too, can be viewed as a distortion since the foreign direct investment is not taking place on the basis of lower costs or other advantages. Rather, it takes place as a means to circumvent trade restrictions much the same way that recent protection directed against the Japanese has led to large increases in Japanese foreign direct investment in the United States and in Western Europe.

Finally, attention is focused on the actions that MNEs themselves may take if they are subject to periodic episodes of extraterritoriality. Potentially large damage may be done to the way in which MNEs allocate their resources on a world-wide basis. If multinational firms find increasing difficulty in being allowed to ship goods from one subsidiary to another, they will have to scale down efforts to integrate their world-wide activities. Increasingly in the last decade, MNEs have been promoting specialisation in their subsidiaries in order to take advantage of scale economies. One way is to integrate vertically, whereby outputs from one subsidiary are used as inputs in another subsidiary. The other way is through horizontal integration, whereby particular products are allocated to a given subsidiary which produces these on a regional or even global basis.[27] When the horizontal integration includes the assigning of research and development activity to the subsidiary manufacturing a particular group of products, it is called world or global product mandating (WPM). Canada, in particular, has been anxious to obtain WPMs so as to make its manufacturing sector more efficient.[28]

United States-based multinationals will be reluctant to continue this specialisation if restrictions are placed by the United States (or other countries) on what may be exported to whom. Such interference with the division of labour among subsidiaries will lead to a decline in both intra-industry and intra-firm international trade.

In fact, the sanctions act very much like protection in their impact on international trade. It can be recalled that the extreme protection of the 1930s exacerbated the Great Depression. At the moment, the world finds itself at a cross roads. On the one hand, the General Agreement on Tariffs and Trade (GATT) Tokyo Round is reducing tariffs over a wide range of products in a series of eight annual cuts ending in 1987. On the other hand, many cases of new non-tariff barriers are showing up with rapid frequency. The recently concluded export restraint agree-

Europe are good examples.[29] The sanctions are one more weight on the side of protectionism. In addition, the fact that the sanctions were directed at a particular country helps indirectly to undermine the non-discriminatory basis of the GATT. It became increasingly difficult for the United States to be a convincing and staunch supporter of GATT while it practiced discrimination in trade.

Having outlined the negative effects of the pipeline sanctions for US exports, royalties from licensing, foreign direct investment and the ways in which US-based MNEs can allocate their resources on a world-wide basis, it can be seen that the potential for damage to international trade and investment is considerable. Thus, it is no wonder that US business on the whole has been hostile to the sanctions. Such hostility, of course, worsens government-business relations which is another cost of the pipeline sanctions to the Reagan Administration.

Other Longer-Term Effects

Besides the direct impact on US-owned firms, there will be other long-term effects on the United States. These include: (1) lower levels of foreign direct investment in the United States; (2) possible extended use of extraterritoriality by other countries; and (3) the desire for compensation in some form from Western Europeans who suffered losses because of the pipeline sanctions.

There will be costs to the United States of actions by foreign firms operating or potentially operating in the United States. First, if the United States continues to be prone to imposing export bans on non-strategic goods in peace time, foreign multinationals will hesitate in establishing plants in the United States which would serve an export market that could be the subject of an embargo. Thus, foreign direct investment in the United States could be curtailed. However, the reduction is likely to be small.

Existing foreign multinationals operating in the United States might also more frequently become subject to applications of extraterritoriality if these source countries copy the US lead in pursuing extraterritoriality. For example, during the Falklands/Malvinas crisis the United Kingdom could have called upon UK-based firms operating in the United States not to ship goods to Argentina, or told UK-owned banks operating in the United States not to make loans to its adversary.[30] An escalation of extraterritoriality cannot be ruled out if the United States does not practice some restraint.

Another factor worthy of consideration on the cost side is an implicit demand for compensation on the part of the Europeans for the losses incurred as a result of shipments which were delayed by the halt in US exports. Given that the Europeans feel that the pipeline embargo was totally unjustified, they will likely use their claims in pressing other issues with the United States, thereby weakening the latter's bargaining position. No doubt the NATO Alliance was strained by the pipeline episode, and efforts will be needed to mend fences.[31]

For the Europeans, the pipeline sanctions were particularly difficult to accept in light of the earlier US decision to extend the grain agreement with the Soviet Union at the strong urging of its farmers.[32] A noted US economist, Lester C. Thurow, observed that 'to stop Europe from exporting machinery while we continued to export grain is simply hypocrisy of the highest order'.[33] The impression was that the United States was willing to impose burdens on European workers who are dependent on sales of equipment for the pipeline 'but it (was) unwilling to impose similar burdens on farmers at home'.[34] Thus, the sanctions could be construed as a 'beggar thy neighbour' policy.

The United States tried to claim that the grain purchases required the use of the Soviet Union's scarce foreign currency and made the Soviet Union more dependent on the United States, whereas the gas provided foreign exchange to the Soviet Union. Richard N. Cooper, a Harvard University economist, suggested in testimony to the Senate Sub-Committee that such reasoning 'represents a version to a mercantilistic fallacy that money (in this case foreign exchange) helps an economy but goods do not'.[35] Moreover, the claim lost even more of its credibility when the United States provided subsidies for the grain sale. Milton Friedman pointed out that it is 'one thing to sell the Soviets goods for hard cash, a very different thing to subsidize the export of goods through cheap credit guaranteed by government'.[36]

Lessons for the United States

With the costs of the pipeline sanctions fairly high and, at least in retrospect, a view that the probability of success was quite low, why did the United States Administration take the steps? Perhaps it misjudged the probabilities, or perhaps it felt so strongly about the issue that it was willing to take a course of action with only a minimal chance of success. However, the pipeline case must be put into the context of prior application of extraterritoriality by the United States. In part, the United States Administration may have been following previous procedures. Rosenthal and Knighton indicate that the United States in the post-war period has generally followed 'an aggressive approach to extraterritorial enforcement'. They suggest that:

> one reason is foreign trade has not, traditionally, been a significant component of gross national product in the U.S. economy....If your primary concern is the regulation of your internal market and you are not particularly dependent upon foreign trade, you need be less concerned about the negative effects that expansive regulation will have on your own economy or on the reactions of other nations. As a corollary, the wealthier and more powerful you are, the more difficult it is for others to resist your actions. Power, and satisfaction in its exercise, explains much. U.S. extraterritoriality increased as the United States became an international power, and as European nations were especially dependent upon the United States for economic assistance...[37]

Thus for the United States with its lesser dependence upon foreign trade and its unrivaled economic power, the relative and absolute costs of extraterritoriality were much lower than for other nations. While this may still be true to some extent, international trade has become much more important to the United States, and its relative international power has declined. For example, its technological lead is not nearly as formidable as before, and it clearly is no longer a leader in many fields. The United States can no longer afford to view the rest of the Western world as dependent upon it, but rather must consider the reality of interdependence. These shifts in turn bring about a change in the balance of costs and benefits to the United States of using economic pressure. In fact, the pipeline debacle, according to Rosenthal, may make the United States in the future less prone to using economic regulations for political aims in times of peace.[38]

The pipeline case is in fact somewhat similar to the Freuhauf France case of the mid-1960s. Freuhauf France, 70 per cent owned by its US parent, had sub-contracted to supply semi-trailers to Berliet, a French company, which was to ship them to China. At the same time, the United States had an embargo on trade with China. The United States Treasury instructed the US parent to cancel the contract. The French government insisted that the shipment be made and had a temporary administrator appointed 'to secure the implementation of the Berliet contract in the interest of the company'.[39] The United States backed down and accepted the fact that, since the US subsidiary was temporarily not controlled by the parent, no action would be taken against the parent company or the US directors of the French subsidiary. The major difference between 1965 and 1982 is that the costs to the United States of its attempts to stop the exports have become far greater.

Conclusions

The sanctions failed to have any significant impact on the construction of the pipeline for three reasons:

1. The embargo came too late to prevent the US technology from becoming available to US overseas subsidiaries and to US licensees whose output could not be controlled by the United States. However, even if the sanctions had been invoked earlier, the technology was such that it could either be obtained elsewhere or developed. Hence, the sanctions at most would have merely led to delay and some cost escalation.
2. The regulations trampled too much on what host countries felt were their rights. These countries completely rejected the application of extraterritorality in this instance since the goods in question were not strategic and the sanctions in part were imposed retroactively.
3. The Western Europeans also viewed the sanctions as being hypocritical on the part of the United States. While European-based producers were supposed to halt their pipeline-related exports to the Soviet Union, the United States was content to increase its grain shipments to the Soviet Union at the behest of US farmers. The Europeans saw no reason to bear major economic costs without compensation while the United States continued to ship grain.

The fact that the sanctions were a failure and that they were subsequently lifted by the United States probably had the salutary effect of mitigating the long-term costs of the policy. Had the policy achieved its objectives, the cost to the United States in forgone exports, in lost royalties due to the switching from US technology, in strengthening competitors of US-based MNEs, in greater hostility to US direct foreign investment abroad, in the obstacles to the rationalisation of production by US-based MNEs, and in the greater application of policies involving extraterritoriality on the part of other countries would have been far greater. The failure of the sanctions illustrated that the United States was severely limited in its ability to control exports by foreign subsidiaries of US firms and by licensees of US technology. The experience with the pipeline sanctions may make the United States more sensitive in the future to the risks inherent in applying its own laws in other countries for foreign policy purposes, and hence may try to impose its will over other countries with less frequency. If it does not, there could be serious distortions to international trade and investment.

Notes

1. Edward A. Hewett, 'The Pipe Connection: Issues for the Alliance', The Brookings Review I(1) Fall 1982, pp. 15-20.
2. Ibid., p. 18.
3. Ibid.
4. Ibid., p. 19.
5. Ibid.
6. Douglas E. Rosenthal and William M. Knighton, National Laws and International Commerce: The Problems of Extraterritoriality, Chatham House Papers 17 (Royal Institute of International Affairs, London, 1983), pp. 60-1.
7. Newsweek, 26 July p. 60.
8. Hewett, 'The Pipe Connection', p. 20.
9. New York Times, 14 Nov. p. 1.
10. Ibid.
11. Ibid.
12. Ibid.
13. Lionel H. Olmer, Prepared Statement, Hearings on the Implications of U.S. Export Controls Related to the Soviet Gas Pipeline, Economic Relations with the Soviet Union, Sub-Committee on International Economic Policy, United States Government Printing Office, (Washington, D.C., 30 July 1982), p. 11.
14. Erskine C. Chapman, Prepared Statement, Hearings on United States Assertion of Extraterritoriality with Respect to the Soviet-European Pipeline, Sub-Committee on International Economic Policy, United States Government Printing Office, (Washington, D.C., 3 March 1982), pp. 10-12.
15. United States Senate, Economic Relations with the Soviet Union, Hearings Before the Sub-Committee on International Economic Policy and the Committee on Foreign Relations, Ninety-Seventh Congress, Second Session (United States Government Printing Office, Washington, D.C., 1982).
16. John H. Dunning, International Production and the Multinational Firm (London, Allen and Unwin, 1981); Bernard M. Wolf, 'Industrial Diversification and Internationalization: Some Empirical Evidence', The Journal of Industrial Economics XXVI-2 December 1977), pp. 177-91.
17. Bernard M. Wolf, 'World Product Mandates and Freer Canada-United States Trade', in Alan Rugman (ed.), Multinationals and Technology Transfer: The Canadian Experience (Praeger, New York, 1983).
18. The Economist, 30 October 1982, pp. 16, 19.
19. The Economist, 19 February 1983, p. 44.
20. Rosenthal and Knighton, National Laws, p. 82.

21. Josh Moskau, 'Reagan's Sanctions: Conflict by Accident', Europe II-3 (Autumn 1982), pp. 12-18.
22. Richard N. Cooper, Prepared Statement, Hearings on Economic Policy Toward the Soviet Union, Economic Relations with the Soviet Union on Foreign Relations, United States Government Printing Office, Washington, D.C., 1982) p. 158.
23. Rosenthal and Knighton, National Laws, p. 63.
24. The Economist, 30 October 1982, p. 16.
25. Rosenthal and Knighton, National Laws, pp. 30-1.
26. Ibid, pp. 30-31.
27. John H. Dunning, 'Changes in the Level and Strategy of International Production: The Last 100 Years', in Mark Casson (ed.), The Growth of International Business, (London, England: George Allen & Unwin, London), pp. 84-139.
28. Wolf, 'World Product Mandates'.
29. The Economist, 19 February 1983, pp. 11-22.
30. The Economist, 30 October 1982, p. 19.
31. William R. Cline, 'Reciprocity': A New Approach to World Trade Policy?', Policy Analyses in International Economics II (Institute for International Economics, Washington, D.C., 1982), p. 22.
32. Globe and Mail, 4 Jan. 1982, p. B16.
33. Newsweek, 26 July 1982, p. 59.
34. Newsweek, 26 July 1982, p. 59.
35. Cooper, Hearings on Economic Policy Towards the Soviet Union, p. 158.
36. Newsweek, 15 November 1982, p. 90.
37. Rosenthal and Knighton, National Laws, p. 9.
38. Globe and Mail, 19 January 1983, p. B2.
39. A. H. Herman, Conflicts of National Laws with International Business Activity (British-North American Committee, London, 1982), p. 34.

PART V

IMPACT OF ECONOMIC SANCTIONS ON THIRD PARTIES

Chapter Twelve

THE IMPACT OF THE ARAB BOYCOTT OF ISRAEL ON THE UNITED STATES AND CANADA

Howard Stanislawski

The Arab economic boycott of Israel introduced extended forms of discriminatory and restrictive trade conditions into Western economic and political life. These provisions were applied to actual or potential commercial partners resident or based in third party states (neither Israel nor any of the Arab League states) and led to a number of statutory, regulatory and investigatory responses in the United States, Canada and European states.[1] This chapter will examine the impact of the Arab economic boycott of Israel on the United States and Canada, reviewing the data compiled in each country, the statutory and regulatory responses to the boycott undertaken in each, and the practical consequences, as far as they can be discerned, of those attempts at statutory and/or regulatory remedy.

The Arab Economic Boycott of Israel

The boycott operation under examination in this paper has its origins in the earliest decades of Jewish-Arab strife in British Mandatory Palestine. In a series of conferences and decisions between 1922 and 1937, boycotts were declared by Arabs in Palestine and by the World Islamic Conference of Jewish 'goods, products, and commercial premises' in Palestine, and such a boycott was declared to be a 'patriotic duty'.[2] At the founding of the Arab League in 1944, one of its stated objectives was to 'frustrate further Jewish economic development in Palestine by means of a boycott against Zionist produce',[3] and Arab League states undertook to prevent the introduction into their countries of Jewish-produced goods.[4] In 1946 a Permanent Boycott Committee was established by the Arab League Council, and it quickly detailed the mechanism of implementing the boycott. A Central Boycott Office (CBO) was established, with each Arab League state responsible for its own boycott operation and overall co-ordination of the boycott of Jewish goods and services assigned to the CBO.

After the establishment of the State of Israel in May 1948, the boycott of Jewish goods and services became a boycott of Israeli goods and services, and the CBO headquarters was moved to Damascus, Syria. In April 1950 a basic change in the scope and policy of the boycott began, extending it from a direct or primary boycott into secondary and tertiary dimensions.[5] By September 1952 the Arab League Council's recommendations entailed the boycott of all companies with branches in Israel and the surveillance of all land, sea and air communications and trade contravening boycott regulations.[6] From that time to the present, third party states and firms have been confronted with problems of extraterritoriality or compulsion in the extended forms of boycott compliance.

In this paper, the following categories of boycott activities will be utilised:

1. The primary boycott is a direct boycott of Israel and Israeli goods and services by Arab states, firms and individuals, by which those Arab states, firms and individuals refuse to do business with Israel. As such, it presents no immediate problem of extra-territoriality or compulsion of third party states.
2. The secondary boycott is an attempt by Arab states, firms or individuals to pressure firms of other countries to refrain from dealing with Israel or Zionists,[7] or to end certain relationships with Israel or Zionists, as a condition of trade with Arab states, firms or individuals. This requirement in effect compels an uninvolved third party state to engage in a boycott against a country with which it may have friendly relations and against which it may not wish to engage in any such action.
3. The tertiary boycott is an attempt by Arab states, firms or individuals to prevent firms of uninvolved third party states from dealing with firms of their own or other similarly uninvolved third party states because of the latter's relationship with Israel or Zionists, as a condition of doing business with Arab states, firms or individuals. This requirement in effect seeks to compel an uninvolved third party state to engage in a boycott against another uninvolved third party with whom or which it may have no quarrel whatever.
4. A fourth type of boycott, or voluntary boycott (also known as a 'shadow boycott' or 'chilling effect'), has come into being as a result of a logical extension of the implications of the secondary and tertiary boycotts. In such cases, firms simply decline to deal with Israel or Zionist-related firms or individuals in any way, even to the point of rejecting attractive and

available business possibilities, for fear of antagonising present or prospective Arab clients.

While application of boycott regulations vary in rigour from one Arab jurisdiction to another, there are basic criteria which are common to all states subscribing to the Arab League's resolutions on the question and accepting the applicability of the provisions of the 'General Principles for the Boycott of Israel', published by the League of Arab States, Central Boycott Office.[8] Third party firms or individuals seeking to engage in business with Arab states, firms or individuals are asked to provide information about their activities; alternatively, information or suspicions about their activities may already have been compiled by the CBO or any of its contributors. Failure to respond to a request for information, the provision of information deemed unacceptable under the boycott regulations, or the presence of suspicions that need not even be cited can lead to the blacklisting of the third party firm. The CBO seeks to invoke boycott restrictions against a firm which:

1. has a main or branch plant in Israel;
2. has an assembly plant in Israel, including firms whose agents assemble their products in Israel, even by their own special arrangements;
3. is assembling in Israel the major portion of the product it is selling to Arab states;
4. maintains general agencies or main offices in Israel;
5. provides Israeli companies with the right to use its trade names or manufacturing processes;
6. holds shares in Israeli companies;
7. renders consultative services and technical expertise to Israeli factories;
8. has directors or managers who are members of joint foreign-Israeli chambers of commerce;
9. acts either as an agent for Israeli companies or as a principal importer of Israeli products outside of Israel;
10. takes part in prospecting for natural resources within Israel;
11. declines to answer questionnaires from Arab authorities requesting information on the nature of its relations with Israel;
12. incorporates in its own products components produced by a blacklisted company;
13. utilises or employs the services or facilities of blacklisted shipping or insurance companies;
14. is pro-Zionist or employs Zionists in high positions;
15. has participated in Jewish organisations or contributed funds to groups active in or on behalf of Israel;
16. directly or indirectly helps Israel's economic growth or war potential;

17. manufactures, anywhere in the world, goods of Israeli-made material or components;
18. sells goods anywhere that are identical to goods imported from Israel (to prevent re-export);
19. invests in any blacklisted company;
20. sells stock to citizens of Israel;
21. appoints an Israeli as a corporate officer;
22. lends money or provides any financial aid in any form to Israeli entities; or
23. takes part in or supports propaganda activities on behalf of Israel.[9]

These many provisions require certification in order to qualify for third party-Arab commerce. Documents involved may be as simple as a 'negative certificate of origin', stipulating that none of the goods involved in a transaction are of Israeli origin, in whole or in part, or as complex as a whole series of attestations to any number of the above items. These many stipulations can be invoked in secondary boycott terms or in tertiary boycott terms. Thus, a third party can be asked to provide any or all of such assurances about itself; it can also be asked to refrain from dealing with any other third party firm which has not passed the same test clearly.

Requests by Arab states, firms or individuals that third party states, firms or individuals comply with boycott-related requests can occur at various phases in a transaction. The request can be made prior to contracts being signed, in the form of a questionnaire or a specific assurance sought as a precondition of trade. It can be required in the actual contractual documents. It can be required in the governing requirements necessary for making payment on the letter of credit utlilised to complete the transaction.[10]

Many different types of boycott clauses have been discovered in US contracts. A 1976 congressional report listed seven types of clauses it had discovered:

1. origin-of-goods clause (referred to above as a negative certificate of origin);
2. Israeli clause, providing assurances regarding the absence of any ongoing contractual relationship with Israel, business in Israel or general contribution to the Israeli economy;
3. shipping clause, stipulating that the vessels transiting cargo are not blacklisted and/or will not call at any Israeli port;
4. insurance clause, stipulating that blacklisted insurance companies will not be used in insuring cargoes;
5. blacklisted companies clause, stipulating that the company itself is not blacklisted and/or none of its

parents or subsidiaries are blacklisted and/or it does not or will not do business with a blacklisted company;
6. religion/ethnic clause, stipulating the nationality or religion of personnel to be hired for particular contracts, stipulating activities or memberships in or donations to Jewish organisations, or stipulating references to individuals' beliefs in Zionism, such as 'Zionist tendencies'; and
7. general clause, also known as an omnibus clause, requiring a stipulation that an exporter will 'observe all the rules of the Arab boycott' or 'otherwise comply with the boycott'.[11]

A Canadian non-governmental report discovered the use in Canada of the same seven types of boycott clauses.[12]

The United States Experience

The most extensive investigations of the impact of Arab boycott practices have been undertaken by committees of the United States Congress, and it is in the statutes and regulations of US governments on both the federal and state levels that the discriminatory and restrictive trade impacts of the boycott have been most clearly addressed. While State Department responses in the 1950s were initially tepid, congressional resolutions regarded Arab boycott activity as inimical to US interests and values as early as 1956.[13] A series of boycott-related incidents in the 1950s and 1960s further aroused US reaction. In 1956 Brown and Williamson Tobacco Company stopped selling its US brands to Israel because of 'the very grave and serious threats by certain of the Arab countries'.[14] Coca-Cola, Ford Motor Company, Xerox Corporation, Miles Laboratories, and Topps Chewing Gum were all blacklisted in the 1960s because of relations with Israel.[15] In 1956 American Express closed its offices in Israel, declaring publicly that the closure was based on commercial considerations. The Israeli government stated, however, that it was convinced beyond any doubt that the American Express action had resulted from Arab boycott threats. Within a short period of time after the matter became public, American Express negotiated a reopening of its Israel operations.[16]

Successful resistance to Arab boycott pressures was undertaken by Hilton Hotels Corporation. In 1961, when Hilton was in the final stages of negotiations to build a hotel in Tel Aviv, it received a letter from the Secretary of the American-Arab Association for Commerce and Industry in New York, which threatened the company with the loss of its holdings in Egypt and the end of any plan it might have had for Tunisia, Iraq, Jordan and other Arab countries.[17] In his reply, Conrad Hilton wrote:

> what the Committee proposes is absolutely counter to the principles we live by and which we hold most dear...the principles of Americanism...(and)...the principles under which the Hilton Hotels Corporation goes about the world, establishing hotels so that people of all nations can gather in peace....Our corporation finds it shocking that the Committee should invoke the threat of boycott condemnation in the case of our contract with the people of Israel. Does the Committee also propose to boycott the United States government because it maintains diplomatic relations with Israel?[18]

Refusal to comply with the boycott in this case, as in others that have also been documented, yielded no punitive action. Hilton Hotels continued with its expansion into both Israel and the Arab world without hindrance or further incident.

These and other examples of the impact on US commerce of the Arab boycott prompted governmental action. In 1960 the State Department protested Kuwaiti requests of US firms that they clarify their relations with Israel or face blacklisting.[19] In the same year, the Douglas-Hays Amendment to the Mutual Security Act expressed the sense of Congress as opposed to economic wars, including boycotts, blockages and restrictions on the use of international waterways.[20] Between 1960 and 1965, the State Department permitted the authentication of documents furnished for boycott purposes, unless they were addressed to the Central Boycott Office or contained declarations of creed.[21] After considerable activity, Congress passed an amendment of the Export Administration Act (EAA) of 1965, which required all US exporters to report to the Commerce Department the receipt and nature of any boycott-related request which had the effect of furthering or supporting the Arab boycott. At this time, Section 3(5) of the EAA was passed, stating that

> It is the policy of the United States to oppose restrictive trade practices or boycotts fostered or imposed by foreign countries against other countries friendly to the United States and to encourage and request domestic concerns engaged in the export of articles, materials, supplies, or information, to refuse to take any action, including the furnishing of information or the signing of agreements, which has the effect of furthering or supporting restrictive trade practices or boycotts fostered or imposed by any foreign countries against any country friendly to the United

States.[22]

The principled statement was purely recommendatory. The reporting mechanism required reports. Between October 1965 and February 1967, US firms reported the receipt of 9,281 requests for information from Arab boycott offices, including 4,815 requests for negative certificates of origin, 3,349 for certification that carrying vessels were not blacklisted, 97 for certification that the exporter had no subsidiaries or financial interests in Israel, and 559 miscellaneous requests.[23] Subsequent Commerce Department announcements reduced the overall coverage of this reporting requirement.[24] While the US government had expressed its principled opposition to boycott demands, Commerce Department personnel and documentation continued to disseminate trade information and tender materials containing boycott references.[25]

In the decade following the enactment of the 1965 statute, US-Arab trade increased considerably. By 1971, US exports to 18 Arab states totalled US $1 billion. This increased to US $5.4 billion in 1975, US $6.9 billion in 1976, US $7.15 billion in 1977, and US $8.36 billion in 1978.[26]

By 1974 it was obvious that the 1965 EAA provisions were doing little to prevent US compliance with the boycott. In that year only 785 reports on boycott requests were filed by US companies, and it became clear that many companies were not bothering to file. In the first three quarters of 1974, companies that were filing admitted that they had complied with the Arab demands 50-60 per cent of the time; the other companies did not indicate how they had responded to the requests received. In the final quarter of 1974, companies reporting indicated 80 per cent compliance.[27]

During the 94th Congress (1975-76), ten anti-boycott amendments to the EAA were introduced, together with twelve other anti-boycott bills intoduced as amendments to other legislative items.[28] In March 1975 an investigation into domestic effects of the boycott began under the aegis of the House of Representatives Subcommittee on Oversight and Investigation, chaired by Rep. John E. Moss of California.[29]

Senator Franch Church's Subcommittee on Multinational Corporations held detailed hearings and released to the public the Saudi 'Directory of Boycotted Companies and Establishments' which listed 1,500 US companies on a 1970 blacklist.[30] Senator Church's subcommittee also heard testimony from Colonel William L. Durham, deputy director for military construction for the Army Corps of Engineers, who admitted that the Corps excluded Jews from assignments to Saudi Arabia. He admitted that it is generally known among contractors that a prerequisite for securing a contract in Saudi Arabia is a work visa, and that a company need not apply for a visa or for selection by the Corps if it has Jewish personnel and/or employees of Israeli nationality in key positions.[31]

In response to these pressures, on 26 February 1975 President Ford denounced Arab attempts to utilise discriminatory provisions in doing business with the United States and ordered studies of the boycott's incidence in the United States of its role within the US military services and of the possibilities of dealing with the boycott through antitrust law, civil rights law, or international law.[32]

On 25 November 1975, in an attempt to forestall legislation and pursuant to the studies undertaken in March, President Ford tightened the 1965 Commerce Department's monitoring mechanism, which required all companies to report all requests received and prohibited compliance by US firms with discriminatory clauses. In subsequent months, presidential directives further broadened this programme, requiring banks, freight forwarders and insurance companies to file reports; requiring the inclusion of indications of the responses provided by US firms to boycott requests opening the reports to public inspection (after 7 October 1976); and requiring the Commerce Department to cease disseminating notices of trade opportunities that required boycott compliance.[33]

As a result of these new provisions and the inquiries of the Moss and other subcommittees, substantial information began to be developed or disseminated regarding the incidence of boycott requests in the United States. For example, in the one-year period from 1 October 1975 to 1 October 1976, 3,477 exporters, banks, freight forwarders, insurers and carriers reported the receipt of 169,710 boycott-related requests in connection with 97,491 transactions, with a total value of $7.7 billion. Fifteen per cent of these 169,710 requests were classed discriminatory on the basis of race, religion or national origin. Forty-one per cent involved negative certificates of origin. Just over 33 per cent requested non-blacklisted certifications with respect to carriers or airlines. Thirteen per cent non-blacklisted certification with respect to the manufacturer, supplier or vendor.[34]

In late August 1976, both the Senate and the House of Representatives passed slightly different versions of a comprehensive anti-boycott package, which was to form part of the EAA (which had come up for renewal). A last minute filibuster by Senator John Tower of Texas prevented the appointment of a Conference Committee until the congressional session adjourned for the 1976 elections. Since the EAA expired on 30 September 1976, President Ford was required to continue its existing monitoring and anti-boycott provisions under executive authority bestowed by the Trading with the Enemy Act.[35]

The 94th Congress did, however, pass a significant piece of limited anti-boycott legislation. The Tax Reform Act (TRA) of 1976 contained an amendment authored by Senator Abraham Ribocoff of Connecticut, which denied to US corporations complying with secondary and tertiary boycott clauses (as defined by Treasury regulations) foreign tax credits, tax benefits for domestic international sales corporations (DISCs) and deferral of taxation on foreign income derived by corporations from business in countries requiring boycott participation.[36]

In additon to this legislative initiative, the executive branch undertook a test case to assess the applicability of US antitrust law in cases of tertiary boycotts. In early 1976 the Justice Department charged Bechtel Corporation, a large private construction company, with implementing an agreement to refuse to deal with US subcontractors blacklisted by Arab states and to require all of its US subcontractors to refuse to deal with blacklisted firms. The Justice Department suit argued that Bechtel thus engaged in a conspiracy in restraint of trade contrary to the antitrust provisons of the Sherman Act. On 10 January 1977 Betchel agreed to a settlement, entering into a consent agreement in which it vowed not to participate in such activities in the future. In the agreement, Betchtel said that it would not perform or enforce any provisions providing for the boycott of a US person or firm; would not require any other person or firm to boycott any US blacklisted person; would not sign within the United States any agreement which provides for a boycott; and would not exclude from lists of possible suppliers any US blacklisted firms.[37] While Bechtel subsequently sought to extricate itself from the terms of this consent agreement, appeals have upheld the agreement and Bechtel has remained bound by its provisons.

While these federal initiatives were being undertaken, civil liberties and human rights groups, Jewish organisations, and others seeking anti-boycott legislation undertook activity on the state level to encourage state legislatures to enact their own anti-boycott statutes. Since banking is subject to state regulation, state anti-boycott provisons were able to deal with the important letter of credit aspect of boycott compliance in the United States.

Between 1975 and 1977, wide-ranging anti-boycott statutes were passed by 13 US states. Beginning with New York, whose statute became effective on 1 January 1976, significant measures were enacted in Illinois, Ohio, Maryland, Massachusetts, California, Florida, New Jersey, Minnesota, Washington, Oregon, North Carolina and Connecticut. Anti-boycott legislation was proposed in many other states, including Pennsylvania, Texas, Missouri and Michigan (in all of which it passed one house); and Rhode Island, Georgia and Louisiana (in which the passage of their bills was rendered moot by the enactment of the EAA amendments of 1977, which specifically stated that the act was pre-empting state anti-boycott laws).[38]

In addition to these statutes, executive orders and city council ordinances were passed in a variety of jurisdictions, further strengthening anti-boycott coverage in US law.[39]

State anti-boycott statutes substantively expanded anti-boycott coverage in the United States, and at the same time created an incentive to federal legislators seeking an equalisation of anti-boycott coverage across the country. As well, specific provisions of certain state anti-boycott statutes motivated corporation and interest group action. For example, in response to specific provisions in the California statutes relating to coverage of letters of credit, the California-based Bank of America reportedly began to petition for federal anti-boycott legislation so that national standardisation would prevent the creation of competitive advantages and disadvantages with respect to boycott compliance depending upon the state in which any given corporation was based.[40]

Under the provisions of the EAA of 1977 (renewed 1979), state anti-boycott statutes were specifically pre-empted; non pre-emption is most likely possible only in cases where such provisions were expressly included in the state statutes. In addition, most state anti-boycott statutes did not contain sunset or expiry provisions, and while the EAA normally is in effect for only two or three years, a theoretical possiblility exists that the anti-boycott provisions of the EAA might at some future date expire. At that time, pre-emption might no longer apply, and state anti-boycott provisions might return into effect. Recent legal arguments have suggested that the pre-emption provisions of the EAA may not be as far-reaching as originally believed. In any case, the question of pre-emption will be a matter for judicial interpetation and decison.[41]

Throughout the process of both federal and state consideration of anti-boycott statutes, dire predictions of grave financial disaster to ensue as a consequence of negative Arab reaction to the statutes' enactment were frequently offered. From the very beginning of all of these legislative efforts, however, economic data indicated that little if any trade was lost as a consequence of anti-boycott laws; rather, the data showed, convincingly, that trade continued to increase in a proportion commensurate with previous increases and in a manner consistent with anticipated increases in a context devoid of anti-boycott action.[42]

While the state and municipal initiatives were continuing, federal activity accelerated. Federal legal authorities acknowledged the potential applicability of the Civil Rights Act of 1964 to limited and specific types of cases involving employer-employee discrimination pursuant to secondary and tertiary boycott requests, but it was clear that more extensive and broader legislation was necessary.[43] From 1977 to 1979 the focus of federal attention was primarily on the enactment of comprehensive anti-boycott legislation under the provisions of the EAA, which was administered by the Department of Commerce, and supplementarily on the protection and preservation of the anti-boycott precedent created by the Bechtel consent decree of January 1977. Continuing efforts were also made to protect the coverage provided by the TRA of 1976 and to standardise its regulations with subsequent anti-boycott legislation.

During the 1976 presidential election campaign, Jimmy Carter proclaimed himself committed unequivocally to anti-boycott legislation. After his election, however, Carter Administration officials argued in favour of a limited anti-boycott approach, which only selectively regulated secondary boycott problems.[44] The new Administration argued against the strong anti-boycott proposals being considered by the Senate and House committees. Congress affirmed its intention to proceed with those strong versions despite Administration opposition; consequently, the Administration argued for the inclusion in the proposed bills of provisions being advocated by business groups, which insisted on the need for broad exceptions for unilateral selection of goods and services, for compliance with host-country laws, for limited US extraterritorial reach, for pre-emption with respect to state laws, and for limited reporting.[45]

A major battle loomed between those backing Congressional anti-boycott legislative proposals, including human rights bodies and Jewish organisations, and other major US corporate interests supported by officials of the Carter Administration, the latter being limited in the scope of opposition available to them by President Carter's prior commitment to anti-boycott legislation. To resolve the major difference between these interests, to allow for the acceptance of legitimate interests held by those on both sides in the legislation that was becoming inevitable, and to minimise political damage that could result from a public showdown on the question, the Administration, national Jewish organisations and major corporate interests turned to a new and remarkable effort to resolve the problem - negotiations aimed at achieving a joint statement of principles, which were held between national Jewish organisations and the Business Roundtable, a group composed of the chief executives of 180 of the largest US corporations.[46]

In early 1977, after a period of negotiations, misunderstandings and renewed negotiations between the

Business Roundtable and Jewish organisations, a joint statement of principles was carefully developed that satisfied the basic concerns and requirements of the two sides. The Jewish organisations sought to allow for the inclusion of as few exceptions to the general principles as possible and to construe these exceptions in as narrow a manner as possible. At the same time, they wanted the extraterritorial reach of the statute to be as broad as possible to prevent any circumvention of its provisions through the use of subsidiaries based and/or registered abroad. The Business Roundtable sought the broadest possible exceptions and the narrowest possible extraterritorial application.[47]

In April 1977 the compromise reached between the parties involved acceptance by the Jewish groups of the permissibility of two basic categories of exceptions: US corporations were to be permitted to accede to the unilateral selection by Arab clients of sub-contracted goods or services, insofar as the unilateral selection process did not indicate a pattern of boycott compliance; and US corporations were to be permitted to comply with the local law of the country in which they were resident in the acquisition and importation of goods or services for their own use, though not for resale. The 'Memorandum of Agreement between Business Roundtable and Major Jewish Organizations on Anti-Boycott Amendments and Interpretation of S69, Pending Bill to Extend Export Administration Act' of 26 April 1977 supported legislation to impose the following restrictions:

1. prohibit all forms of religious or ethnic discrimination arising out of a foreign boycott;
2. prohibit US firms from refusing to do business with a boycotted company as a condition of doing business in another country;
3. prohibit US firms from acting as enforcers of a foreign boycott;
4. prohibit US firms from responding to requests for boycott-related information;
5. prohibit the use of negative certificates of origin within one year of the statute's enactment.[48]

A new EAA, incorporating amendments proposed by the memorandum, was signed into law on 22 June 1977. Its provisions, implemented by detailed Department of Commerce regulations, prohibit compliance by US persons with secondary and tertiary boycott conditions. A compulsory, comprehensive reporting mechanism was established, which required that all cases of boycott requests be reported to the Secretary of Commerce, together with information regarding the disposition of those requests, and that the information thus compiled would be available to the public.[49] The EAA amendments of 1977 constitute the most extensive set of anti-boycott provisions enacted in any jurisdiction in the world. As such, they served as a model for anti-boycott legislative efforts elsewhere, especially in Canada.

Throughout debates on enactment of anti-boycott legislation in the United States, pro-Arab forces and corporate spokesmen opposed to anti-boycott legislation issued dire warnings about the potential effects on trade of such statutes. In a series of newspaper advertisements designed to arouse opposition to anti-boycott efforts, Mobil Oil raised the spectre of a loss to the United States of Arab oil if legislation were enacted.[50] Dresser Industries of Dallas, Texas, bought two full pages in the Wall Street Journal in April 1977 to predict that '500,000 jobs hang in the balance as Congress considers more boycott legislation'.[51]

The experience of US export trade with the Arab world since the enactment of anti-boycott statutes has indicated a contrary experience. As early as 14 September 1978, Deputy Assistant Secretary of Commerce Stanley J. Marcuss spoke in Chicago, saying:

> last year's gloomy predictions that passage of the foreign boycott provisions of the Export Administration Amendments would cost thousands of US jobs and severely damage US-Arab trade have not materialized. On the contrary, since the passage of the law, there has been a significant increase in US exports to the 14 Near East/North African boycotting nations.[52]

In April 1978 Burhan Dajani, Secretary-General of the General Union of Arab Chambers of Commerce, Industry, and Agriculture, told a Washington business conference that

> business on both sides has been able to live with these laws. It has been possible to continue the flow of trade.[53]

In 1978 US exports to Arab boycotting states totalled US $8.36 billion, an increase of 16.1 per cent over the 1977 total and one that was higher than the increases of the previous two years. Ironically, during that period, US exports to the three most zealous supporters of the boycott - Libya, Syria and Iraq - increased by 34 per cent in 1978, a fact even more noteworthy because none of these states purchased any US military equipment or armaments.[54]

The available evidence indicates that the major impact of US anti-boycott legislation has been on the Arab states' boycott practices themselves and has led to significant revisions in boycott practices. On 22 February 1977, prior to the enactment of the EAA but in the midst of its consideration by Congress, the Journal of Commerce reported that all the Arab states, with the exception of Iraq, had dropped their requirement for the provision of negative certificates of origin.[55] Stories reporting the weakening of boycott provisions and the rewarding of contractual documents to avoid violating US laws appeared widely in the following months.[56] These economic conclusions were to prove important in Canadian considerations of anti-boycott proposals, though far from determinant.

In September 1979, with little publicity and even less oposition, the EAA was extended for a four-year period, its anti-boycott provisions remaining unchanged. In its implementation, the anti-boycott provisions of the EAA and the TRA have revealed substantial patterns of compliance with the law, together with an apparently increasing determination on the part of US officials to penalise those contravening its various provisions. Throughout these periods of implementation, US exports to Arab boycotting states have continued their previous patterns of increase.

The EAA's anti-boycott provisons are enforced through the activities of the Office of Anti-boycott Compliance (OAC) of the US Department of Commerce, which investigates, undertakes legal actions and provides all the supportive material relevant to implementation of the statutory and regulatory anti-boycott system. In the 1980 fiscal year, the OAC initiated approximately 130 investigations of potential violations and took compliance actions against twelve companies (many for repeated numbers of violations).[57] Ten companies entered into consent agreements with the Department of Commerce, paying US $128,500 in fines for alleged violations and agreeing to develop and implement internal compliance programs to deter further violations. In that year, the OAC received reports of 37,737 restrictive trade practice requests (received from boycotting countries by 1,778 US firms) in 30,500 transactions, with a total value of US $14 billion. Transactions containing prohibited actions totalled 3,047, with a value of US $5.9 billion. Parties reporting these transactions included banks, freight forwarders and insurers, as well as exporters themselves.

In the 1981 fiscal year, 140 investigations were completed, which resulted in the issue of 74 warning letters, three charging letters, and 20 settlement agreements.[58] These 20 companies agreed to pay fines totalling US $385,500, with the largest such settlement involving the 3M Company of St. Paul, Minnesota, and nine of its foreign and domestic subsidiaries, which paid fines of US $137,500 and undertook an extensive compliance programe. In that year, the OAC saw a 23 per cent rise in the numbers of transactions and requests received. A total of 2,118 firms filed reports on 41,659 transactions, with total value rising to US $17.3 billion. A total of 50,204 restrictive trade practice or boycott requests were reported, with banks constituting the largest single category of such reporters. Most requests in this year originated from Kuwait (57 per cent), followed by Saudi Arabia, the United Arab Emirates, Qatar, and Iraq. Transactions requesting prohibited actions totalled 3,219, with a dollar value of US $5.6 billion.

During 1981 US exports to Arab boycotting countries continued to rise, with an overall increase of 25.3 per cent over 1980 figures. Saudi Arabia increased its purchases by 27 per cent. Sales to Iraq jumped by 26.1 per cent and to Libya by 59.8 per cent.[59] Total dollar value of exports increased from US $8.6 billion in 1979 to US $10.3 billion in 1980 and to US $12.9 billion in 1981.

In mid-1982 the US Department of the Treasury issued a report on compliance with the TRA's antiboycott provisions for 1978 and 1979. Since the TRA requires the forfeit by US taxpayers of certain tax benefits and credits, including credits for foreign taxes, deferral of taxes on foreign subsidiaries' earnings and on DISC earnings, taxpayers were required to calculate the size of the benefits lost because of participation or co-operation in the Arab boycott of Israel.[60]

Despite the anti-boycott laws, then, US exports to Arab boycotting states continued to increase significantly. The arms, health care, oil and gas processing, telephone and construction sectors remain major areas for US sales, with arms and health care contracts frequently entailing expenditures of one billion dollars and more. In the first three quarters of 1982, US exports to 13 Arab boycotting countries increased overall by 8.6 per cent to US $10.4 billion, which was over the comparable period in 1981, with exports to Saudi Arabia increasing by 22.6 per cent to US $6.7 billion. In that period, for the first time in more than ten years, the United States achieved a favourable balance of trade with the Arab states, with the dollar value of Saudi exports to the United States (almost entirely composed of oil-related exports) exceeded by US exports to Saudi Arabia.[61] While Saudi purchases continued their substantial increases, US imports of Saudi oil decreased by more than 50 per cent from 1980 to 1982.

In its actions during the 1982 fiscal year, the OAC roughened its approach by substantially increasing the sizes of its per offence fines, and 48 US companies were charged with boycott-related offences. The OAC collected about US $640,000 in fines, including US $189,000 for a record fine given to the Philadelphia National Bank for alleged delays in reporting to the OAC its receipt of 220 letters of credit containing anti-Israel provisions.[62]

The United States, Canada and the Arab Boycott

The US-Arab relationship has grown dramatically since 1973, notwithstanding the extension of boycotting activities to new areas[63] and the enactment and implementation in 1976 and 1977 of rigorous anti-boycott legislation by the Congress. Data collected both prior and subsequent to the introduction of the anti-boycott statutes and regulations indicate that the reciprocal profitability of the US-Arab relationship has continued unabated, with economic factors extraneous to the Arab-Israeli dispute constituting the most significant influences on trade between these states. While the US share of certain specific markets appears to have declined as Japanese and South Korean firms have acquired the expertise, contacts and cost-effective techniques to offer competitively advantageous terms of trade, there is little if any credible evidence that this reflects any boycott-related set of considerations. Substantial alterations in boycott clause terminology have been provided by Arab boycotting states so as to make compliance with US law simpler and much less problematic. In every respect, then, the operations of the US anti-boycott statutory and regulatory system appear to be working successfully, with discriminatory and restrictive trade provisions contrary to US policy rendered illegal, their incidence sharply reduced, offenders punished and US commerce continuing to enjoy the fruits of reciprocally beneficial economic interaction that is free from burdensome and politically unacceptable boycott provisions.

The Canadian Experience

The Canadian experience with the Arab boycott of Israel is one marked by far less substantial governmental documentation of the extent of the problem, far less substantial federal governmental willingness to act to prevent the involvement of Canadians in the Arab boycott system, and virtually unceasing efforts by federal governmental officials to stymie the development of any apparatus that could act with the power of law to control and curtail boycott activities generally regarded by political leaders in Canada as offensive and contrary to Canadian values and practices.

For many years, despite apparent acquiescence by Canadians and Canadian companies in many and varied aspects of Arab boycott requirements, the Canadian government undertook no response of any kind to those pressures. Boycott stipulations were not perceived as significantly intrusive into the Canadian economy, nor were they viewed as causing any serious damage to the Israeli economy. Canada pursued a general economic policy of seeking to maximise all trading opportunities, and contracts of all sorts were pursued by Canadian firms with the support of the Canadian government. Canada only declined to pursue such opportunities when they involved engaging in business with countries which were the objects of UN-sponsored or UN-approved international boycotts. As part of its normal support role, Canadian government personnel abroad forwarded to Canadian firms any and all information relating to transactions, including those known to contain boycott clauses, and Canadian government publications provided information to Canadians on how to comply with boycott stipulations.[64]

The Arab boycott became a more significant Canadian public policy concern in the period following the 1973 Yom Kippur War in the Middle East and the oil price increases and oil embargo that followed. In late April 1975, the Hon. Herb Gray (who had previously been but was not at that time in the federal Cabinet) revealed that the Export Development Corporation (EDC), an important federal Crown Corporation that provided both financing and insurance coverage for export transactions, had been giving export insurance coverage for certain transactions with Arab states, knowing that those transactions were proceeding on terms that included compliance with Arab boycott conditions. He asked the government if it would continue to allow governmental agencies and departments knowingly to participate in contracts containing such discriminatory and restrictive trade provisions. On 8 May 1975, Prime Minister Pierre Elliott Trudeau stated in the House of Commons: 'I think it is sufficient to say that this type of practice is alien to everything the government stands for and indeed to what in general Canadian ethics stand for'.[65] However, this statement of principle was not translated into a statement of policy and policy guidelines aimed at dealing with the Arab boycott question. A statement on 2 June 1975 by Alastair Gillespie, then Minister of Industry, Trade and Commerce (ITC), which committed the government no longer to permit the EDC to ensure discriminatory boycott clauses, was apparently not implemented.[66]

After a lobbying campaign, intense by Canadian standards, on 21 October 1976, the federal government announced an anti-boycott policy to be administered not by means of legislation, but by means of administrative guidelines. This policy, it was stated, could deny government services, support and facilities to companies for specific transactions containing certain types of boycott clauses, which would,

> in connection with the provision of any boycott, require a Canadian firm to: engage in discrimination based on the race, national or ethnic origin or religion of any Canadian or other individual; refuse to purchase from or sell to any other Canadian firm; refuse to sell Canadian goods to any country; or refrain from

purchases from any country.[67]

The policy announcement also stated that the government would require all Canadians to report to the government on their experiences with boycott requests and would make public the names of firms signing unacceptable clauses. While initially this policy seemed attractive to anti-boycott activists, its subsequent haphazard application by ITC, the many loopholes in it that soon became apparent and a number of ex post facto reinterpretations of the policy for the purpose of widening those loopholes, led to intensified lobbying for comprehensive anti-boycott legislation. The January 1977 report of the Commission on Economic Coercion and Discrimination, a citizen's panel composed of distinguished Canadians from all major political parties, served to arouse further large-scale public activity on the issue.[68]

In the midst of the furor of reaction occasioned by the publication of the commission's report, ITC on 21 January 1977 quietly released its guidelines implementing the 21 October 1976 government policy statement.[69] The guidelines were brief - only eight short paragraphs in length - but they made it clear that the policy statement had been watered down considerably. The guidelines appeared to be based on the narrowest possible interpretations and definitions of the four types of clauses mentioned in the October statement, the acceptance of which would result in loss of government support and facilities. They indicated that governmental assistance would be denied only after contracts were actually concluded and signed. Thus, Canadian trade commissioners abroad would continue to forward trade opportunity information on transactions containing boycott clauses that were a direct and clear contravention of Canadian government policy. Promotional services, market information, and all facilities would continue to be made available for any transaction, as long as the boycott clauses, known to be required, were not yet signed. The vast majority of boycott clauses requested from Canadian firms would continue to be acceptable under the parameters of these guidelines; no loss of government assistance would result from acceptance of them.

The reporting mechanism clearly called for in the government's policy statement was simply abandoned in the guidelines. Canadian firms would not have to report anything at all to the federal government regarding their receipt of boycott requests. The guidelines only indicated that ITC officers abroad would report to headquarters in Ottawa those instances of firms approaching them for aid with contracts containing Canadian governmentally unacceptable boycott clauses; that was all. Industry, Trade and Commerce officers in Ottawa would keep track of cases they heard about, and semi-annual reports of the information at their disposal would be made. Thus, a primary objective of the policy statement was not applied. In addition, EDC indicated that the guidelines it would be applying were not necessarily the same as those to be applied by ITC.

The means of publicising the guidelines chosen by ITC officials were also very unusual. In fact, there were none. The document was available only upon request. If firms did not ask for the information, it was not disseminated. As an article in the Financial Post stated, 'The Department is making few efforts to publicize its new rules. That may be because the rules deal only with parts of the policy - and they seem to contain some sizeable loopholes'.[70]

In January and February 1977 Canadian banks offered two reactions to the charges regarding banks' involvement in boycott operations contained in the Cotler Report and to the issuing of the ITC guidelines. Some banks denied any complicity with the boycott and stated their eagerness to receive detailed and definitive governmental guidelines on procedures that were to be followed. In public communications responding to the Cotler Report, officials of the Toronto-Dominion Bank, Bank of Montreal and the Canadian Imperial Bank of Commerce described the technical financial character of their banks' role, which was devoid of any moral or foreign policy implication.[71]

The second type of banking response was more encouraging to those seeking significant anti-boycott action. Officials of the Royal Bank of Canada stated that that bank had not knowingly 'negotiated any letters of credit including terms and conditions commonly referred to as secondary and tertiary boycott provisions', and they stated that the bank 'will not negotiate any letters of credit in the future which might include such terms'.[72] In public statements and letters to individuals with interests in the Royal Bank, its officials restated their commitment to the terms of the government's anti-boycott policy and urged the government to contribute clear and definitive guidelines in implementation of its policy. Pending such developments, the bank made clear that

> the Royal Bank will not:
> When acting as a third party or agent for foreign banks with respect to Canadian exports, process letters of credit containing restrictive clauses requiring certification of discriminatory policies and practices on the part of the exporting company. These would include policies of refusal to purchase from or sale to any other Canadian firm; refusal to sell Canadian goods to any country with which Canada has trade relations; or refusal to purchase from any such country.[73]

While controversy swirled around the federal government's anti-boycott stance, human rights agencies in Canada began to take a strong interest in the question. At its sixth annual conference in Banff, Alberta, in early June 1977, the Canadian Association of Statutory Human Rights Agencies (CASHRA) passed two resolutions on the Arab boycott, calling on the federal government to pass anti-boycott legislation and on provincial human rights agencies to oppose the Arab boycott and seek to influence their respective provincial governments to do so as well. In late September 1977, the Canadian Labour Congress declared itself in support of the CASHRA resolutions and called for anti-boycott legislation to be passed and implemented.

In the midst of these demands, the Conservative Premier of Ontario, William Davis, announced his intention of introducing provincial anti-boycott legislation, should federal inaction continue. During the Ontario election campaign in the summer of 1977, Mr Davis committed himself to early introduction of such legislation, and his Liberal party and New Democratic Party opponents supported that initiative. In December 1977 the first draft on Ontario's anti-boycott bill was introduced. With some revisions, it was signed into law on 8 November 1978.

While Ontario initiatives were underway, the federal Liberal government of Pierre Trudeau was subjected to continuing criticism by the press and the Jewish community for what was perceived to be its weak policy on the issue. Bureaucratic and business pressures were all arrayed against any significant federal anti-boycott activity; indeed, there had been business pressure on the Ontario government to refrain from pursuing its initiative. Large-scale bureaucratic and business pressures developed against any new federal anti-boycott initiatives. However, the release of the first and second reports of the federal government's anti-boycott policy on 10 February 1978 (covering the period from 31 October 1976 to 31 July 1977) and on 30 May 1978 (covering the period of 1 August 1977 to 31 January 1978) created major controversies, which illustrated clearly the major deficiences of coverage by the programme and galvanised public opinion against the government. With an election looming in the months ahead, the federal government felt compelled to undertake some new action on this issue, and in August 1978 it announced a significant tightening of the terms of its anti-boycott policy, together with a pledge to enact legislation establishing a compulsory, comprehensive reporting mechanism regarding the receipt of boycott requests with boycott clauses. Companies that agreed to sign boycott clauses would be named publicly. While such legislation would not have outlawed compliance with boycott provisions but would merely have created possible disincentives to such action because of a fear of embarrassment from public disclosure, anti-boycott activists greeted the pledge warmly and awaited its introduction and enactment.

The House of Commons reconvened in October 1978, but Bill C-32, the reporting legislation, was not introduced until the middle of December, and it was not brought back for second reading and subsequent consideration. Despite the government's pledge to enact the bill, the Minister of Industry, Trade and Commerce, Jack Horner, whose department was to have been responsible for its implementation, repeatedly made clear his opposition to any anti-boycott programme, which was based on his fear of trade losses. He attacked the Ontario anti-boycott law, arguing that Ontario had already lost trade because of its initiative; however, he was unable to provide any documentation supporting that allegation, and ministers of the Ontario government asserted that Horner's claims were totally untrue. In the immediate pre-electoral period of March 1979, Horner's statements opposing any anti-boycott initiative embarrased the federal government, and extraordinary manoeuvres were examined with a view to expediting passage of the bill in one day. These did not succeed, and the bill died on the order paper upon the dissolution of the House of Commons on 26 March 1979. The last few months of the then-Liberal government saw the tabling in December 1978 of the third semi-annual report on the government's policy, which covers the period from 1 February 1978 to 31 July 1978.[74] The report indicated that no firms had been denied federal assistance in that period for contravention of government policy.

During the 1979 election campaign, the Liberal party promised to reintroduce Bill C-32. The Progressive Conservative party and New Democratic Party repeatedly, forcefully and publicly called for the introduction and enactment of comprehensive anti-boycott legislation, along the lines of the US and Ontario statutes. The election of a Conservative government on 22 May 1979 gave rise to expectations that such legislation would be forthcoming within several months of the opening of the new Parliament.

Between 25 April 1979 and late October of that year, the Conservative party and (later) government found itself in the midst of a major national controversy involving PC Leader Joe Clark's campaign pledge to move the Canadian Embassy in Israel from Tel Aviv to Jerusalem. Developments during that controversy occasioned very significant implications for the anti-boycott policies of all political parties in Canada, especially so for the Conservative party in power, which, as a consequence of the Jerusalem controversy as well as its pre-existing inclinations with regard to the need for an absence of constraints on business activities, led it to refuse to consider anti-boycott legislation during its brief, nine-month tenure in office. On 14 December 1979 the government of Prime Minister Joe Clark was defeated in the House of Commons, and in the elections that followed two months later, the Liberals and Pierre Trudeau were returned to power. Under the new Trudeau government, no new announcements, investigations or initiatives took place on the issue of the Arab boycott or its significance in Canada.

Because of the unwillingness of successive federal governments of Canada to undertake any serious, wide-ranging and publicly available analyses and estimates of the impact of the Arab boycott on Canadians, inferences of its significance often had to be derived from assessment of US data and their extension to the Canadian context, which suggested the likelihood of a wide-spread impact in Canada of the boycott system - a perception that was bolstered by the documentation and findings of the January 1977 Cotler report. While boycott-related data remain generally inaccessible, the federal government does, of course, release overall export trade information. Those figures indicate that Canadian exports to Arab Middle East states (excluding North Africa) rose from approximately $460 million in 1977 to $556 million in 1978, to $560 million in 1979, to $738 million in 1980, and to $1.011 billion in 1981. Canadian exports to six Arab North African states (including Egypt) totalled $300 million in 1977, $313 million in 1978, $403 million in 1979, $727 million in 1980, and $816 million in 1981.[75] The implementation of the very limited federal anti-boycott programme and the enactment of the Ontario anti-boycott statute do not on the surface appear to have given rise to any significant adverse impact on Canadian exports to these states.

Federal Semi-annual Reports

The federal semi-annual reports did make evident some details about the government's policy and programme. The first semi-annual report stated that the government viewed negative certificates of origin, a main document required by secondary boycott clauses, as acceptable within the Canadian government's policy (a policy abandoned only with the August 1978 changes in the implementing guidelines). It established distinction between clauses that it regarded as 'statements of fact', and thus permissible, and those which were 'statements of intent', and therefore contrary to policy. Clauses involving tertiary boycott provisions, which stated that blacklisted ships could not be used for the transit of cargo to Arab states, were viewed as acceptable in an ex post facto ruling that noted that there were no Canadian vessels in such businesses and that there were no Canadians who could be damaged by such clauses. In the first report, ITC wrote that its officials had discovered 24 boycott-related undertakings in 80 transactions coming to their attention; EDC indicated that it had issued loans and insurance coverage totalling approximately $250 to Arab boycotting states, with no reductions as consequence of boycott clauses. No exporter, it is important to stress once again, was obliged to show his contracts to ITC officials or to EDC officials for insurance purposes; thus, even in transactions with which the federal government had some contact, there was no assurance that it would ever see relevant information. The likelihood existed, as well, that other contracts were being signed with which federal authorities had less contact, and perhaps even no contact at all.[76]

In the second semi-annual report, the federal government again reported the application of its policy in a manner that sought to avoid the denial of service or the naming of firms for contravening policy provision. This report stated that 26 boycott-related undertakings had been discovered among 87 transactions and that EDC insurance policy coverage totalling $90 million had been implemented. No firms lost governmental assistance in this period either.[77]

In the third semi-annual report, 38 boycott-related undertakings were discovered among 92 transactions, and no firms lost government support because the vast majority of the clauses were being renegotiated into governmentally acceptable form. EDC insurance policies totalling over $1 billion in coverage were issued to boycotting states.[78]

Although the three semi-annual reports offered substantial evidence of the minimalist manner in which the federal government was pursuing its minimalist, non-legislated policy, they offered a paucity of information on specific contracts. Overall export data as has already been noted, made clear that Canadian trade with Arab boycotting states was increasing substantially. United States data, reduced in scope to account for Canadian economic differentials, suggested that boycott clauses should have been appearing in large numbers. Yet the federal government made no effort to obtain appropriate data, and limited its efforts to the small number of cases in which contract clauses were actually shown to ITC officials, obligating them to take note of that information for inclusion in the reports. Since the publication of the third report, no further reports or information have been made public; nonetheless, departmental officials have insisted that they have been compiled on a regular basis and made available to Cabinet and Ministers of the government.

Ontario's Anti-boycott Statute

The most apparent success of anti-boycott activity in Canada took place in the province of Ontario, under the leadership of its Conservative Premier, William Davis, who was supported by the provincial Liberal party and New Democratic Party and their caucuses. During the election campaign of the summer of 1977, all three major political parties pledged themselves to introduce and pass provincial anti-boycott legislation. A minority Conservative government was elected, and on 16 December 1977 Premier Davis introduced 'the Discriminatory Business Practices Act of 1977'. The introduction of this proposal was made on the last day of the 1977 legislative session, when the bill died on the order paper. However, since many business representations that argued against anti-boycott legislation had been made to Premier Davis, he wished to introduce the bill and allow time for public discussion of its contents prior to its reintroduction in the next legislative session. In his statement introducing the bill, Premier Davis recalled his various commitments to introduce a bill to

> make it clear that, as far as Ontario was concerned, economic boycotts which prejudice citizens of this province by virtue of their ethnic background, religious affiliation, or freely expressed views will not be tolerated by this legislature and the people of Ontario.[79]

During the winter and spring of 1978, business and ethnic community representations on the bill were received by the Ontario government. On 8 June 1978 a slightly amended version of the bill was reintroduced in the Legislature. From 18 to 28 September 1978 the Standing Committee on the Administration of Justice held two full weeks of hearings on the bill, which was known as Bill 112, received testimony from a wide variety of groups, individuals and firms, and revised a number of the provisions of the bill. These hearings constituted the most detailed public exposition and examination of the Arab boycott undertaken in Canada.[80]

Among the many witnesses appearing before the Committee, an official of the Arab League delegation to the United Nations testified that Saudi Arabia discriminated in its entry policies against Jews, the chairman of the Commission on Economic Coercion and Discrimination testified in detail regarding the implementation of the boycott system in Canada, trade groups expressed their support for the bill in principle and their concerns about certain technical points of its provisions (concerns that were abated by textual corrections during the hearing process), Jewish and

Arab groups presented their perspectives on the bill, and a number of banking officials and businessmen gave detailed testimony regarding their experiences with boycott provisions.[81]

On 29 September 1978 the committee completed its detailed study of Bill 112, approved its provisions and returned it to the Legislature for the third and final reading. On 7 November the bill received its third reading and the support of all parties in the Legislature. Two days later, it was enacted into law and became the first anti-boycott statute in effect in Canada.

An Act to Prohibit Discrimination in Business Relationships, the formal title for Bill 112, prohibits secondary and tertiary restrictive trade and discriminatory boycott provisions from being agreed to in Ontario, prohibits the furnishing of information related to such boycott requests, establishes a compulsory, comprehensive reporting mechanism to monitor its implementation, requires annual public reports on its implementation, utlilizes the existing investigatory and regulatory apparatus of the Ontario Business Practices Act, allows for recourse to the courts and the right to compensation for damages arising from the act's contravention, makes boycott provisions that had been previously accepted in Ontario contracts into nullities that are severable from the contract, disqualifies those contravening the act from receiving Crown contracts for five years, provides fines of up to $5,000 for individuals and up to $50,000 for corporations for each offense, and stipulates that in cases of corporate convictions, directors, officers, servants or agents of the corporation responsible for the offences are considered parties to it.[82]

Soon after the enactment of the bill, indications began to be received that it was being implemented successfully. A boycott report filed in the United States with the US Department of Commerce by AC Monk and Company of Farmville, North Carolina, regarding the sale of tobacco from its Canadian subsidiary in Tillsonburg, Ontario, to Iraq contained a letter from the Canadian Imperial Bank of Commerce which indicated that the letter of credit provided by the Rafidain Bank of Baghdad could not be negotiated 'as the credit contains clauses which contravene Ontario Bill 112....'[83] On 12 September 1979 Ontario Attorney-General Roy McMurtry publicly stated:

> our former federal government made a number of gloomy predictions as to what was going to happen to Ontario's trade in the Middle East as a result of the anti-boycott legislation. Our legislation has been in force for...a year and there is absolutely no evidence to support the federal government's concerns. Our trade with the Middle East is steadily increasing and

> that...was the experience of the United States since the passing of their own anti-discrimination legislation.[84]

Recent Canadian Developments

Since the presentation of its third semi-annual report, the federal government of Canada has declined to pursue investigations or to release any further information on boycott-related incidents. In the absence of any Canadian equivalent of the US Freedom of Information Act, and given the tradition of reticence on the part of the government regarding the provision of information on its activities in the foreign economic policy sector, it has proven to be very difficult to obtain information on this problem. Parliamentary committees, not known in general for their investigative skills or perseverance, have yielded very sparse returns from the occasional questions raised there with reference to the boycott issue. In the autumn of 1982, the Standing Senate Committee on Foreign Affairs held a series of hearings on Canadian relations with the Middle East and North Africa, yielding little more than repetitions by governmental officials of the anti-boycott policy and assurances that it was working well, without the provision of any data whatever in this regard.[85]

Export Development Corporation officials, throughout the period of the federal anti-boycott policy's implementation, have tended to downplay the significance of the issue and argue that it has presented them with no problems. In that regard, Mr Sylvain Cloutier, the Chairman and President of the EDC, told the Senate Committee on 25 November 1982 that

> In doing business in certain countries in...[the Middle East], exports are sometimes faced with boycott inquiries. We at EDC recognize that international boycotts are a factor in doing business in these regions. We are, of course, fully aware of the government's policy on boycotts...and strictly administer that policy in the context of our export support services. To date, however, we have found that the boycott question has not had a great impact on our business, primarily because the exporter is generally already aware of, and has conformed with, government policy.[86]

That is all the EDC has to say about the Arab boycott issue in its testimony before the Senate.

Despite the generally unrevealing nature of Canadian governmental hearings with regard to the boycott issue, and despite strong preferences within the federal government that boycott-related incidents not become known, developments occasionally surface which offer a glimpse of an apparently slipshod approach in the federal government to the implementation of its policy. On 2 December 1982 the Globe and Mail reported a series of direct contraventions of federal anti-boycott policy by a Crown corporation, the Canadian Dairy Commission (CDC), which negotiated a sale of skim milk to Libya. The Arab purchasers asked for the inclusion of prohibited boycott clauses, and a letter of credit containing such clauses was expected. To facilitate the transaction and attempt to distance the government somewhat from a set of clear contraventions of its own policy, a Quebec farmers' co-operative was used to sign the contract, though the co-operative had effectively no connection with negotiating or undertaking the sale. In testimony before the House of Commons Public Accounts Committee, CDC Chairman Gilles Choquette confirmed the transaction, the boycott clauses and the attempt at circumvention.[87]

The Canadian anti-boycott system is thus composed of a strong anti-boycott statute in Ontario which is obviously limited in its coverage to that province, a weak anti-boycott policy on the federal level and a continuing lack of willingness of federal officials to seek out or provide even the most basic information of the impact of the boycott in Canada. While the US experience and the limited data available in Canada would suggest wide-spread compliance and complicity with the Arab boycott in Canada, determined federal governmental efforts have apparently stymied the development of new initiatives in this regard. As a public policy issue, the boycott question has experienced periods of peak public interest and governmental attention, especially in late 1976, early 1977, the summer of 1978 and early 1979. In recent years, the disinterest which federal governmental officials would seem to prefer the public to manifest on this issue has apparently triumphed over the occasional public involvement that has asserted itself in the past in this issue area.

Conclusion

The US and Canadian experiences with the Arab boycott of Israel illustrate dramatic differences of orientation, perspective and policy-making at work in these two countries. While they were subjected to similar threatening arguments that anti-boycott action would lead to major economic losses for each country, the two governments responded in substantially different ways. The US response indicated that refusal to comply with the boycott's provisions led not to economic losses but to Arab alterations in the texts of boycott clauses, together with a continuation of increasing export trade with Arab states. The US political process incorporated policy inputs from a variety of interest groups - economic, ethnic, human rights, labour and others - and developed policy outputs which appeared to deal effectively with the problem.

The Canadian response essentially entailed the most limited possible reaction to the problem. The Canadian policy process was also subjected to a wide variety of interest group inputs but responded very differently to them. The government was determined to reduce to an absolute minimum any public scrutiny of the issue, and it was essentially successful in its efforts to refrain from taking any risks that might adversely affect profit considerations.

This comparison of responses raises significant questions regarding the public policy process in the two countries and the approaches taken by each to the utilisation of statutory and regulatory approaches to public policy problems in the foreign policy sector.

Also, much can be learned from these experiences in responding to future instances of transactional economic boycotts which seek to utilise coercive secondary and tertiary provisions to alter the nature of relations between states.

Notes

1. For the experiences of the United Kingdom, France, Holland and other Western and Northern European states, see H. Stanislawski, 'Elites, Domestic Interest Groups, and International Interests in the Canadian Foreign Policy Decision-Making Process: The Arab Economic Boycott of Canadians and Canadian Companies Doing Business with Israel', Ph.D. dissertation, Brandeis University, February 1981, pp. 126-41.

2. Dan S. Chill, The Arab Boycott of Israel: Economic Agression (Praeger, New York, 1976), p 1; and W. H. Nelson and T. Prittle, The Economic War against the Jews (Random House, New York, 1977), p. 47.

3. Donald L. Losman, International Economic Sanctions: The Cases of Cuba, Israel, and Rhodesia (Albuquerque Press, University of New Mexico, 1979), p. 47.

4. Chill, The Arab Boycott, p. 1; and Nelson and Prittie, The Economic War, p. 103.

5. Nancy Turck, 'The Arab Boycott of Israel', Foreign Affairs 55(3) (April 1977), p. 474. Also see Report of the Subcommittee on Oversight and Intelligence of the Committee on Interstate and Foreign Commerce of the US House of Representatives, chairman, Representative John Moss (US Government Printing Office, Washington, D.C., 1976), p. 20.

6. Chill, The Arab Boycott, p. 2.

7. The presumption that the term 'Zionist' is understood to comprehend all Jews, unless otherwise shown, was confirmed by Sheik Ahmed Zaki al-Yamami in a press conference in Ottawa, Canada, on 28 June 1978. See Stanislawski, 'Elites and Interests', pp. 115-18. Also see Report of the Commission on Economic Coercion and Discrimination, chairman, Irwin Cotler (Commission on Economic Coercion and Discrimination, Montreal, 1977) (hereinafter cited as Cotler Report), app. 3, app. 22. Also see US Department of State document, Division of Language Services (translation), L. S. No. 34448 T-C/R, Arabic, 1972 (hereinafter cited as General Principles).

8. General Principles.

9. See Chill, The Arab Boycott, pp. 4-5. Also see Turck, 'The Arab Boycott of Israel', pp. 475-8, and General Principles.

10. See Stainislawski, 'Elites and Interests', pp. 120-5.

11. Moss Report, pp. 32-3.

12. Cotler Report, pp. 13-14.

13. Chill, The Arab Boycott, p. 48.

14. Nelson and Prittle, The Economic War, pp. 51-2.

15. Ibid., pp. 50-4. Also see Turck, 'The Arab Boycott of Israel', p. 475.

16. Nelson and Prittle, The Economic War, pp. 56-7.

17. Ibid., pp. 179-80.

18. Ibid., pp. 180-1.

19. Chill, The Arab Boycott, p. 48.

20. Ibid., pp. 48-9.

21. Ibid., p. 49.

22. Turck, 'The Arab Boycott of Israel', p. 484.

23. Chill, The Arab Boycott, p. 50.

24. Ibid.

25. Ibid., pp. 50-1.

26. Turck, 'The Arab Boycott of Israel', p. 485.

27. Chill, The Arab Boycott.

28. Turck, p. 485.

29. The Moss Report.

30. Chill, The Arab Boycott, p. 53.

31. Ibid., p. 53.

32. Ibid., p. 54.

33. Turck, 'The Arab Boycott of Israel', pp. 485-6.

34. Ibid., p. 485.

35. Ibid., p. 486.

36. For provision of the Ribicoff Amendment, see Tax Reform Act of 1976, Sections 999, 999a, 999b, 999c 999d, 999e and 999f; and the Internal Revenue Code, amending P-L 94-455. For detailed regulations of the TRA, see Federal Register, 5 January 1977, 42,3; 1 March 1977, 42,20; 17 August 1977, 42,159.

37. Washington Post, 11 Jan. 1977.

38. Illinois law: Public Act 79-963 (H.B. 25900), (H.B. 2591), Public Act 79-964, and Public Act 79-965 (H.B. 2592), became law 12 September 1975.
Massachusetts law: Amended General Laws by inserting chapter 151E - Prohibitions on Certain Discrimination in Business, enacted August 1976, effective January 1977.
California laws: Assembly Bill 2553, enacted July 1976, amended Section 52 of the Civil Code and added to Section 51.5 of the Civil Code; Assembly Bill 3080, enacted September 1976, amended Business and Professions Code, adding Sections 16721 and 16721.5.
Ohio law: Sub. H.B. No. 1358, enacted 1 July 1976, effective 1 October 1976, amending Sections 1331.01, 1331.03, 1331.08, 1331.10, 1331.11, 1331.99, 1707.44, 2307.382, and enacting Sections 1129.11, 1153.05 of the Revised Code.
New York law: A.1640-B Cal. No 636, S. 6411, enacted May 1975, effective 1 January 1976.
North Carolina law: Senate Bill 515; Foreign Trade Boycott Bill; adding to General Statutes, chapter 75B, passed April 1977, effective 1 January 1978.
Washington law: S. Bill No. 2906, an act relating to freedom from discrimination in commerce, amending section 2, chapter 183, laws of 1949, as amended by section 1, chapter 32, laws of 1974 and RCW 49.60.030, passed May 1977.
Oregon law: H. B. 2562, an act relating to civil rights, passed March 1977.
Minnesota law: SF No. 125, amending Minn. Statutes 1976, Section 325.8018, subdivision 2, and chapter 325, by adding Section 325.80155, passed May 1977.

39. E. G. Massachusetts Executive Order No. 130, 1976, p. 1; and New York Int. No. 187-A, City Council of New York.

40. For an examination of the banking situation, see New York Times, 12 Sept. 1976.

41. See Boycott Report, vol. 6, no. 6, p. 5.

42. See 'Israeli Boycott Losing its Grip', New York Times, 12 June 1978; 'Anti-boycott law: a quiet success, US News and World Report, 26 June 1978. Also see Petro-economic File, July 1978; Newsday, 30 May 1978, and New York Times, 12 Oct. 1976.

43. For an examination of the civil rights applicability question, see 'The Arab Boycott and Title VII', Harvard Civil Rights-Civil Liberties Law Review 12 (1977), pp. 181-205.

44. Henry J. Steiner, 'Pressures and Principles - The Politics of the Antiboycott Legislation', Georgia Journal of International and Comparative Law 8, 3 (1978), pp. 550-1.

45. Ibid., p. 552.

46. See ibid., p. 553.
47. Ibid., pp. 554-5.
48. Michael Beasely, 'Analysis and Application of the Anti-Boycott Provision of the Export Administration Amendments of 1977', Law and Policy in International Business 9 (1977), pp. 930-3.
49. For a detailed report on the provisions of the Export Administration Act of 1977 regarding the Arab boycott, see Stanley J. Marcuss, 'The Arab Boycott Law: The Regulation of International Business Behaviour', Georgia Journal of International and Comparative Law 8 (1978, pp. 559-80.
50. For example, see New York Times 30 Sept. 1976; and Los Angeles Times, 1 Nov. 1976.
51. Wall Street Journal, 14 Apr. 1977.
52. Quoted in American Jewish Committee, 'Impact of US Anti-Boycott Laws', p. 1.
53. Petroeconomic File, July 1978.
54. US Department of Commerce, Commerce Action Group for the Near East, 1978.
55. Journal of Commerce (February 1977).
56. 'US boycott laws seen not affecting trade with Arabs', American Banker (April 1978); Houston Business Journal (29 May 1978); Newsday, 30 May 1977; New York Times, 12 June 1978; US News and World Report, 26 June 1978.
57. US Department of Commerce, II$_t$?national Trade Administration, Office of Export Administration, Washington, D.C., Export Administration Annual Report FY 1980 (1981), pp. 73-86.
58. US Administration, Office of Export Administration, Washington, D.C., Export Administration Annual Report FY 1981 (1982), pp. 75-96.
59. Boycott Report, vol. 6, no. 3 (March 1982), p. 4.
60. Boycott Report, vol. 6, no. 3 (July 1982), pp. 3-4.
61. Boycott Report, vol. 7, no. 1.
62. Wall Street Journal, 9 Dec. 1982.
63. New York Times, 17 Feb. 1983.
64. See, for example, Canada Commerce (June 1973), p. 17.
65. Government of Canada, House of Commons
66. Government of Canada, House of Commons Debates, 2 June 1975.
67. Government of Canada, House of Commons Debates, October 1976.
68. For copies of editorials in Canadian newspapers following the publication of the Cotler Commission Report, see 'Canada and the Arab Boycott: Developments and Pro-

posals' (Canada-Israel Committee, Montreal, 1977).

69. Guidelines from Deputy Minister of the Department of Industry, Trade and Commerce on International Economic Boycotts, 21 January 1977.

70. *Financial Post*, 26 Feb. 1977.

71. Toronto-Dominion Bank statement, Toronto, 14 January 1977; Letter from J. A. Whitney, Bank of Montreal, Montreal, 4 February 1977; Letter from Vivian Korn, Canadian Imperial Bank of Commerce, 22 March 1977.

72. Letter from R. G. P. Styles, General Manager, Metropolitan Toronto, Royal Bank of Canada, to Mr H. Levy, Executive Vice-President, B'nai Brith of Canada, 21 January 1977.

73. Letter from R. G. P. Styles, Royal Bank of Canada, 31 January 1977.

74. Since the writing of this paper in March 1983, only three semi-annual reports have been issued by the federal government of Canada.

75. Senate of Canada, *Hearings of the Standing Committee on Foreign Affairs*, 9 November 1982, p. 27a.

76. See *Report on International Economic Boycotts*, I (Department of Industry, Trade and Commerce and Export Development Corporation, Ottawa, 1978).

77. See *Report on International Economic Boycotts*, II (Department of Industry, Trade and Commerce and Export Development Corporation, Ottawa, 1978).

78. See *Report on International Economic Boycotts*, III (Department of Industry, Trade and Commerce and Export Development Corporation, Ottawa, 1978).

79. Government of Canada, *Ontario Legislature Debates*, 16 December 1977.

80. *Hearings of the Standing Committee on the Administration of Justice of the Legislature of Ontario*, Toronto, 18-28 September 1978.

81. Ibid., p. J 1015-1 to J 1035-2, 28 September 1978.

82. Ontario Legislature, Bill 112, 1978, Sections 5(1), 5(8), 17,6,7,8,9,11,10(2), 10(1), 16(1) and 11(3).

83. US Department of Commerce, *Single Transaction Boycott Report No. 1472197*, received 9 April 1979.

84. Attorney General Roy McMurtry, Speech to Canada-Israel Chamber of Commerce, Toronto, 12 September 1979; text provided by the Office of the Attorney-General.

85. See *Hearings of the Standing Senate Committee on Foreign Affairs*, Ottawa, First Session, 32nd Parliament, 1980-81-82, 9, 18 and 25 November 1982.

86. *Hearings of the Standing Senate Committee on Foreign Affairs*, 25 November 1982.

87. *Globe and Mail*, 2 Dec. 1982.

Chapter Thirteen

EXTRATERRITORIALITY IN UNITED STATES TRADE SANCTIONS

David Leyton-Brown

Economic sanctions are a tool of unquestioned legality in the arsenal of state craft when applied directly by an initiating state against a target state. Legal and political problems arise, however, when the government of the initiating state claims jurisdiction over economic activities within the territory of some third state and, in so doing, undermines or conflicts with the laws and policies of the government of that state. Especially when the two governments differ on the appropriateness of the ends or means involved, an attempt by the initiating state to require compliance with its sanctions by individual or corporate residents of the other state can be perceived as an assault on the interests and even the sovereignty of the latter.

Since the end of the Second World War, the United States has been the most prominent practitioner of peace-time restrictions upon trade and other economic transactions. This policy propensity is no doubt due to a variety of factors, among them being the economic leverage of the US government resulting from the size and power of the US economy, the inclination to use that leverage resulting from the global interests and concerns of a superpower, the relatively low cost associated with economic sanctions because of the historically low importance of international trade to the US economy, and a moral imperative not to carry on normal relations with those whose behaviour is unacceptable. The extraterritorial application of the sanctions has its origin in the determination to maximise the effect of a policy instrument, to treat all US companies and citizens in an equal and non-discriminatory fashion, whether their economic activity is within the United States or in some other country,[1] and to prevent any appearance of evasion of US law by its own firms and citizens. These motivations cannot but conflict with the desire of a host government that subsidiaries of US firms incorporated under its laws be subject to the jurisdiction and direction of its own laws and policies, and not those of the US parent government. This clash of competing claims to jurisdiction is the crux of the extraterritoriality problem.

United States government restrictions on various foreign business activities have fallen into several areas: (1) export controls; (2) controls over dollar assets by foreign banks, and over currency assets held by foreign branches of US banks (e.g. freezing Iranian dollar assets in the European branches of US banks during the hostage crisis); (3) unilateral control to improve foreign practices, such as US foreign anti-bribery legislation, or US anti-Arab boycott regulations which apply to foreign subsidiaries or affiliates with as little as 25 per cent US ownership; and (4) foreign transaction control regulations.[2] This account will be restricted to the first of these categories, namely US restrictions on export practices of foreign companies as a part of a programme of economic sanctions, on the basis either that, because an American is in an ownership or control position in the foreign enterprise, the enterprise is defined as a 'person subject to the jurisdiction of the United States', or that the enterprise has received US technology or components which will be incorporated into its products.

Two principal pieces of US legislation authorise these restrictions. The Trading with the Enemy Act, originally passed in 1917, prohibits economic transactions with proscribed foreign countries by any person subject to the jurisdiction of the United States. The Export Administration Act of 1969, amended in 1979, restricts the export, or re-export, to certain countries of goods and technology originating in the United States.

The Trading with the Enemy Act empowered the President in time of war or declared national emergency to regulate or prohibit all commercial or financial transactions by Americans with certain foreign countries. During the Korean War in 1950, this legislation was invoked to prohibit transactions with China, North Korea and North Vietnam. The Treasury Department was given the responsibility of administering the Foreign Assets Control Regulations to give effect to the embargo. These regulations prohibited all transactions with the three countries by 'any person subject to the jurisdiction of the United States', defined as any citizen or resident of the United States, any corporation organised under the laws of the United States, or 'any partnership, association, corporation or other oganisation wheresoever organised or doing business which is owned or controlled' by an American citizen, resident or corporation, without a specific licence from the Secretary of the Treasury. This clause has been used to bring the export behaviour of foreign subsidiaries or affiliates of US multinational enterprises under the authority of the Trading with the Enemy Act by holding the parent company or US citizens on the foreign subsidiary's board of directors criminally liable for non-compliance.

The notion of control of foreign affiliates has been inclusively interpreted. The Treasury Department obviously enough considers control to rest with US 'persons' when ownership is greater than 50 per cent, but it also recognises that real control can be associated with shareholdings that are considerably smaller. Under various circumstances, the Treasury Department has considered US control of foreign affiliates to be identified by a minimum 10 per cent ownership or by a minimum of one director shared with the parent company.

In 1963, the two-year-old US trade embargo of Cuba was brought under the authority of the Trading with the Enemy Act. The Cuban Assets Control Regulations differed from the Foreign Assets Control Regulations in that there was no prohibition on trade with Cuba in goods of foreign origin by foreign companies owned or controlled by US persons or firms. However, though the regulations differed in form there was little difference in effect, since all US citizens were still prohibited from participating in such transactions. Thus, while a foreign subsidiary of a US company might appear unaffected by the trade ban on Cuba, any US citizen on its board of directors would be prosecuted under the Trading with the Enemy Act if a sale to Cuba did take place. Even an American on the board of a wholly foreign-controlled company seemed subject to the prohibition.[3]

The list of 'enemy' countries proscribed under the Foreign Assets Control Regulations has undergone change over the years. In 1969 the regulations were modified to permit foreign subsidiaries of US firms to export non-strategic goods to China (but not to North Korea or North Vietnam). In keeping with the growing normalisation of relations, restrictions on trade with China were progressively relaxed until, with the establishment of full diplomatic relations in 1978, China became a more accessible market for US exports than the Soviet Union and most of Eastern Europe. In mid-1975, after the Organisation of American States lifted its trade embargo on Cuba, the US government eased the Cuban Assets Control Regulations to allow foreign subsidiaries of US firms to sell non-strategic goods containing not more than 20 per cent of US-made components. Though exports to these two markets have been largely freed from extraterritorial restraint, the Trading with the Enemy Act remains a live issue. Kampuchea and Laos have been added to the proscribed list along with North Korea and Vietnam, and the relatively low importance attached to the trade with these countries does not diminish the fact that the US claim to extraterritorial control over the export practices of firms incorporated in other countries continues.

More recently, the International Emergency Economic Powers Act (IEEPA) has given the President similar authority to apply economic sanctions against a target country in peace time. The major substantial difference between IEEPA and the Trading with the Enemy Act is that under the latter, the United States can 'vest', or take, the property of the enemy, but not so under IEEPA. Trade sanctions authorised under both acts are broadly similar. Indeed the sanctions applied against Iran in the hostage crisis were authorised under IEEPA were substantively comparable to those discussed above.

Control over the re-export of goods and technology of US origin are authorised under the Export Administration Act of 1979, which is the successor to the Export Control Act of 1947. In this way, the United States has shown unusual readiness to use export controls for foreign policy purposes over a widening range of goods.[4] Under the authority of this act, the Department of Commerce requires licences of different kinds for all exports of goods and technical data to different categories of countries. The US government claims its licensing control over re-exports of goods and technology. Trade restrictions of varying severity under the act are presently aimed against such targets as the Soviet Union, Vietnam, Cuba, Kampuchea, South Africa, and countries that violate human rights or support 'international terrorism' (such as Libya).[5] Section 6 of the act authorises the President, for foreign policy reasons, to stop or limit the export 'of any goods, technology or other information subject to the jurisdiction of the United States, or exported by any person subject to the jurisdiction of the United States'. The US government claims its licensing control over re-exports of goods and technology of US origin, no matter how many hands the goods pass through. The act threatens the imposition of penalties including imprisonment for up to ten years, fines of up to $100,000, and denial of export privileges (black-listing of companies from receiving future licences to export or purchase US goods or technology) against any person or company of whatever nationality or residence, however remote from the original export transaction, who fails to observe the control. The ability of the United States to withhold further exports is a powerful penalty that commonly produces compliance, unless the firm is faced with an equal or greater penalty from its own government for failing to conform to national laws and policies. The issue of extraterritoriality is particularly salient in cases where US goods or technology are simply minor (but perhaps necessary) components in a final product produced in the foreign country, sometimes by a domestic firm. In such a case the local government will consider the locally-produced goods eligible for export to any market encouraged or not prohibited by its own policies, but the US government will consider such goods to maintain their US identity.

Some recent regulations issued under IEEPA and the Export Administration Act showed greater sensitivity to foreign sensibilities. The Iranian Assets Control Regulations to give effect to the US embargo on Iran in the hostage crisis, and the Controls on the Export to the USSR of Goods and Technology (for use related to the 1980 Summer Olympics) gave a more restrictive definition of a 'person subject to the jurisdiction of the United States'. For example, the Moscow Olympics regulations defined such a person as a US citizen or resident, or a corporation organised under the laws of the United States, but no longer included foreign subsidiaries in the definition. Furthermore, regulation 385.2(d) stated:

> A person subject to the jurisdiction of the United States who actually authorises, arranges, directs or actually participates in the authorization, arrangement or direction of a particular export transaction may be considered to have performed that transaction, but no person will be deemed to have so participated solely by reason of having an ownership or financial interest in or position with another person.

This seems to release individual US directors of foreign companies from some of the legal liabilities they have earlier faced. However, in the 1982 gas pipeline sanctions, the US government appeared determined to enforce its export controls based on US components and licensed technology despite the opposition of several allied governments to the extent of denying export privileges to six European firms.

Extraterritorial application of these laws has occasionally led to conflict between the governments of the United States and other states where subsidiaries or affiliates of US companies are located.[6] Those cases which occurred in the late 1950s and early 1960s primarily concerned sales to China, while those in the late 1960s and early 1970s mainly involved Cuba. Such cases have been more frequent in Canada,[7] but the same US laws and regulations have been applied with similar effect to block prospective sales by companies in other countries, such as those of Western Europe.

The first Canadian public awareness of the problem came in 1957 when it was charged that the Ford Motor Company of Canada had refused to sell trucks to China because of the threat of legal penalties against its parent. The ensuing dispute resulted in the so-called Diefenbaker-Eisenhower agreement to depoliticise such conflicts and provide for the possibility of exemptions for particular sales. This consultative procedure was used in several cases involving proposed sales to China and later to Cuba, and did succeed in limiting public outcry. Exemptions were received for the sale to China of pulp and paper by the Canadian subsidiary of Rayonnier and for the reconditioning by the Canadian subsidiary of Fairbanks-Morse of locomotives owned by Canadian National Railways for sale to China, but in neither case did the sale actually take place. It has been suggested that some Chinese orders might not have been genuine, but might merely have been ploys to embarrass US subsidiaries in Canada and to aggravate tensions between Canada and the United States.[8] There were no such concerns about Cuban intentions, and many sales were made to Cuba without applying for an exemption, or with an application handled administratively.

On occasion, public attention raised the salience of the cases. In 1965 US-owned milling companies were ordered not to supply flour in connection with a Canadian government wheat sale to the Soviet Union involving the shipment of flour to Cuba and, despite a diplomatic protest and a public ministerial outcry, no exemption was received. Canadian-owned companies were found to fill the order. In 1974 Studebaker applied for an exemption for the sale of locomotives to Cuba by its Montreal subsidiary, MLW-Worthington, but the application was denied. The Canadian government was determined that the sale should proceed regardless, and encouraged (by threatening the loss of government subsidies) the company to proceed. The three US directors on the board of directors of MLW-Worthington either were absent or abstained when the decision was taken, and the sale went through. Similarly in 1975, when Litton Industries did not wish to sell office equipment to Cuba and tried to cancel the contract entered into by the subsidiary, the Canadian government sent a diplomatic note to Washington complaining that Canadian companies were being inhibited by US law, and considered accelerated passage of its proposed Competition Act, which would have made it illegal to refuse a sale in compliance with the demand of a foreign jurisdiction. Though the US government never officially responded to the note, an exemption for the sale was granted.

Similar cases occurred in other allied countries. In 1963 an attempt to sell six Viscount aircraft from the United Kingdom to China was blocked by US export controls since the aircraft was designed to use navigational equipment produced by a UK affiliate of AT & T. Despite the complaints from the UK government, the US government refused to yield and allow the US components to be used. After considerable delay, and at considerable cost, an order for redesigned equipment was placed with a UK-owned electronics company, and the sale of the aircraft was eventually completed.

Two cases in France were particularly notable. In 1965 the Treasury Department ordered the Fruehauf Corporation to prevent its majority-owned subsidiary in France from filling a contract to sell transport trailers to a French truck manufacturer, Berliet, since the final product was to be sold to China. The French minority owners obtained a French court order appointing a provisional administrator for the subsidiary for 90 days (enough time to complete the order), in order to protect the jobs of Frenchmen and the rights of the minority owners. After a month of further legal challenges, diplomatic protests and government-blocked attempts to buy out the minority shareholders, the Treasury Department withdrew its order to the parent because the decision of the French courts had removed the subsidiary from the control of its parent. After the sale was completed, the provisional administrator resigned, and the subsidiary was returned to Fruehauf.

In another significant French case, US controls over US goods and technology were used to block a sale, not to China or some proscribed 'enemy' state, but to the Government of France itself. In 1964 because of its opposition to nuclear proliferation, the US government ordered IBM not to permit its French subsidiary to sell to the French government for use in its nuclear weapons development programme certain large computers manufactured in France but incorporating US components and technology. The dispute was finally resolved two years later when the French government promised not use the computers in its nuclear weapons programme, and the US government allowed the sale to proceed for use solely in peaceful nuclear programmes. The result of this case was to damage the standing of IBM France as a good corporate citizen, to delay but not prevent the development of French nuclear weapons, and to contribute significantly to the determination of the French government to create a French computer company able to compete in France and abroad with IBM. It is also reported to have affected the policy of the French government on subsequent US investment and takeover applications in France, and on the UK's entry to the European Economic Community.[9]

Through to the end of the 1970s, the number of cases where foreign companies were expressly forbidden to export to proscribed countries was small, and little economic harm was visited upon the target country. However, political harm to the relationship between the United States and its allies was more considerable, and certainly out of proportion to the economic importance of the individual cases themselves. It must also be recognised that, though the economic costs to the host countries of the handful of sales which were forbidden were marginal, the opportunity costs of sales never explored and trade forgone cannot be measured.

This then was the situation as the most recent case of extraterritorial application of US trade sanctions unfolded - the sanctions in the Polish crisis intended to block construction of the Soviet gas pipeline to Western Europe. The issue, discussed more completely elsewhere,[10] began with the proposal in 1978 to construct a pipeline to export Soviet natural gas from Siberia to Western Europe. Upon taking office, the Reagan Administration opposed the pipeline as increasing Western European vulnerability to Soviet interruptions of supply and increasing the revenues of the Soviet government available for allocation to military spending. Most Western European governments defended the pipeline as a diversification of European energy dependence on the Middle East and an increase in Soviet reliance on continuation of income earned from gas exports. Then, following the imposition of martial law in Poland on 13 December 1981, President Reagan, on 29 December, under the authority of the Export Administration Act, denied licences for the export of oil and gas equipment and technology from the United States to the Soviet Union. This impaired the ability of European companies to fulfil contracts with the Soviet Union for 125 gas pipeline compressor turbines which were designed to incorporate rotors, nozzles and stator blades produced by General Electric (GE) (and subject to licence by the Commerce Department).[11]

The agreement at the Versailles economic summit in June 1982 for the seven industrialised powers to exercise 'commercial prudence in limiting export credits' to the Soviet Union was publicly belittled by French President Francois Mitterand and FRG Chancellor Helmut Schmidt as in no way hampering their trade. President Reagan, on 18 June 1982, then extended the sanctions to apply to exports to the Soviet Union of oil and gas equipment or technology by US subsidiaries outside the United States and by foreign firms using US technology under licence, even under contracts signed prior to the crisis. This latter provision was the particularly important one because the only alternative to GE as a source of the rotor sets needed for the compressor turbines was the French firm, Alsthom-Atlantique, which was the only European company with a license from GE to make the rotors itself. In the ensuing months six companies, some subsidiaries of US firms like Dresser Industries and some European-owned such as John Brown & Company of Scotland, violated the sanctions by shipping compressors to the Soviet Union and were placed on the 'denial list,' blocking their access to further US components or technology.

In addition to criticising the extraterritorial outreach of the sanctions, European governments (especially that of France) complained about their retroactivity. Europeans challenged the legality of expecting GE's manufacturing associates to abide by new rules that were not a part of the initial licensing arrangements, but the United States counter-argument was that the companies previously agreed to abide by US export control regulations. It is reported that Alsthom-Atlantique's licence agreement with GE was phrased to say that the French company 'will keep itself fully informed of the [export] regulations (including amendments and changes thereto) and agree to comply therewith'.[12]

The escalating dispute between the United States and its European allies was brought to an end on 13 November 1982, when President Reagan lifted the gas pipeline embargo (but not other related sanctions against the Soviet Union such as licensing requirements, controls on access to the United States by Soviet aircraft and shipping, postponement of negotiation of maritime and agricultural agreements, etc.)[13] President Reagan presented his lifting of the sanctions as made possible by the achievement of a broad and substantial agreement among the allies on an overall economic strategy toward the Soviet bloc. In his announcement he said:

> We have agreed not to engage in trade arrangements which contribute to the military or strategic advantage of the USSR or serve to preferentially aid the heavily militarised Soviet economy. In putting these principles into practice, we will give priority attention to trade in high technology products, including those used in oil and gas production. We will also undertake an urgent study of Western energy alternatives as well as the question of dependence on energy imports from the Soviet Union.
>
> In addition, we've agreed on the following immediate actions:
>
> First, each partner has affirmed that no new contracts for the purchase of Soviet natural gas will be signed or approved during the course of our study of alternative Western sources of energy.
> Second, we and our partners will strengthen existing controls on the transfer of strategic items to the Soviet Union.
> Third, we will establish without delay procedures for monitoring financial relations with the Soviet Union and will work to harmonize our export credit policies.[14]

The French government had all along argued that the gas pipeline sanctions were illegal, directed at allies rather than the Soviet Union, and must be ended by the United States without any concessions in return. It immediately announced that France was not a party to the agreement announced by President Reagan in Washington, and that in any event no new agreement on East-West trade had been made. It remains unclear whether the announcement of an overall policy agreement was accurate, or merely a face-saving device to extricate the United States from a worsening relationship with its European allies.

During the last session of Congress, the Reagan Administration sought to amend the Export Administration Act. Proposed changes would have increased the authority of the President to apply trade controls for foreign policy as well as national security purposes. Penalties upon foreign firms for non-compliance would also have been expanded to include denial of access to the US market as well as denial of export privileges. These proposed changes were strongly opposed by Western European and other allied governments, and were the subject of much disagreement in Congress. Eventually, Congress dissolved in December 1984 without enacting the amendments, so the entire legislative process will have to be renewed in the newly-elected Congress. Nonetheless, it appears that the determination of the Reagan Administration to press for these amendements is as great as ever. If this effort succeeds in increasing the number of extraterritorially applied trade sanctions and the penalties for non-compliance, the occasions for dispute between the US and other governments will be bound to increase.

Other than acquiescence in the extraterritorial exercise of US jurisdiction, there are three courses of action open to affected governments: the negotiation of exemptions, passage of countervailing domestic legislation, or harmonisation of policies through some diplomatic settlement.

An exemption procedure was embodied in the Eisenhower-Diefenbaker Joint Statement on Export Policies of 9 July 1958. This so-called Diefenbaker-Eisenhower agreement between the US and Canadian governments resulted from the dispute over the Trading with the Enemy Act in the Ford trucks case of 1957. It reflected the understanding that the Canadian economy should not be disadvantaged by the application of the US regulations, and stated that

> If cases arose in the future where the refusal of orders by companies operating in Canada might have any effect on Canadian economic activity, the United States government would consider favourably exempting the parent company in the United States from the

foreign assets control regulations with respect to such orders.[15]

A consultation procedure was established whereby a US parent company could, with Canadian government support, apply to the Treasury Department for a special licence to exempt its directors from legal liability, thus permitting the Canadian subsidiary to complete the sale. The agreement was intended to depoliticise future conflicts over extraterritorial export controls and to lessen tensions, but not to guarantee freedom of export activity to Canadian subsidiaries. The principle of extraterritoriality was implicitly maintained, and exemptions were only to be considered on a case-by-case basis with no promise of permission. It was, however, made clear that an exemption was more likely to be forthcoming if refusal of the order would have significant detrimental effect on the Canadian economy, and if the order in question could only be filled by a US-owned subsidiary.[16]

Countervailing national legislation has been seen in several countries. In France, the Fruehauf case was settled only by the authority of French courts to remove the subsidiary temporarily from its parent's control and place it in the hands of a provisional administrator. During the gas pipeline dispute, the UK government invoked the Protection of Trading Interests Act of 1980 to threaten prosecution of UK companies that broke their sales contracts in compliance with the US sanctions. Recently, the Canadian government has departed from its traditional response of consultative procedures to obtain exemptions by amending the Combines Investigation Act in 1975 to forbid Canadian companies from implementing foreign judgements, laws or directives which would adversely affect competition, efficiency or trade. Sections 31.5 and 31.6 empower the Restrictive Trade Practices Commission to review and issue legally binding remedial orders respecting the implementation in Canada of such foreign orders with such specified adverse effects. Nevertheless, such countervailing legislation can only confront companies with mutually exclusive and competing legal demands, thus escalating the political tensions, and then only when a firm order is refused for reasons of extraterritoriality. It cannot require or encourage aggressive salesmanship nor solve the problem of trade opportunities forgone because of a desire to avoid the administrative and legal headaches, or to avoid alienating an important customer such as the US government.

The third recourse to the problem of extraterritoriality is a diplomatic settlement, harmonising policies so that there is no clash between the objectives or means of the various governments. Such agreement has been sought, especially by the US government, at successive economic summits and has been presented as the solution to the impasse over the gas pipeline sanctions. However, US policy may be criticised for having failed to anticipate and prepare for some diplomatic fall-back position when the pipeline sanctions were extended. Indeed, if the extension of the sanctions to include subsidiaries and licencees was motivated in any part by the desire to punish various European governments for their reluctance to harmonise their policies on East-West trade with that of the United States, then the US government should be criticised severely for misuse and misdirection of the sanctions instrument.

The problem of extraterritoriality with regard to trade sanctions is clearly more than a legal one. As the gas pipeline dispute is only the most recent to show, the problem is fundamentally a political conflict of goals and interests. A competition between national jurisdictions with regard to a specific export can readily be counterproductive to the attainment of long-run political interests. Issues of extraterritoriality impose opportunity costs and direct economic costs on the host state, and also damage the longer-term economic interests of the United States; itself, through the creation of doubts about the reliability of US-owned firms. The political costs, in terms of the erosion of autonomy of the host state and strained alliance relationships, are less tangible but no less real. Clearly, these problems are best avoided by prior consultation and harmonisation of policies before the imposition of trade sanctions. Where time or policy disagreement does not permit that, it is incumbent upon the US government to show greater sensitivity to the sovereign sensibilities of its allies.

Notes

1. Kingman Brewster Jr., Law and United States Business in Canada (Canadian-American Committee, Canada, 1960), p. 23.
2. Douglas E. Rosenthal and William M. Knights, National Laws and International Commerce, Chatham House Papers 17 (Royal Institute of International Affairs, London, 1982), pp. 6-7.
3. Canada, Foreign Direct Investment in Canada (Gray Report) (Government of Canada, Ottawa, 1972), p. 257.
4. J. F. Murphy and A. T. Downey, 'National Security, Foreign Policy and Individual Rights: The Quandary of United States Export Controls', International and Comparative Law Quarterly, vol. 30 (1981), p. 791.
5. John Felton, 'Congress May Weigh Limits on Presidents' Authority to Impose Trade Restrictions', Congressional Quarterly 357(ii) (20 November 1982), p. 2883.

6. David Leyton-Brown, 'The Multinational Enterprise and Conflict in Canadian-American Relations', International Organization, vol. 28, no. 4 (Autumn 1974); Jack N. Behrman, National Interests and the Multinational Enterprise Prentice Hall, (Englewood Cliffs, N.J., 1970).

7. David Leyton-Brown, 'Extraterritoriality in Canadian-American Relations', International Journal, vol. XXXVI, no. 1 (Winter 1980-81).

8. I. A. Litvak, C. J. Maule and R. D. Robinson, Dual Loyalty (McGraw-Hill of Canada, Toronto, 1971), p. 71.

9. Behrman, National Interests and Multinational Enterprise, p. 105.

10. See Chs. 7 and 11.

11. Jonathan B. Stein, 'U.S., Controls and the Soviet Pipeline', The Washington Quarterly 5(4), (Autumn 1982), p. 54.

12. The Economist, 14 August 1982, p. 59.

13. Felton, 'Congress may Weigh Limits', p. 2884.

14. New York Times, 14 Nov. 1982.

15. Canada House of Commons Debates, 11 July 1958, p. 2142.

16. Brewster, Law and United States Business in Canada, p. 26.

Chapter Fourteen

ECONOMIC SANCTIONS AND ALLIANCE CONSULTATIONS: CANADA, THE UNITED STATES AND THE STRAINS OF 1979-82

John Kirton

Few contentious issues afflicting the Atlantic Alliance have arisen with such wearying predictability as the debate over the proper purposes and processes for imposing economic sanctions on external adversaries. The participants in this debate over the decade have been engaged in a dialogue of the deaf. The United States, as the self-proclaimed and often acknowledged alliance leader, patiently explains the need for 'effective' action and for US responsibility to exercise swift, decisive, unilateral leadership when a clear and present danger threatens. In return the lesser allies, sporting the mantle of multilateralism, plead the obligations of 'consultation'. Their grounds range from the superior wisdom of their insights and instincts in time of crisis, through the very heavy direct burdens they are often asked to bear, to the claim that 'no taxation without representation' is a fundamental principle that all the allies share. United by a belief that 'effectiveness' and 'consultation' are rival claimants on the same fixed pool of US presidential time and attention, the United States and its allies have thus remained imprisoned in the liturgy of their dreary debate.

Scholars have enunciated three iron laws of the economic sanctions process.[1] The first is that sanctions are ineffective in meeting their declared objectives, almost regardless of the rich variety of common goals and individual motives of the sponsors. The second is that sanctions are rendered ineffective by inadequate consultation among, and commitment by, the sanctioners. Many, feeling left out of the initial and ongoing decision-making, take advantage of a sanctions programme, or at least save on the taxes for a 'collective good' to which they feel less-than-equally attached. The third, imprinted in academic consciousness by the spectacle of the League of Nations idly debating while Mussolini invaded Ethiopia, is that the time consuming quest for consultation and unanimity breeds the very ineffectiveness that lesser allies claim it prevents. The only possible escape from these iron laws is through that most elusive phenomenon - a meaningful consultative process that does not consume time once the need for swift and sure sanctioning arises.

To begin to identify such a process, and thus loosen these policy and scholarly deadlocks, it is useful to consider the recent effectiveness of the alliance's sanctions and surrounding consultative processes. Undeterred either by evidence of the ineffectiveness of sanctions or by their memories of discord over embargos of the People's Republic of China and Cuba, members of the Atlantic Alliance have, in the short space of three years, engaged in four major sanctions ventures: Iran, 1979-81; Afghanistan, 1980-81; Poland, 1980-82; and Argentina, 1982. The particular consultative process the allies employed appears to have had little effect on specific sanctions decisions, on the effectiveness of those sanctions, or on the ensuing alliance disagreement about the adequacy of consultations and sanctions.[2] If the degree and form of consultations provide such a poor explanation of outcomes, then how are prompt, effective and harmonious sanctions to be ensured?

The answer lies in the adoption of a broader concept of 'consultation' than has traditionally been employed.[3] Such a broader concept, which has recently been employed in exploring the 'effectiveness' of sanctions, includes both the interchange over specific sanctions in the individual case (the sanctions-specific consultative process) and the preceeding and more general dialogue concerning relations between the allies and the adversary in various situations (the contextual consultative process).[4] In the sanctions-specific consultative process, perfection is hardly possible, for failure to consult and agree can and does strike at any point from prior planning to termination of sanctions.

The secret of success lies in the second realm of the critical consultations occurring before the initial discussions about invoking sanctions take place, and beyond the consultations focused upon the specific sanctions themselves. This contextual consultative process deals with the advance consensus on the boundaries, intensity and probability of common threats, the existing general system of crisis-response mechanisms, alliance communication and international institutions, and even events in the extra-sanctions environment over which the sanctioners have some anticipatory control. Attention to this realm suggests that states contemplating or employing economic sanctions are neither the slaves of the sanctions-specific consultative meachanisms created *ab nihilo*, nor victims of the vagaries of an ever-changing balance of power. Indeed, the experience of the United States and its closest ally, Canada, in these four recent cases suggests that sanctions can be remarkably effective, even without good case-specific consultations. If the key sanctioners are embedded in an institutionalised concert small enough in number yet large enough in scope and legitimacy, they can provide a continuing core around which to build a convergent multilateral response.[5]

Beyond Sanctions-specific Consultation: The Search for an Expanded Conception

The quest for proper consultative procedures for deciding how to impose, apply and end sanctions is likely to be immensely frustrating and ultimately futile. No matter how careful and well-understood the procedures, failures are almost guaranteed. The fragility of the sanctions-specific consultative process stems from a variety of causes.[6] Yet two fundamental features of the timing involved in most sanctions cases are often enough to ensure that the consultative process fails. The first, and most obvious, is that sanctions are imposed swiftly and suddenly in unexpected situations, leaving the lead sanctioner and alliance manager little time to consult. The second, and more important feature, is that most sanctions programmes, while instituted swiftly, last for long periods of time.[7]

The length of time that sanctions endure places enormous burdens on the processes of intra-alliance consultation. The possibility of breakdown increases as the sanctions last. Moreover, after the first flush of enthusiasm and dramatic demonstrations of political resolve, the tedium of technical issues takes over. Here even the most dedicated sanctioner can fall prey to the tyranny of small details as ambiguities arise about where the lines should be drawn, divergent interpretations of the original objectives emerge, and officials discover inventive ways to stretch the rules without being caught. In addition, objectives change, both for the alliance as a whole and, unevenly, for its individual members. Frustration mounts and controls are tightened under the elegant logic of graduated response. Extraneous events - e.g. domestic elections or military invasions - intrude to lower or elevate the sanctions exercise on the priority scale.

Finally, each stage of the sanctions process raises a fresh set of dilemmas for which previous consultative successes and habits may be irrelevant or even counterproductive. The first stage - invoking the sanctions - involves a host of complex judgements about a formidable array of subjects: what states and goods qualify for various categories; what timing is most suitable; what is the purpose and precise target of the sanctions; what form should they take; what level of success is required; and how long should they last. But conscious of the gaze of a defiant adversary, ambivalent allies and an enraged domestic electorate, the alliance leader rapidly succumbs to the deadly logic of 'doing something now'. Decisions to invoke sanctions are almost inherently crisis decisions.

The second stage - applying the sanctions - provides time for consultation and thus ample scope to debate the fine arithmetic of burden-sharing. The applications stage requires a series of more technical decisions: assigning roles to various alliance members; activating restraints through intrusions in the bureaucratic and private sector; monitoring the impact on allies and adversaries; identifying violators; punishing backsliding sanctioners; and extending the sanctions regime should the adversary prove recalcitrant. During these tasks the measure adopted in stage one (invocation) can easily be identified as inequitable by some parties. The demands of internal equity and external solidarity-stability can clash in the debate over permissable amendments. The superior capacity of the alliance leader to monitor compliance can cause resentments.

The third stage - terminating the sanctions - demands decisions about whether it is legitimate to raise the subject of ending the sanctions, at least publicly: about when and how termination should occur (e.g. all at once or in stages); and whether it should be kept possible to reinvoke the sanctions. Here there are real advantages to being neither the first nor the last in the termination game, a fact which places heavy demands on the consultative process to provide precise information about who is likely to move how much and when. Compounding these problems are inherent ambiguities about whether the real political objectives of the sanctions - often changed, forgotten or never initially specified - have actually been accomplished.

These time-based causes of failure help explain the differences among the four cases. Indeed it is striking that the shortest cases - Iran and Argentina - were those where maximum effectiveness and minimum discord were evident.[8] Yet as these cases were also the ones in which the sanctions-specific consultative process was the least well developed, the cause of their success lies elsewhere - in the realm of those convergence breeding devices of the contextual consultative process.

Various components of this broader, 'contextual consensus' can be identified. The first and most proximate is the consensus among allies about the boundaries, and probability of threats that might require common action. In the discussions on such subjects (which can range from formal targets contingency planning to an informal sharing of perspectives) economic sanctions may or may not be identified or discussed as a preferred or possible response. To be useful, these efforts at prior consensus require that participants know the range and weighting of relevant opinion.

Alliance Consultation

This question of whose views count how much can be answered effectively by a second pre-sanctions consultative stage - the network of channels for consultation and communication which exist for subjects more general than and apart from sanctions, and which give institutionalised expression to which players fit where within the game. As institutions, these channels provide an existing infrastructure through which communications can rapidly be transmitted and skilled secretariats to which technical tasks can be delegated. More importantly, they provide legitimacy, predictability and reliability - a strong agreement about and practical presumption in favour of the rules of the game and the relevance of various players. When developed into a strong regime or codified body of international law, they provide a ready calculus by which to measure the severity of various threats, and hence justifications for strong countermeasures.

Third, it helps in defining threats to have a ready referent by which to predict which threats the international system is likely to breed, and to calculate severity. The possibilities for random events which profoundly disrupt the inter-allied communications, consultation and sanctions process are considerable. Yet two features of the structure of the international system are capable of being absorbed in advance. The first is the distribution of power among states, which suggests whether a given network of channels of communication is likely to be sufficient for and sustainable during the sanctions and consultative task. The second is the stability of the structure of power in the international system, which determines whether threats overwhelm, or are overwhelmed by, the existing structure. If the structure is highly stable, even major threats can be quickly absorbed and identified as sufficiently serious to warrant a forceful response. If the network of channels is largely the institutionalised expression of the real balance of power in the system, it can sustain the demands imposed by the burden of technical consultation at later stages. In short, a concert of principal powers defending and defining a stable international order provides the best guarantee that effective consultations will subsequently occur.

Iran, 1979-1981: Success Through the System

The US and allied sanctions imposed against Iran from 1979 to 1981 have been judged by knowledgeable observers to have been highly effective means of securing release of the US hostages and affirming the sanctity of a fundamental aspect of international law. Robert Carswell, Deputy Secretary of the US Treasury from 1977-81, concludes: 'the degree of leverage the sanctions exerted - whatever its exact weight - depended on a high degree of co-operation by other countries'.[9]

This easy conclusion, beguilingly flattering to US allies, masks, however, a deeper reality. Upon close examination, the deliberate, case-specific process of consultation was neither prominent nor effective.[10] Consultation was notably absent in the first ten days after the US hostages were seized in Tehran on 4 November 1979. The consultative process grew only gradually until April 1980, when the United States unveiled a comprehensive sanctions programme that the French press described as an 'ultimatum' to the allies. Ultimately what save the sanctions, if not the diplomatic reputation of the Carter Administration, were three forces from the realm of the 'before and beyond' - a network of strong international institutions which the Carter Administration used in a major way from the outset, an existing structure for broader 'alliance' consultation capable of adaptation to provide the minimum effective consensus required to enforce US unilateralism, and two extrasystemic events - the failure of the US rescue mission and the Soviet invasion of Afghanistan - which gave the Western alliance the geopolitical obligation to sustain the actions of its US member.

The strength of these broader forces is indicated by the heavy incentives for failure which pervaded the case-focused consultative process from January 1979, when the Shah fell, to the summer of 1981, when allied sanctions were lifted. There were few consultations between the United States and its allies over possible events in Iran and Western reactions prior to the seizure of the hostages. United States shock at the fall of the Shah indicated its lack of anticipating that problems in Iran were sufficiently serious to warrant advance allied planning.

Moreover, the measures taken by the United States in the first ten days after the embassy seizure were essentially unilateral. The United States began by banning oil imports from Iran and on 14 November announced a freeze on all Iranian assets in the United States and controlled by US banks, firms and individuals abroad. This latter action was taken with little consideration of the long-standing concern of allies to such assertions of US extraterritoriality, precisely how much of .Iran's assets were blocked by the measures, or a rigorous assessment of cost effectiveness. The original order also applied to Iranian accounts in other currencies held by US banks abroad, but rapid and vigorous complaints by host governments and a US calculation that the amounts were small led the United States to rescind the order. United States overtures soliciting allied governments to take similar measures were rebuffed. While the ten day interval had allowed the United States to select a potentially effective sanctions instrument, its decision process was driven and dominated by a host of considerations far removed from 'effectivenss' and 'consultation'. These included a trade embargo imposed by US longshoremen, the need for some forceful action by the United States, a reluctance to employ risky political or military means, the demands of demonstrating leadership, and a calculation that consultations with allies would take too long and secure too little. Indeed, the key catalyst was a hollow threat by Iran to 'attack the dollar' by withdrawing its reserves from US currency accounts. This led the United States to respond in a similar way (with financial measures) with a target of preventing the precise Iranian threat (blocking the accounts).

There are few signs of meaningful advance consultation at subsequent stages as the United States, saturated with media attention and entering a US presidential election campaign, steadily escalated its response. It expelled 183 Iranian diplomats on 12 December, suspended diplomatic relations and imposed trade sanctions on 7 April 1980, imposed additional sanctions and threatened military action on 17 April, and carried out its ill-fated rescue mission on 25 April.

It was only a few days before the rescue mission that the United States' major allies took any meaningful sanctioning actions - a further incentive for the US sanctions programme to fail. They had reluctantly acquiesced in US financial sanctions, but their approach to further economic and diplomatic sanctions was conditioned by several considerations: a fear that Iran would be driven into chaos or the Soviet bloc; the presence of large numbers of their national and commercial interests in Iran; a general preference for diplomatic means; and a much greater dependence on Iranian oil, deposits and markets than the United States. As a result, the sanctions of the European allies lagged considerably behind those of the United States, in both time and severity.

The response of the United States most proximate ally, Canada, was equally mild. Prior to November 1979 Canada had taken few actions to indicate its displeasure with the new Iranian regime. In January 1979 it had evacuated Canadian nationals and in February relaxed the criteria for student work permits and immigration of relatives for Iranians in Canada. Yet in the same month it formally recognised the provisional government of Iran and accepted representational duties on behalf of the recently closed Israeli mission in Tehran.

After the seizure of the hostages on 4 November, the pace quickened moderately. On 6 November the House of Commons unanimously passed a resolution condemning the action. Canada also made known its displeasure directly to Iran and offered to help US citizens in Iran in any way possible. As part of this pledge, Canada's embassy in

Tehran continued to function normally. Yet when asked on 3 December if Canada would join the United States in refusing to import oil from Iran (which by then represented only about 10 per cent of Canada's imports), Prime Minister Clark promised only to consider the matter. He emphasised throughout that Canada's goal was not only to support the United States, but to mobilise international opinion to influence officials in Iran.

Canada's most well-known action came on 28 January when it temporarily suspended the operations of its embassy in Iran as a means of facilitating the escape of six US diplomats whom it had been sheltering.[11] Cabinet had approved the issuance of Canadian passports to these individuals on 4 January. From the inception of the crisis, Canada had kept the US government closely informed about the situation of these diplomats and events in Iran. Yet this particular role played by Canada secured for it no greater than normal access to or influence over US policy on Iran, either before or after the escape of the US diplomats. Canada clearly stated that the removal of its embassy personnel did not represent a breaking or suspending of diplomatic relations with Iran, which would continue through other channels. Indeed, Prime Minister Clark was quick to point to hopeful signs that Iran's attitude toward the hostages was moderating.

After the 7 April imposition of sanctions and suspensions of diplomatic relations by the United States, Canada's response strengthened only a little. Prime Minister Trudeau expressed Canda's understanding of the US suspension of diplomatic relations and promised that Canada would consider further measures. Yet on 15 April the new Secretary of State for External Affairs, Mark MacGuigan, declared that it would not be meaningful for Canada to copy the United States and sever diplomatic relations. On 23 April Canada announced a mild series of initial sanctions and its consideration of further trade measures if the hostage crisis was not over by 17 May.[12]

After the failure of the US raid on 25 April, Canada was quick to express its belief that the mission was a defensive rescue raid rather than a military operation and offered its sympathy. Almost a month later, on 22 May, Canada's second stage of sanctions was invoked when Canada placed controls on the exports of goods to Iran, with exemptions for food, medical supplies and other humanitarian products.

Canada's only other action came when the drop in oil from Iran technically triggered the International Energy Agency (IEA) emergency-sharing mechanism. Canada, though particularly harmed by the mechanism and emphasising the global oil surplus, joined with its allies to confine its actions to tests of the mechanism. In January 1981 both the Prime Minister and the Commons congratulated the United States and Algeria for their roles in securing the release of the hostages. On 3 March Canada's sanctions were lifted, although its embassy remained closed.

A further incentive for failure in the sanctions process was the US dominance over the negotiation of the January 1981 Algiers agreement. While the United States had been in close touch with private actors in allied countries, it alone conducted the negotiations with Iran. Although no allied government wanted to accept responsibility for the failure of the negotiations, they had several fears about loans that Iran declared it would not pay and repayment-sharing agreements. Although the final solution was made possible when Iran reduced its cash demands and offered to repay loans (which consumed a considerable amount of the block funds in 'Eurodollar' accounts), it was achieved by a very narrow margin.

Finally, there was a further, potentially fatal incentive to failure in this case - the extraterritoriality of the US actions. Extraterritoriality for Canada was an issue of sovereignty which, as shown in the Cuba and China cases, could take precedence over national security considerations. Here extraterritoriality was disguised and diminished by the US reliance on the convenience of the New York clearing accounts and by the fact that, to make this action effective, the allies merely had to do nothing rather than take action. But US manipulation of its historically-generated centrality in a multilateral system could well have served as an additional irritant and certainly did not eliminate the extraterritoriality. For Canada, at least the threat to sovereignty remained, which required a higher trump to induce Ottawa to depart from its historic concerns. That higher threat came from Iran's violation of one of the most fundamental precepts of international law and community - the integrity of the diplomatic system and the principle of diplomatic immunity on which it rests.[13] While virtually every other state concurred in this judgement, for Canada, the special claims of consultation were trumped by the special historic centrality given to international law (rather than national principles) and by the special responsibility Canada had as the place of sanctuary for the six US diplomats in Tehran.

Moreover, international law was backed by international organisations, as the United States went immediately to the latter and confined its demands to what they would easily bear. The United States asked only for the return of its hostages and, at a secondary level, the protection of some US property claims against Iran. This gave it broadly-shared systemic and national interests (the latter with the many states which had diplomats or property and loans in Iran). The United States chose initial sanctions measures which placed all the real future costs on the United States. By focusing on international institutions, it demonstrated its reliance on peaceful means. Within a month of the US financial sanctions, the International Court of Justice had unanimously declared Iran's actions illegal and asked for the hostages to be freed. By 13 January 1980 the Security Council of the United Nations had shown itself prepared to vote sanctions and was stopped from doing so only by a Soviet veto. During the following two months, the United States allowed UN mediation efforts to unfold. Only after they had clearly failed were the US economic sanctions of April unveiled.

Additionally, while the Soviet Union may have formally immobilised authoritative UN action, there were supplementary, and equally effective, institutionalised channels in place, to which the issue, under US guidance, quickly flowed. The most important of these - the Western Economic Summit Seven - was first invoked as early as December 1979 when high level US officials visited the United Kingdom, France, the Federal Republic of Germany, Italy and Japan (as well as Switzerland) to discuss possible sanctions that these countries might impose.[14]

For Canada, the summit seven channel ultimately proved to be central, but only after, and as reinforced by, supplementary channels and institutions. On a practical level, Canadian consultation on Iran began as early as January 1979 when Ambassador Taylor, after discussions with other Western representatives, oversaw an airlift of Canadians and other nationals out of Iran. He also held discussions with other friendly embassies in Iran concerning contingency plans. Immediately after the US embassy seizure, Taylor played a particularly active part in assembling representatives of the diplomatic corps in Iran.

On a policy level, Canada's first response was to rely on international institutions. In February 1979 Canada reacted to the prospect of a curtailment of oil imports from Iran, from which it received 24 per cent of its imported supplies, by relying on the existing emergency mechanism of the IEA.[15]

After the hostage taking, Commonwealth representatives convened in London on 27 November at Canada's initiative to appeal to Iran to release the hostages, to express their commitment to international law, and to declare their support for the mediatory efforts of the Secretary-General of the United Nations. On the same day in Ottawa, Canada's Secretary of State for External Affairs convened a meeting of the ambassadors of francophone countries for the same purposes. Following this, Canada focused on NATO and participated in the 13 December foreign ministers' statements that declared the hostage taking illegal and 'totally unacceptable'. On 30 December Canada's foreign minister spoke to the United Nations Security Council to express Canada's outrage at Iran's action, admiration for US restraint, conviction of the seriousness of the issue and support for the previous call of both the Security Council and International Court of Justice for Iran to release the hostages. Canada also warned that should the Secretary-General's forthcoming mediation effort fail, Canada would support the use of sanctions under the United Nations Charter.

By the beginning of April, with the UN mission clearly a failure, Canada consulted other Western nations and participated in a discussion of the details of possible sanctions at a meeting in Sardinia of senior economic officials from nine countries. Although this meeting was designed to prepare the Venice Western Economic Summit, Canada pressed for a consensus on economic sanctions. As a result of these discussions, Canada announced its initial series of measures. It is noteworthy that these measures were described as 'in parallel' with the actions announced by the EEC foreign ministers the previous day, aimed at enforcing international law, and part of a concerted international response. Indeed, it further promised that future trade measures would also be taken in concert with like-minded states.

On 23 April 1980, two days before the failed US rescue mission in Iran, Secretary of State Cyrus Vance visited Ottawa. During the visit Vance discussed in detail possible actions to deal with the situation in Iran. Canada, however, was given no advance notice of the rescue operation, and Prime Minister Trudeau told Vance that Canada opposed any military action by the United States in Iran.

It is the process underlying the introduction and passage of Canada's Iran Sanctions Act that most poignantly captures the importance of the international institutional network. The Soviet veto of the UN draft demanding 'specific sanctions against Iran' had posed a problem for Canada, which had the legal basis to impose only sanctions approved by the United Nations. The Soviet veto not only meant the administrative inconvenience of a separate act at a busy time, but raised the question whether Canada - in some respects for the first time - should resort to sanctions not formally authorized by the United Nations.

Canada's decision to proceed was based on the grave Iranian violation of international law, the unanimous condemnation of the UN Security Council, and the need to implement the measures of the vetoed Security Council draft resolution of 10 January (which the Canadian bill closely resembled). It further flowed from the lengthy delay in responding to the US request for sanctions (to allow a cohesive and pragmatic administration to emerge in Iran), and the graduated response begun on 23 April. Another factor was the decision of appropriate measures in concert with, and the co-ordination of Canada's actions with, the European Community, Japan and Australia (in the need to demonstrate to the United States the solidarity of the international community). A final factor was a desire to avoid the hostility of the Iranian people and maintain a humanitarian stance, yet signal that breaches of international law erode co-operative links with the international community. This led to provisions for the automatic expiry of sanctions after one year, repeal of the bill when the hostages were released, and a promise of efforts to renew relations with Iran in that event.

Finally, due allowance must be made for the role of forces emanating from the structure of the international system. The Soviet invasion of Afghanistan in late December 1979 arguably led to the Soviet veto of 13 January 1980 (and hence Canada's agony about whether to participate in a non-UN mandated sanctions regime) and to the US determination to move to non-diplomatic and financial instruments. United States warnings of military actions in April likely prompted the first Canadian sanctions action, as Canada pursued its traditional policy of constraining forceful and unilateral US behaviour by publicly accommodating moves. It is equally likely that the failure of the US rescue raid prompted Canada to join with its European summit allies in a united front to compensate for the loss of US and hence Western prestige.

Afghanistan, 1979-1982: Failure through Frustration

In the opinion of knowledgeable US scholars and authors, the Afghanistan grain embargo lives on as the clearest modern instance of failure in the effectiveness of economic sanctions. Those responsible are among United States' allies and friends who defied or subverted the US programme.[16] In turn, the allies respond that their lapses derive directly from the failure of the United States at virtually every stage. Given this massive failure of consultation, the interesting qustion is not why key allies such as Canada and France sanctioned so little for so short a time relative to the United States, but why they did so much for so long compared to everyone else. Again, the answer lies in the realm of the 'before and beyond'.

Prior to the Soviet Union's Christmas Day 1979 invasion of Afghanistan, the United States had made two approaches to its allies about the emerging situation: one through bilateral messages, and the other through a discussion among NATO permanent representatives.[17] Designed to get allies seized with the issue and to issue warnings to the Soviet Union, these meetings saw the United States neither indicate what it would do in the event of an invasion nor solicit commitments from allies.

After the invasion, the United States Under-Secretary of State Warren Christopher flew to London (and Brussels) on 27 December to inform officials of various countries, including Canada, of what the United States had decided. This focus, and the rather general nature of the discussions, provoked considerable unhappiness among the Europeans. However, after a six-hour meeting on 31 December with officials from the United Kingdom, France, the Federal Republic of Germany, Italy and Canada, Christopher announced an allied review of relations with the Soviet Union and an agreement to press for discussions at the United Nations. The following day an emergency meeting of NATO on East-West relations set up working groups, received US promises of consultation and heard a West German proposal for a boycott of the Olympics to take place that summer in Moscow. In addition, the United States secured a general agreement that there ought to be unspecified steps taken to demonstrate Western disapproval of the Soviet action. By 2 January the United States believed that there was a strong allied consensus for UN action as a result of Christopher's meetings. This feeling was confirmed the next day when 43 nations called for a UN meeting and the United States backed a European and Third World proposal to take the issue to the Security Council.

This institutionally-embedded general consensus was vital, given the sanctions specific unilateralism that came two days later on. On 4 January, President Carter announced that the United States would embargo 17 million metric tons (mmt) of grain to the Soviet Union, store the excess grain in the United States, and pay US farmers full market price for it. In additon, he said that he had received assurance from the other grain exporters that they would not make up the differences. Amidst reports that conclusions had been held with all European allies, White House officials added that Argentina was 'sympathetic' and that specific assurance had been received from Australia and Canada. In the case of Canada, such a pronouncement appears to have been premature. Prior to the invasion, Canadian External Affairs officials had watched the early signs of mounting tension in the region with growing concern. Their accounts of NATO meetings, their information exchanges with the United States and their own intelligence community had indicated a troop concentration in the southern Soviet Union that was not normal. At this time, the perception of Canada's senior officialdom was dominated by a vision of a 'crescent of uncertainty' extending from Africa through to the Middle East to Afghanistan that was plagued by instability. As a result, Afghanistan was seen as one of a number of troublesome situations and one that no one felt was the most likely to erupt. Indeed, the preferred candidate was Iran, where officials, who recalled

Soviet actions in the 1950s, felt that the Soviet Union might take direct action to control the disintegration that had followed the overthrow of the Shah. This estimate, and an historic tendency to withstand a flood of US demarches on East-West relations until time and perspective dictated which one was truly serious, made for a minimal anticipatory response.

Although there was an initial, unifying horror at what the Soviet Union had done, differences of perspective and calculation quickly emerged. In particular, there was a considerable debate within Ottawa about the Soviet motives for the intervention, what the Soviet Union's next move was likely to be, and what kind of Western actions were most likely to achieve a desired result. Allan MacKinnon, the Minister of National Defence, saw it as a component of a malevolent world-wide Communist design. Secretary of State for External Affairs Flora MacDonald, reacting quickly to the invasion, tended to view the Soviet objective as a grab at oil in Iran and adjacent regions. Her officials were sceptical and felt that Soviet objectives had more to do with Afghanistan itself, the Brezhnev doctrine, instability in Iran and Soviet fear that the revival of Islamic fundamentalism would spread, perhaps even to the Soviet Union. In addition, they calculated, Afghanistan had presented an all too inviting target of opportunity that was ripe for intervention, given the Soviet Union's previous machinations over the preceding half decade, and the failure of the Carter Administration to take significant moves to signal that Afghanistan was important to the United States and the West.

Despite these uncertainties, forces flowing from the structure of the international system generated a convergent Canadian response. The sheer shock of the invasion prompted MacDonald and other ministers to conclude immediately that Canada must do something, even as the public, perhaps viewing rapid US responses, called for something to be done. A second impetus was the US request itself. At the time, Canadians, apart from those few who knew the Canadian embassy in Iran was providing sanctuary to US diplomats, had looked upon developments in Iran with a sense of frustration which stemmed from their perceived inability to do anything to help the US in that part of the world. Such a feeling predisposed Canadian ministers in particular to respond favourably to a US call over Afghanistan, particularly as the events in the latter country demonstrated the United States' defensiveness and need for support in the region as a whole.

In defining Canada's response, however, Canadian decision-makers operated under several constraints. The first was a feeling that Canadian objectives were not simply to contain the Soviet Union, but perhaps equally, in the light of US agitation, to prevent US leaders from doing anything rash. A second was a recognition that their European allies shared a similar view of what the objectives of the Western response should be. While recognising that calling for a Soviet pull out was a necessary posture that could command Canada's public adherence, Ottawa remained massively sceptical that anything the West could do would achieve such a goal. Aided by Europeans, they thus defined their objectives, in practise, as raising the cost to the Soviet Union of undertaking additional actions elsewhere and, in particular, of moving into Iran or Turkey. Concern over Canada's own relationship with the Soviet Union also entered into the decisional equation.

By the time of the President's grain embargo announcement, the Canadian government had been informed of US thinking in the Christopher consultations in London and Brussels and subsequent NATO deliberations, perhaps in high-level telephone calls on the evening of 27 December and through a more routine diplomatic note of 3 January. On that date the US embassy in Ottawa received instructions at a fairly low level to consent to inform their External Affairs counterparts that the United States was considering a grain embargo, to ask if the Canadians thought it was a good idea, and to inquire if they were inclined to support it. A day later, just prior to the President's announcement, US Agriculture Department officials contacted exporting nations, including, as the first step, Canadian officials in the Grains Group, to inform them of US actions, and to invite them to Washington on 12 January for a meeting of grain exporting nations.

Thus on 4 January in his weekly press conference Prime Minister Clark could announce only a condemnation of Soviet action, a refusal to recognise the new regime in Afghanistan, the termination of Canada's two aid programmes in the country (consisting of a hydroelectric and educational project together valued at $3.1 million), and the withdrawal of its aid personnel. The following day NATO began discussing joint steps to support the United States, although only the United Kingdom seemed firm in its support. Yet following a Soviet veto of the Security Council resolution and its transmittal to the General Assembly, France, the United Kingdom and the Federal Republic of Germany pledged on 8 January not to increase grain sales to make up the US shortfall. Australia provided a similar pledge. Both France and the Federal Republic of Germany, which feared the impact of trade sanctions and serious damage to East-West relations, continued to be more hesitant than the United Kingdom, with France declaring no reduction in her traditional exports. Argentina was even more recalcitrant; it offered to attend a meeting of grain exporters in Washington which the United States had called for 12 January, but given the lack of prior consultation, refused to participate in an embargo. At the end of that meeting, the United States was able to announce that all Western countries that were represented supported the embargo and that Argentina had pledged not to take advantage of the situation. Two days later the US push for active measures received further multilateral support when the General Assembly voted 104-18 against the Soviet Union and the World Bank stopped disbursing funds for development projects in Afghanistan.

Yet from this point on, consensus and momentum quickly eroded. By 15 January Argentina and the United States were publicly offering differing versions of the former's promises. The following day Japan announced that it would not impose sanctions on the Soviet Union, Brazil declared that it was not involved in the embargo, and France became embroiled in a dispute with the United States over France's proposal to sell meat and butter to the Soviet Union.

In late January the Canadian Cabinet focused on Canada's inclusion in the grain embargo. As a result of differences in the crop-year between Canada and the other major exporters (with Canada's crop-year falling later in the calendar year), other countries had settled their negotiations with the Soviet Union for 1980, whereas Canada had a group of representatives about to leave for Moscow to complete sales discussions for the current crop year. Given the recently completed American and Australian experiences, Canada held high expectations of signing a huge contract for the fall of 1980. Although it became clear at the 12 January meeting that Canada's negotiations would be permitted to continue, the question arose of what historical levels would constitute guidelines for the negotiations. Initially, a hasty Canadian estimate was 3.0 to 3.5 mmt. Now Cabinet approval was given for 3.5 to 3.8 mmt up to 31 July. And in February Canada signed a contract to sell more than half of the 3.19 mmt of grain already authorised for the Soviet Union for the eleven months of the 1979-80 crop-year.

Fuelled by these moves and with the appearance of unanimity unravelling under the impact of French and Argentine actions, the US government began to cast a more critical eye on Canadian sales. To a considerable extent, US frustration with its Canadian ally stemmed from the distinctly different approach to the Soviet Union that arose in Ottawa when Pierre Trudeau's Liberal majority government replaced Joe Clark's Conservative minority government on 19 February. In late February the Liberals began a review of all Canadian actions. A month later they had confirmed all decisions, save for that on the proposed Olympic boycott. They thus set, for the time being, the grain sale level at

3.8 mmt.

As summer approached, disagreement arose over Canada's plan for grain exports in the new crop year beginning 1 August. On 11 June Ottawa announced its decision to abide by Canada's original promise not to sell grain in excess of 'normal and traditional levels'. But with the Soviet acquisition of new suppliers, US hustling for new markets, and the end of the crop-year two months away, Cabinet was unable to set an official sales ceiling to give the embargo visible clout. Canadian experts laid the blame for the problem on the US Department of Agriculture, which produced low estimates of Soviet import demand. Moscow was getting all the grain it wanted, but given delivery problems, long lead times and a barley shortage, the Canadian Wheat Board could not compete for non-traditional markets. As well, the grain industry was worried over the potential long-term erosion of Canada's international market position as a result of the embargo.

Later in June, at the economic summit of allied leaders in Venice, Trudeau merely repeated to Carter Canada's general commitment on trade restrictions for the next crop year. With the approach of the 1 August date, Canada announced that it could sell up to 5 million metric tons in 1980-81, depending on shipping capacity and crop size. With the other factors taken into consideration - continued leaking of US grain through Eastern Europe, record sales for Australia and Argentina, no impact felt by the Soviet Union, no withdrawal from Afghanistan - Canada's support for the embargo dwindled.

Within this maze of complex calculations and shifting positions, the behaviour of the United States itself occupied a primary place. Canadian support for the embargo remained relatively firm during the spring, despite the lack of prior US consultation and the continuing massive US sales to the Soviet Union (2.5 mmt under the former US agreement and sales through Eastern Europe). It eroded considerably during the summer as US grain leaked into international markets, as US domestic support eroded, and as presidential candidate Reagan pledged an end to the embargo. And it evaporated in the autumn when the United States proceeded to sell 8 mmt to the Soviet Union and assault traditional Canadian markets in China and elsewhere.

That Canada provided such strong support in the initial phase can be traced to two major factors. The first is that the only high-level consultations prior to the 4 January embargo, however unsatisfactory and general, did focus on the six key members of the Western Economic Summit Seven and steered the US action into NATO and UN channels. Second, the simultaneous shocks of Iran and Afghanistan gave the major Western allies a security interest in acting to support a US president under siege, to prevent further Soviet incursions into the 'arc of crisis' and possibly to prevent a perception that their weak response to Iran may have tempted the Soviet Union to move on Afghanistan. At any rate, it is striking that within the grain exporters group, the United States' most faithful suppporters (Canada and France) were members of the Summit 7, while the most recalcitrant (Australia and Argentina) were middle powers with no responsibilities for Western security or global balance. Thus the Afghanistan grain embargo ultimately failed not because the channels and obligations of the summit members were impotent, (as the legacy of the Venice summit suggests), but because its two most loyal members - Canada and France - controlled less of the grain flow to the Soviet Union and the Argentine and Australian outsiders, and the highly leaky United States itself.[18]

Poland 1980-1982: Success through the Six

The logic of the Summit Seven grouping became apparent in the initial stages and subsequent inter-allied disagreements in the Polish crisis. The United States attempted to activate and apply the general alliance consensus directly to possible sanctions over Poland before the crisis broke. It also adopted almost precisely the proper set of players and procedures for this purpose. The subsequent US failure to prevail against its fellow summitteers on the pipelines sanctions component of the crisis merely underscored the weight of the summit group.[19]

The consultations of the six major Western powers over Poland (the summitteers, minus Japan) over Poland had their origins in US acceptance of the inadequacy of the consultations over Afghanistan. In January of 1980 Vance had travelled to Europe for allied discussions over Afganistan but, given the election campaign in progress in Canada, had been unable to stop off in Ottawa on his return voyage for ministerial-level consultations. As a result, on his return to Washington he invited the Canadian Ambassador to the State Department as a substitute. During the course of the conversation which centred on the problems of consultation over Afghanistan, the idea emerged of having follow-up sessions on Afghanistan and successor problems, as well as inviting the Washington ambassadors of the other Summit Six countries (usually representing the most senior and skilled diplomats in their countries' corps) to these gatherings. Given the sensitivities surrounding such an 'inner club,' the gatherings took place in secret in a highly informal seminar-like atmosphere after office hours in Vance's office. During the course of half a dozen meetings, the participants did much to identify different points of view that had emerged over Afghanistan, develop a shared recognition of the problem emerging there and in Poland, and harmonise perspectives where possible.

Although the gatherings ended when Secretary Muskie replaced Vance, their legacy was apparent in the initial public response of the allies to the growing tensions in Poland in the autumn of 1980. In responding to the increasing tension in December of 1980, Prime Minister Trudeau noted that he was consulting the leaders of France and the Federal Republic of Germany and emphasised the need for the allies to present a united front, because they had not done so in Afghanistan. On 9 December he spoke of forthcoming NATO and OECD meetings as the proper fora in which a co-ordinated allied position should be defined. On 15 December he declared Canada's full support for the NATO position of 'a strong and appropriate reaction to any intensification of the crisis in Poland'. Indeed, as late as June 1981 the Prime Minister could state that the NATO consultation on European issues had improved greatly and was promoting stability and balance, although situations outside Europe remained to be dealt with by emergency arrangements and Western summits.

The finely developed structure of consultation created against the contingency of a Soviet invasion of Poland was not, however, fully transferable to the unexpected event of martial law imposed from within on 13 December 1981. As a result, dissension soon began to appear. By late December the United States had curtailed credits, high technology sales, government food aid, civil aviation and fishing rights, and subsequently prospects of a Soviet-American summit and strategic arms talks were deferred. Although in early January NATO foreign ministers declared that the Soviets were involved in the Polish crisis, the consensus went no further. In Madrid, the Federal Republic of Germany and the United States disagreed over the continuance of the Conference on Security and Co-operation in Europe. The United Kingdom in early February reduced technological co-operation and fishing quotas for the Soviet Union and Poland, but the Federal Republic of Germany and France refused to follow.

With the summit powers divided in this fashion, Canada adopted an intermediate position. After surprisingly favourable initial comments, Prime Minister Trudeau's statements on the crisis quickly began to resemble those emanating from Washington. Yet on the issue of sanctions Canada remained, with the West Germans, on the 'dovish' end of the alliance spectrum. While several factors contributed to this stance - including Trudeau's special bilateral relationship with Helmut Schmidt - the legacy of the previous consensus was prominent among them. Throughout the crisis Canada continued to argue for holding more punitive measures in reserve for the situation against which the planning of the six had been directed and which may, in some small measure, have deterred a Soviet military invasion of Poland.[20]

The Falklands/Malvinas, 1982: Success without the Superpower

The British-inaugurated embargo of Argentina following the latter's invasion of the Falklands/Malvinas on 2 April 1982 provides further evidence of the strength of the Summit Seven channel. In this instance, it had the ability to withstand the refusal of its leading member, the United States, to associate itself with the collective regime. Throughout the crisis Canada's response demonstrated clearly how the views of the Summit Seven majority, reinforced by international law and organisation and the adequacy of sanctions-specific consultation, predominated in the Canadian calculation over concern with US positions. For one of the few times in its history, Canada was definitely prepared to invoke economic sanctions that were significantly more stringent than those of the United States.[21]

On the day of the Argentine invasion, Canada's response was swift and sure. The Secretary of State for External Affairs pronounced the invasion 'deeply shocking', particularly as it violated a 1976 United Nations General Assembly resolution on the dispute which Argentina had supported. Within three days Canada had recalled its ambassador from Buenos Aires, embargoed all military shipments to Argentina and cancelled official visits. After consultation with the British High Commissioner, it began to consider further measures. Two days later the minister noted that Canada's measures were 'exactly parallel' to those of the Federal Republic of Germany and surpassed in severity only by those of the United Kingdom and New Zealand. Following this logic, on 12 April Canada imposed a ban on all imports from Argentina and export credits for any new commercial transactions with that country.

In comparative perspective (which dominated the Canadian vision), these measures went well beyond those taken by the United States. They were precisely parallel to those taken by the European Community (as the minister endlessly emphasised) and by Australia and New Zealand. Unlike the European Community sanctions, which were authorised for short, fixed periods, Canada's sanctions were adopted without a specified terminal date.

In the Falklands/Malvinas case the logic of the existing channels received no strong reinforcement from directly compatible Canadian interests or from extrasystemic pressures. It did, however, receive a considerable assist from Canadian concern with the effectiveness of international law and organisation. This consideration, signalled in Canada's first statement, was legitimised for Canada the following day when the UN Security Council, in a 10 to 1 vote, demanded an immediate cessation of hostilities and Argentinian withdrawal. When Argentina flouted this resolution by actually strengthening its garrison, Canada introduced sanctions out of a 'principal concern' to contribute to the UN Charter and international law.

During the ensuing months Canada's emphasis on international law and organisation continued. Canada declared that the issue of sovereignty over the Falklands/Malvinas was a matter for decision by an arbitration tribunal, the International Court of Justice or negotiations between the parties, in accordance with its initial support for Security Council resolution 502 on the subject. It associated itself, when invited, with a Peruvian initiative for a negotiated settlement, on the sole condition that Canada's involvement be acceptable to both parties in the dispute. And Canada similarly offered to assist the UN Secretary-General in his subsequent efforts.

Curiously enough, the strength of Canada's commitment to international law was reflected in Canada's refusal to halt exports of nuclear fuel rod bundles to Argentina. The Canadian defence went well beyond the usual argument centred on the sanctity of existing contracts and actual ownership of the bundles and constituent uranium. It was based on the argument that delivery was guaranteed under a bilateral nuclear agreement with Argentina that provided unusually strong safeguards and that provided Canada with the right of inspection by the International Atomic Energy Agency.

Conclusion

Writing in the winter of 1981-82 about the US sanctions in Iran, Robert Carswell concluded his analysis with the following advice to his countrymen:

> when the next international emergency arises, U.S. policy-makers should exhaust every possible avenue of multilateral co-operation before considering unilateral sanctions - and should be prepared to accept even substantial modification of what the United States itself might deem desirable in order to achieve a united front with other major industrialized countries (and with key regional nations if necessary)....The United States can no longer afford the luxury or cost of leadership when our allies do not follow.[22]

The analysis in this chapter suggests that Carswell is only partly correct. Certainly his stress on involving or adapting existing avenues of co-operation is well taken, as these can powerfully compensate for deficiences in the technicalities of sanctions-specific consultation and add the reinforcing legitimacy of existing international law. He is clearly accurate in his assessment that the United States no longer has sufficiently predominant capability in most issue areas or overall to afford the risk and subsequent costs of going it alone.

Yet in its search for a broader coalition and consensus, it need not launch an indiscriminate quest for every possible avenue and every member which happens to appear in every multilateral framework so discovered. Indeed, it can confine its search to the seven industrialised world's principal powers, which in the concert of the Western Economic Summit have proven themselves capable of acting as the 'executive committee' of the OECD and in some respects of NATO as well. A sanctioning power might even be able to get away with only six of the summit seven, even if, for some purposes, the missing member is the United States.

Notes

The author is an Associate Professor of Political Science at the University of Toronto and Co-director of its Centre for International Studies project on Canada-U.S. Institutional Relations of which this chapter forms a part. Appreciation is extended to the Donner Canadian Foundation for financial support, and to Tom Mito, Blair Dimock and Sarah Saunders for research assistance.

1. K. J. Holsti, International Politics: A Framework for Analysis, 3rd edition, (Prentice-Hall, Englewood Cliffs, N.J., 1977) pp. 242-72.

2. In the case of Iran, little consultation led to a heavy programme of sanctions, with high effectiveness and few allied complaints; in the case of Afghanistan, low consultation led to heavy sanctions, but with little effectiveness and much complaint; in the case of Poland, high consultation produced light sanctions, with low effectiveness and many complaints; in the case of Argentina, low consultation generated heavy sanctions with high effectiveness and little discord.

3. Left unaddressed is the explanatory relevance of such more general and less policy-relevant factors as the severity of the transgression being punished, the fragility of the international order and the prevailing international distribution of power.

4. On the broader conception of 'effectivenss', see, for example, James Barber, 'Economic Sanctions as a Policy Instrument', International Affairs, 55 (July 1979), pp 367-84.

5. In these four test cases (Iran, Afghanistan, Poland, Argentina), the degree and form for case specific

consultation varied widely. So did the severity of the sanctions selected, their effectiveness and the satisfaction with the process employed and results obtained. These four cases also have the advantage of occurring at close intervals (thereby allowing important environmental variables to be held constant), simultaneously (thereby having partly-fused decision-making processes and the potential for trade-offs among cases), and sequentially in direct succession (thereby permitting the process of decisional learning to be assessed). Conclusions must remain suggestive, however, given the small number of cases and the lesser attention devoted to the two most recent ones, for which reliable information remains limited.

The focus on the Canada-United States component of these cases in instructive in four ways. The two states represent the polar ends of the consultation continium, with the United States being the superpower perenially pleading the demands of leadership and effectiveness, and Canada being the smallest ally big enough to matter (that is, a state whose compliance is important enough to the effectiveness of a sanctions programme that it should be able to extract consultation commitments in return). The pronounced interdependence and ideal of a 'special relationship' between the two countries has generated an abundance of special sanctions problems (such as transshipment, spare parts substitution and extraterritoriality), special expectations of consultation on the part of Canada, and special expectations of compliance on the part of the United States. The long history of sanctions disputes between the two countries, notably those over China and Cuba, has given Canada a claim to be an alliance leader in the dilemmas of coping with US unilateralism, calling as a right for greater consultation, and creatively devising ways by which the latter task might be accomplished. For Canada, these four cases confirm a historic change in Canada's approach to economic sanctions that were begun in 1974, in which the small, open, trade-dependent non-compliance over China and Cuba, adopted sanctions as a routine instrument of statecraft for at least a decade.

6. Most of the major causes, apart from the time related ones, stem ultimately from characteristics of the external environment.

7. The short-term application of sanctions may be sufficient for some purposes - e.g. signalling resolve, declaring illegitimacy, defining the area in which other states should stay out. Yet most purposes demand that the sanctioners be prepared to settle down for the long haul: to convince leaders and citizens of the 'outlaw country', after the initial outburst of national solidarity in both societies, that there is no future under existing policies, and to enforce the slow economic strangulation and stag-

nation of their country to this end.

8. Robert Carswell, 'Economic Sanctions and the Iran Experience', Foreign Affairs 60 (Winter 1981-82), p. 264.

9. This analysis of the Iran case is based primarly on interviews with senior officials in Ottawa in 1981 and 1982 and in Washington in 1981. Much useful additional detail about US calculations has come from the memoir material of the Carter Administration, notably Jimmy Carter, Keeping Faith (Bantam, Toronto, 1982); Cyrus Vance, Hard Choices: Critical Years in American's Foreign Policy (Simon and Schuster, New York, 1983); Zbigniew Brzezinski, Power and Principle (Farrar, Stratus, Groux, 1983); and Hamilton Jordan, Crisis (Berkley Books, New York, 1982).

10. Only in the second week of April did the European Community members and Japan temporarily withdraw their ambassadors from Iran. By 20 April the United Kingdom, the Federal Republic of Germany and the Netherlands seemed seemed prepared to join a collective effort, but French intransigence appeared likely to doom this effort. On 22 April the Community did announce measures, which were centred on a denial of military exports and new export credits to Iran. Japan's response was to freeze the price that it paid for imported Iranian oil and later, to stop Iranian oil imports. Only Portugal at that stage went as far as the United States in banning trade with Iran.

11. This episode is described in Jean Pelletier, The Canadian Caper (Paperjacks, Markham, 1981). See also Jeffrey Simpson, Discipline of Power (Personal Library, Toronto, 1980).

12. The initial sanctions included a denial of student visas to Iranians outside Canada, the removal of one Iranian diplomat from Ottawa, a denial of military export permits and export development and corporation credits, and advisory to oil companies to cease purchases of Iranian oil, and a similar advisory to Canadian companies not to enter into new export and service contracts until the hostages were released.

13. L. C. Green, 'The Tehran Embassy Incident and International Law', Behind the Headlines 38 (1980).

14. On the role of the summit see George de Menil and Anthony M. Solomon, Economic Summitry, (New York Council on Foreign Relations, 1983); Robert Putnam and Nicholas Baryne, Hanging Together: The Seven-Power Summits (Harvard University Press, Cambridge, Mass., 1984).

15. Canada also pursued bilateral negotiations with Mexico and Venezuela for additional supplies and resisted Exxon's efforts to divert Canadian-destined crude from Canada under Exxon's private sector emergency-sharing scheme.

16. See, for example, Robert Paarlberg, 'Lessons of the Grain Embargo', Foreign Affairs 59 (Autumn 1980), p.

149.

17. This analysis is based primarily on the interview programmes listed in note 9.

18. On the Venice summit, see Carter, _Keeping Faith_, p. 538.

19. Adam Bromke et al., _Canada's Response to the Polish Crisis_ (Canadian Institute of International Affairs, Toronto, 1982).

20. Alexander Haig, _Caveat_ (MacMillan, New York, 1984).

21. This account is based primarily on _International Canada_, Government of Canada, House of Commons, _Debates_, 1 June 1982, pp. 17779-17981.

22. Carswell, 'Economic Sanctions and the Iran Experience', p. 265.

PART VI

THE UTILITY OF ECONOMIC SANCTIONS

Chapter Fifteen

THE UTILITY OF ECONOMIC SANCTIONS AS A POLICY INSTRUMENT

Lawrence J. Brady

The utility of economic sanctions is a broad topic, which must be narrowed considerably if we are to make useful statements about sanctions as policies. We cannot generalise about sanctions as though they were all alike and will all have predictable results. In actual fact, there are an infinite number of possible variants in the conditions under which sanctions might be imposed and in the results they might have.

People often think of sanctions as standing in a category by themselves. When we examine the nature of sanctions more closely, however, we find that they actually belong to a large family of economic instruments that are occasionally used for foreign policy reasons.

We can easily document the instances in which a threat to deny an economic benefit is used to gain political leverage. Contracts, markets, credits and other assets are frequently offered in return for political favours, by individuals as well as governments. Sanctions are no more than one form of economic denial, in which an existing rather than a potential benefit is denied the target country in response to unacceptable conduct in the international community. Unless we allow governments only to promote and not to regulate trade in the national interest, they will continue to utilise sanctions to some degree for foreign policy purposes.

Broadly speaking, economic sanctions include a wide range of penalties such as: embargoes on financial and commercial dealings; restrictions on the use of transport; and restricted communications of all kinds. A ban on imports from the target nation is intended to produce a shortage of foreign exchange, unemployment in export industries and reduced use of industrial capacity. A ban on exports to the target nation is intended to deprive it of essential commodities.

Financial sanctions can deny the target country access to foreign capital and money markets. A ban on transport can physically isolate the target country and harm it economically. A disruption of communications can have serious economic effects as well as produce a sense of psychological isolation.

The Goals of Sanctions

There are several possible foreign policy objectives that may be sought by imposing economic sanctions in response to a threat or misconduct by another country. The generally accepted goal is to influence the conduct of the political actors in another country who refuse to conform to accepted norms of international conduct. This is done by inflicting an economic punishment on those actors, which can have political side-effects. It can be difficult to inflict such a punishment unless the economic privation is especially harsh and is imposed in co-operation with other nations. If economic sanctions are not imposed in a co-operative fashion, the target nation can turn to alternative sources of economic sustenance, and may not suffer enough to motivate a change in behaviour.

Other objectives when imposing economic sanctions include:

1. to bring about a diplomatic loss of face;
2. to signal the target country that the resolve to resist its aggression is not lacking;
3. to signal the target country that its conduct is considered unacceptable by some, and to raise the possibility that others will condemn such behaviour;
4. to reduce the possibility of military conflict;
5. to alter the status of the target country as a dominant supplier of critical resources to friends and allies; and
6. to reduce other forms of economic leverage that may be used by a potential adversary to harm the national interests of the initiator.

It should be remembered that sanctions are rarely, if ever, applied with one narrow goal in mind. They always constitute an effort to achieve some or all of the goals mentioned above. In this sense, they are complex political instruments. Their complexity is enhanced by the fact that economic sanctions are by definition applied as response to aggressive behaviour rather than an offensive coercive action. They are used when other avenues of response have been exhausted, or when it is perceived that other forms of response will be futile.

Economic sanctions can bring about a loss of face by undermining, over time, the legitimacy of a particular government. The United States has for many years maintained economic embargoes on all products and technical data to the governments of North Korea, Vietnam, Kampuchea, and Cuba. These embargoes were applied in response to efforts by these countries to export revolution to countries around them. In this sense, the sanctions are designed to undermine the legitimacy of those governments' conduct.

Economic sanctions such as those applied by the United States against Libya are designed to express the resolve of the United States to oppose Libyan support for terrorism. In this way, economic sanctions signal another country that the resolve to resist is not lacking and warns the offender that the response could be escalated if the conduct were to get any worse.

Economic sanctions are all designed to point out unacceptable behaviour. With time, sanctions are extremely effective if one by one other countries begin to agree that certain conduct cannot be tolerated. The longer the conduct persists, the higher the chance that other countries will begin to sympathise with certain sanctions and offer to help make them more effective.

The most important general goal of economic sanctions is to reduce the possibility of precipitate military response to actions in the international community. In relations among nations, international incidents of aggression will progressively raise tension levels until they reach their highest point, which is war. If there is no outlet for the outrage and tension at the lower end of the spectrum, they could set off a military reaction at some indeterminable point.

Let us examine this explanation on the basis of experience. The United States evinced little reaction to the events in the Horn of Africa, Yemen, Latin America and the Middle East during the 1970s. On 24 December 1979 the Soviet Union invaded Afghanistan, putting it about 400 hundred miles from the tip of the Arabian Peninsula. This action contravened standard Soviet behaviour up to that point, which was basically to use surrogate revolutionaries, not the Red Army, in actions against other countries. The United States responded with a partial embargo on grain, which achieved partial success by causing the Soviet Union to purchase higher priced grain elsewhere, to engage in distress slaughtering and to purchase grain from several producers, which is always less efficient than purchasing from one principal producer. This action relieved some of the accumulated outrage building in the United States toward Soviet behaviour, although only a real change in Soviet conduct could achieve a permanent reduction in tensions. The Soviet Union did not change its menacing behaviour in response to the grain embargo. Nevertheless, whether we agree as students of international relations and policy-makers that the sanctions were effective, we cannot underestimate the importance of these sanctions in lowering the threshold of tension in the international system. It may be better that we spar on the economic battlefield than the military one.

In addition to the goals I have just briefly described - diplomatic loss of face, signal of resolve, signal that at least one country and possibly others over time disapprove of the target government's behaviour, and reduction of chances that the response will be military - I listed two other goals. Those were to alter the status of the target country as a dominant supplier of critical resources and to reduce other forms of possibly harmful economic leverage.

These last two goals are unusual, perhaps, and apply directly to the economic sanctions imposed by the United States against the Soviet pipeline from Siberia to Europe. We must focus on the goals of these sanctions for one moment because they were different from the other list of sanctions I mentioned. They differed in that they targeted a long-term potential adversary and they had a direct impact on the economies of our friends and allies who were helping to construct the pipeline.

The concern about reliance on the critical resources of the Soviet Union was not new. The United States and NATO had opposed energy co-operation with the Soviet Union for years prior to the signing of the first energy agreement with the Soviet Union in 1972. During detente, security opposition to such co-operation virtually disappeared.

But Soviet actions since 1979 gradually convinced the Reagan Administration that such a sanguine outlook on energy co-operation with the Soviet Union was perhaps not wise. It has taken the better part of two years to turn this realisation into active policy. But this is understandable if we think about how difficult it is to modify the basic principles of co-operation and exchange that had been the basis for Western detente with the Soviet Union. Europe, Japan and the United States are still struggling to redefine and modify those principles in accordance with the kind of quid pro quo we expect from the Soviet Union.

As you are aware, the United States imposed sanctions due to Soviet proxy actions in Poland. However, our objectives in this instance were far more than tactical or temporary. Rather we sought to build a consensus for cautious economic and trade relations with a hostile state bent upon global domination. When we lifted the sanctions we did so because we were able to persuade our European allies to take a closer look at their growing economic relationship with the Soviet Union and to co-operate with us in redefining a cohesive Western approach to the entire East-West economic agenda.

The Reagan Administration has clearly adopted the approach that the entire East-West economic relationship should be re-examined. Certain quid pro quos should be identified and areas in which trade is bestowing extraordinary economic leverage on the Soviet Union, such as in oil and gas and export credits, must be studied in order to perhaps inhibit that leverage.

The perception of some is that the pipeline sanctions were not effective in delaying the pipeline and were lifted without receiving anything in return. But the Reagan Administration does not share this perception. It views the pipeline sanctions in the context of making some very significant long-term changes in East-West economic policies in the future. This became the context when the sanctions were lifted and the Europeans signed agreements to form a working group on East-West economic relations which would undertake several comprehensive studies on the entire spectrum of East-West economics.

Achieving Broad Goals

It is quite true that in order to inflict the maximum economic price on a target country, economic sanctions must not be breached by alternate suppliers. However, it would be naive to expect every alternative supplier to observe an embargo. Some will have political differences or economic motives, and sometimes effective pressure will be applied on alternate suppliers by the target country. Economic sanctions such as the ones concerning the pipeline can have economic consequences for our allies, which will work to vitiate support for the goals of the sanctions. Only if the sanctions can contribute to long-term foreign policy perceptions and understanding, as the pipeline sanctions have, can they still be defended. Again, with time, if the conduct of the Soviet Union does not change, there is the growing possibility that other countries will support these long-term goals.

One hundred per cent effectiveness cannot be sought when applying economic sanctions. The initiator must also be ready to pay an economic price. All sanctions affect economic interest groups in the initiating country. Exporters lose contracts which would strengthen the health of the economy. These costs, however, must be weighed against the national interests and the future costs to US society if the contested behaviour is condoned or allowed to go on unopposed.

Conclusion

In sum, economic sanctions will always be one of the instruments used on occasion by national governments in response to threats and aggression by actors in the international system. The effectiveness of sanctions will never be 100 per cent, and the economic sacrifices made to carry out the policy will always be a source of controversy.

Nevertheless, sanctions do accomplish important foreign policy objectives. They express the feelings of a nation when other responses are futile. They punish the offending nation in several ways: by depriving it of diplomatic face and legitimacy; by posing the threat of gradual ostracism and isolation; by altering status in the economic community; and by denying certain kinds of economic power. All of these foreign policy objectives are worth while because they can be achieved without the use of military force, if there is sufficient co-operation.

Chapter Sixteen

LESSONS AND POLICY CONSIDERATIONS ABOUT ECONOMIC SANCTIONS

David Leyton-Brown

Economic sanctions are almost never solely responsible for the outcome produced in an international conflict, but they may be important contributory factors. Much of the confusion and controversy about the utility of international economic sanctions stems from confusion about the purposes which they can and are intended to serve. Five analytically distinct but not mutually exclusive goals may be pursued by economic sanctions. Clarification of these interrelated but separate purposes leads to the understanding that different objectives are but achieved by different instruments, and should be judged by different criteria as to their success or failure.

1. To punish transgression. The first purpose of sanctions, both conceptually and historically, is punitive. Whether based on legal or utilitarian considerations, the thrust of this approach is to make a wrong-doer suffer a penalty for his act. It is analogous to sentencing a burglar to a term in jail for his crime, not in the hope that he will be rehabilitated by the uplifting environment of the penitentiary, but in punishment for the offense. The imposition of economic sanctions in this spirit serves to define unacceptable behaviour, either unilaterally or multilaterally, and thus serves to contribute to the establishment of internationally accepted standards of legitimated conduct.

Sanctions designed for punitive purposes should be short, sharp and to the point. As in the domestic legal system, the punishment should fit the crime. Just as capital punishment is an inappropriate penalty for minor crimes, so too must the severity and duration of economic sanctions be tailored to the magnitude of the offence. Punitive sanctions succeed if the norms of acceptable behaviour are reaffirmed and strengthened, and the violator is effectively punished.

2. To deter future action. Economic sanctions are not only intended to punish those who have acted unacceptably in the past. They are also intended to deter those actors and others from engaging in similar behaviour in the

future.

Sanctions designed for deterrent purposes should be explicit, proportionate to the act being deterred, and credible, with regard to the costs to be incurred and the certainty of application. Like all deterrents, success can never be securely measured, since the offending behaviour might not have taken place in any event. The only true test is one of failure, but even that is ambiguous, since the deterrent itself can paradoxically have invited the behaviour it was intended to prevent by contributing to a climate of escalating hostility. Despite these conceptual difficulties, one might judge the deterrent purposes of sanctions to have been successful in a particular case so long as future undesired behaviour was avoided, even if the outcome in the immediate case was unfavourable.

3. To compel a change in behaviour. The types of changes encompassed within this category are numerous and disparate. Indeed, the range is so great that a strong argument could be made for subdividing the category into two or more separate purposes. However, all of the purposes involve a coercive attempt to compel others to alter the status quo, be it a specific policy, the outcome of military conflict or negotiation, or the nature of the political regime itself. The specific objectives can range from minor policy changes, such as the resumption of negotiations or the release of hostages, to major policy changes, such as the withdrawal of troops or the cessation of hostilities, to the destabilisation of a government, to the overthrow of the entire social, economic and political basis of a regime. Goals of forcing a strong, self-sufficient state to change the fundamental identity of its society, or even to abandon major policies associated with its vital interests, are virtually impossible of realisation. Economic sanctions alone are hardly likely to compel the Soviet Union to give up Communism, South Africa to end the apartheid system, or Western Europe to convert to Islam. Specific minor policies, not related to the vital interests of the state concerned or of the goverment in power, can more readily be affected by economic sanctions, but even there there is a problem. If sanctions are explicitly and publicly imposed to bring about a policy change, it becomes politically much more difficult for the target government to comply, for it will be seen by its own citizens and by others to have yielded to foreign pressure. Compellent purposes of sanctions are the most difficult to achieve, especially for changes to important policies. However, failure to bring about a desired change does not mean that some other purpose may not have been realised.

4. To restrict economic and military capabilities. Sanctions may be designed to deny the target access to technology and the benefits of comparative advantage in a trading

system, and to force the target to produce goods itself less efficiently, and thus at higher social cost and a slower rate of economic growth. This all can have the effect of making it more costly and time-consuming for the target to pursue its policies. Ongoing export controls aimed at the Soviet Union or the People's Republic of China fall in this category. Success is very hard to gauge, since in almost every case the proscribed technology is eventually acquired and the economic or military activities are undertaken, though perhaps somewhat later and at greater cost. Resources diverted, inefficiencies imposed and opportunities forgone are the measure of success, and they are very hard to quantify.

5. To signal resolve. Economic sanctions can be used to send a message to the target and to one's own domestic population. To the target, economic sanctions can communicate outrage, firmness and solidarity. In the face of a provocative act which requires a response, economic sanctions are stronger than mere rhetoric, but not as costly or prone to escalation as military action. Out of the range of available policy responses, economic sanctions, when well designed and well applied, can be a useful alternative to military force, and indeed can work to contain or prevent the subsequent use of force by the target. When other states join in the sanctions, the signal of resolve is not just unilateral but multilateral, and the unity thus demonstrated can have substantial effect on future developments.

In this connection, the issue of costs to the initiator must be raised. Despite sceptical images of 'shooting oneself in the foot', the seriousness of the signal of resolve can be strengthened by the willingness of the initiator to incur some costs in the process. This phenomenon is reminiscent of the argument in early deterrence theory that the credibility and effectiveness of a deterrent threat could be enhanced if its execution involved some cost to the party issuing the threat.[1] Collective goods literature argues for the importance of an alliance leader initiating action and bearing a higher share of the cost.[2] In most East-West sanctions cases, and in several other instances, the United States has played that role. The signal of alliance solidarity requires the design of sanctions so that there is general acceptance of the equality of sacrifice and not resentment at unequal burden-sharing.

Perhaps even more important than the signal to the target is the signal to one's own domestic population. This domestic dimension is an inescapable part of the objective in every sanctions case. It may be important for the government to act in a conflict situation, but in domestic political terms it is more important for the government to be seen to be acting. Economic sanctions are often intended to defuse pressures for more extreme action, and to satisfy others that the government is acting firmly. There is a danger that this objective may contradict others. Designing sanctions for domestic consumption rather than an impact on the target and presenting them to the public with an exaggerated description of their intended and anticipated effects can undercut the other purposes, and, in the long-term, can lead to public disillusionment and a possible public backlash of opinion. Still, this purpose for economic sanctions can be judged to have been fulfilled successfully if public opinion broadly supports the action, regardless of whether any other objectives are met.

This review of the purposes of economic sanctions makes it clear that sanctions are rarely, if ever, designed to pursue one and only one objective, but that some one or more of the purposes will take priority in each case. Even partial success can mean that one or more of these goals is realised through a low-cost alternative to military force which can both signal and build resolve, unity and legitimacy.

Of course, economic sanctions do not always succeed, even in terms of a limited set of purposes. Unsuccessful sanctions can result in such consequences as the forced development of the economic infrastructure and alternative sources of supply for the target, which will lead to reduced economic leverage by the initiator in any future conflict, or a signal of ineffectivness and disunity rather than resolve. The cases studied in this book are loaded toward failure because they concentrate on situations of large, economically self-sufficient targets with important policy goals, or else on targets with big powerful friends, which are the least compliant categories. Nonetheless, these cases illustrate a number of problems associated with the failure of economic sanctions.

In some cases there are problems with economic sanctions because of confusion about the objectives pursued. If the sanctions instrument is intended to serve too many purposes at the same time, or if it is not clear that there is any purpose at all other than being seen to do something, general satisfaction with the outcome is unlikely. The more elusive and ambiguous the goal, the less are the chances of success. One can hardly succeed without knowing what one realistically hopes to accomplish.

In other cases, objectives are not successfully met because the target is not sufficiently susceptible to the pressure applied. Where the target is economically strong and self-sufficient, such as in the Soviet Union or China, the effect of economic sanctions may be felt, but is unlikely to compel a policy change. Where the target's economy is able to respond flexibly by import substitution, trade diversification or shifting the economic burden to a disadvantaged social group, such as the blacks in Rhodesia, economic sanctions may fail to have the desired harsh impact. If another powerful state is prepared to offset the economic costs of the sanctions, as the Soviet Union was for Cuba or Poland, the target will be less vulnerable to the intended effects, and sanctions may only serve to drive the target into the arms of that other state and make it dependent upon that support. Regardless of the economic effect on the target, the political effect can be counter-productive if sanctions increase the spirit of resistance of the target population, as in Cuba or Rhodesia. The determination to stand firm and not bow to pressure can increase the political strength of the domestic regime.

In some cases, problems arise even though the objectives are clear and the target is susceptible to pressure because the desired effects are not attainable through measures and under unilateral or multilateral control. In an interdependent world, trade sanctions are often porous, since many sources of supply or channels of access are beyond total control. Alternate suppliers can often be found to replace those abiding by economic sanctions. In some cases, as in Rhodesia, commercial greed will impel firms from the sanctioning country to violate the sanctions in pursuit of swift and substantial profits. The activities of subsidiaries of multinational enterprises in the target country (as in Rhodesia and South Africa) or in alternative supplier countries (as in Arab oil embargo) can frustrate the sanctions policies of initiating governments. Technology is often available from subsidiaries, licensees, and competitors at only slightly greater cost, as in the pipeline sanctions. For these and similar reasons, the desired objectives may simply not be attainable.

Problems can also arise with regard to disagreements among allies about the design, implementation and termination of sanctions. In some cases, as perhaps in the pipeline sanctions, this collateral damage can be far greater than the economic costs imposed on the target. Differing motives of the participating states coupled with dissatisfaction with the relative burdens borne by the allies can provide an opportunity for the target to manipulate allied differences and even to gain politically from the entire episode. In such a case, sanctions can send entirely the wrong signal. Rather than solidarity and resolve, they may indicate only disunity and ineffectiveness. Such disunity can result from inadequate consultation among allies which take allied compliance for granted, as in the US announcement of the grain embargo to which other grain-exporting countries were expected to conform. Even more troubling is the perception or reality of uneven distribution of the costs of the sanctions among allies. In the gas pipeline sanctions, European allies considered that their economies were expected to bear the cost of sanctions against the

Soviet Union through the extraterritorial enforcement of US jurisdiction, while US grain sales to the Soviet Union continued unabated. In the earlier grain embargo, aggressive US grain exports into non-Soviet markets led foreign competitors to redirect some of their exports to the Soviet Union.

The effectiveness of sanctions can be undermined by concerns about the equitable distribution of burdens not only among allies, but also among groups within the domestic population of the initiating country. If particular industries (such as farming in the grain embargo) or regions feel unfairly singled out, their resentment can rapidly become political opposition to the continuation of the sanctions. Apart from the short-term loss of export sales to individual firms, there can be long-term negative effects on those firms and on the industry of the initiating country as a whole. International competitiveness can be diminished as alternative foreign production is encouraged, a reputation for reliability of supply can be impaired, and the receptivity to foreign investment can be reduced. These costs of shooting oneself in the foot provide fertile ground for domestic opposition to sanctions if they do not enjoy swift success. Public opinion can readily become disillusioned and demand a return to business as usual if the objectives of the sanctions are not quickly realised, and especially if the anticipated effects were initially overstated. Attempts to rally popular support for the imposition of economic sanctions by exaggerated claims of anticipated success can all too easily prove counter-productive, as they invite a popular backlash.

Finally, many problems have arisen about the termination of economic sanctions once they have been imposed. If this is not prepared for in advance, it can cause problems of alliance co-ordination and can send undesired signals to the target and to one's own population. If punitive sanctions are clearly intended to be imposed for a fixed time period, they can be lifted automatically at the end of that time without incident. But if the declared purpose of sanctions is to compel a policy change and the policy remains unchanged, then to lift the sanctions, even after an extended period of time, may signal approval or at least acceptance of the previously undesirable policy. At the very least, it will signal retreat by the initiator from an ineffectual posture. If not carefully thought out in advance, it can be harder to get out of sanctions than to get in.

Policy Planning

This assessment of the purposes which may be served by economic sanctions and the problems which may arise from inadequate design and implementation makes possible a number of policy considerations which should be taken into account in planning for the effective use of sanctions:

1. Be clear which of the variety objectives the sanctions are intended to achieve. Different purposes are best pursued by sanctions of differing kind, severity and duration. More importantly, only if the goals of the exercise are clear can sanctions be designed, imposed, adjusted and evaluated.
2. Be clear that the target is susceptible to the intended effects. Sanctions should be designed expeditiously so that a sufficiently severe effect will be felt by the target, and so that the intended signal, related to the purpose of the sanctions, is received.
3. Be clear that the objective is attainable through unilateral or multilateral action. Robert Browning once wrote that a man's reach should exceed his grasp, or what's a heaven for? That poetic phrase is a fine philosophy of life, but a poor prescription for economic sanctions. Sanctions must be designed so that the desired objective can realistically be achieved by measures under the control of the initiating country or countries.
4. Consult adequately with allies. The support and participation of allies must not be taken for granted, whether or not it is essential to the achievement of the objective. Consultation can ensure that allies understand, accept and share the objective and will not engage in offsetting action. Consultation can serve a damage limitation function by minimising comfort to the enemy from alliance disunity. Sanctions should be designed and implemented so as not to impose unnecessary or unacceptable costs upon allies.
5. Be sensitive to domestic support. Sanctions should be designed and implemented so as not to impose unnecessary costs upon particular domestic groups. The declared purpose and anticipated effect of economic sanctions should not be exaggerated to the domestic audience. Overselling sanctions initially breeds disillusionment, and ultimately domestic opposition to the continuation of the particular sanctions and to the use of sanctions in future cases.
6. Plan ahead for the eventual termination of the sanctions. This advance planning cannot be too detailed, or it will rigidify the sanctions, making it impossible for governments to respond to un-

expected developments, and taking the conduct and termination of the sanctions out of the control of the initiators. This could prove a disincentive to the use of sanctions at all. But failure to anticipate the conditions under which the sanctions will be lifted, and to communicate that expectation to the public, invites disagreement over the suitability of that action and disillusionment with the result.

Due attention to these policy precepts can minimise the negative effects of international economic sanctions and maximise their utility.

Notes

1. Thomas Schelling, The Strategy of Conflict, (Oxford University Press, New York, 1963).

2. See, for example, Mancur Olson and R. Zeckhauser, 'An Economic Theory of Alliances', Review of Economic Statistics, 1966; and D. B. Bobrow and R. T. Kudrle, 'Energy R&D: in Tepid Pursuit of Collective Goods', International Organization 33(2), (Spring 1979).

LIST OF CONTRIBUTORS

ANGLIN, Douglas G
Department of Political Science
Carleton University
Ottawa, Ontario, Canada

BRADY, Lawrence J
Assistant Secretary of Commerce
United States Government
Washington, D.C., USA

DEWITT, David B
Department of Political Science
York University
Toronto, Ontario, Canada

EVANS, Paul M
Department of Political Science
York University
Toronto, Ontario, Canada

FALKENHEIM, Peggy
Office of International Cooperation
University of Toronto
Toronto, Ontario, Canada

KIRTON, John
Department of Political Science
University of Toronto
Toronto, Ontario, Canada

LEYTON-BROWN, David
Department of Political Science
York University and
Associate Director
Research Programme in Strategic Studies
York University
Toronto, Ontario, Canada

LICKLIDER, Roy
Department of Political Science
Rutgers University
New Brunswick, New Jersey, USA

MARANTZ, Paul
Department of Political Science
University of British Columbia
Vancouver, British Columbia, Canada

List of Contributors

NOSSAL, Kim
Department of Political Science
McMaster University
Hamilton, Ontario, Canada

PAARLBERG, Robert
Department of Political Science
Wellesley College
Wellesley, Massachusetts, USA

ROCA, Sergio
Department of Economics
Adelphi University
Garden City, New York, USA

STANISLAWSKI, Howard
Department of Political Science
Wellesley College
Wellesley, Massachusetts, USA

WOLF, Bernard M
Faculty of Administrative Studies
York University
Toronto, Ontario, Canada

SUBJECT INDEX

SUBJECT INDEX